Prisons under
protest

CRIME, JUSTICE AND SOCIAL POLICY
Series Editors: Phil Scraton, Joe Sim and Paula Skidmore

Titles in the series include:

Prisons under protest

Phil Scraton
Joe Sim
Paula Skidmore

Open University Press
MILTON KEYNES · PHILADELPHIA

Open University Press
Celtic Court
22 Ballmoor
Buckingham
MK18 1XW

and
1900 Frost Road, Suite 101
Bristol, PA 19007, US

First Published 1991

British Library Cataloguing in Publication Data
Scraton, Phil
  Prisons under protest. —(Crime, justice and social
  policy)
  1. Great Britain. Prisons
  I. Title   II. Sim, Joe   III. Skidmore, Paula   IV. Series
  365.942

  ISBN 0-335-15181-7
  ISBN 0-335-15180-9 pbk

Library of Congress Cataloging-in-Publication Data
Scraton, Phil.
    Prisons under protest / Phil Scraton, Joe Sim, Paula Skidmore.
      p.   cm. —(Crime, justice, and social policy)
    Includes bibliographical references and index.
    ISBN 0-335-15181-7 (hb). —ISBN 0-335-15180-9 (pb)
    1. Prisons—Great Britain.   2. Prison riots—Great Britain.
  I. Sim, Joe.   II. Skidmore, Paula, 1963–   .   III. Title.
  IV. Series.
  HV9647.S37   1991
  365'.941—dc20
                                        91-10521
                                           CIP

Typeset by Rowland Phototypesetting Ltd
Bury St Edmunds, Suffolk
Printed in Great Britain by St Edmundsbury Press Ltd
Bury St Edmunds, Suffolk

Contents

Foreword

In a society where satellites are deployed to eavesdrop on communications thousands of miles away, it is almost tragic that we have neglected, indeed almost forgotten how, to listen to and heed the voices of those locked away for transgressions against 'our' rules and whom many dismiss with the utmost contempt. This book is unequivocally about the unheard voice of the underdog.

It is ironic that it is the voice of the incarcerated that pulls us back to examine what we are doing to each other. An increasing number of angry young men have in recent years taken to the roofs of our prisons and raised their anguished voices in a guttural cry of despair. The authors of this book, critical criminologists, have decided that enough is enough; that there is a need to listen to this alternative voice. They have researched the way in which the media have been manipulated by politicians and prison authorities to give a sanitized version of what is going on within our prison walls. This book is a powerful indictment of our so-called democracy. The contents vividly remind us that there is another story which, until now, has remained untold – that of the prisoner.

Peterhead is a high security prison rich in convict mythology. Some serving prisoners can still remember when guards were armed with rifles and prisoners wounded or shot at – this in a society which prides itself on a civilian police force that remains, for the most part, unarmed. Set in a bleak part of the north of Scotland, the prison is infamous for its institutional brutality. As the Scottish equivalent of its American cousin, Alcatraz, Peterhead accumulated a large number of young, long-term prisoners. Contained in a regime which treated them abominably, they were stripped of their self-respect and dignity. Inevitably, with a powerful symbolism, they took to the roofs of the prison in order to share their despair with the public at large, thus allowing an uncaring public to see the way in which some prison officers were brutalizing them with impunity. They highlighted the inhumane way the system ignored any formal complaints made by prisoners about maltreatment. They focused attention on the way their families were abused and mistreated when visiting them. This was not the voice of whingeing, pleading submissives. It was the dignified voice of a self-sacrificing group seeking justice. Many of them have since been harshly punished for the action they took. All of them feel it was worth it.

In essence, this is the story of a system that failed to learn from experience. What happened in Peterhead was the first spark of a long fuse that ignited and exploded throughout the British penal system, ending in Strangeways. The authors have, piece by piece, fitted together a jigsaw, adding their weighty academic credibility to a body of evidence that leaves no room for doubt. The writing had been on the wall for a long time and no one in authority cared to read and, more importantly, act on it. This cost all of us dearly. In the end, it took the roof off the penal system and that can be no bad thing.

Jimmy Boyle
Edinburgh

Preface

On 1 April 1990 prisoners at Strangeways jail, Manchester, took control of the prison and destroyed much of the fabric of the buildings. The month-long protest, with its near-hysterical media coverage alleging butchery and carnage in the prison, was unprecedented in its scale and severity. Official responses were confused and contradictory, revealing poor communications and a clear lack of understanding of the motivations and context of contemporary prison protest. As helicopters shone high beams on to the rooftops and blasted Wagner across Manchester's night sky, the public was assured that the circus was part of an informed longer-term psychological strategy geared to breaking the prisoners' resilience. Frustrated prison officers, clad in riot gear, beat their shields and chanted 'beast' to those on the roof, demanding a short, sharp end to the protest. Government ministers and prison service officials appeared surprised at the severity of the protest, the destruction of the rat-infested buildings and the strength of the resistance daily demonstrated to the world by the men on the roof. But Strangeways represented the culmination of years of prison protest in England and Wales. The only surprise expressed by campaign groups, penal reformers and prisoner organizations was that it had not happened sooner. Further, as they continually asserted, it could have happened at any one of several main prisons.

The incidents at Strangeways and at other English penal establishments during the same month were reported and received as a unique aberration. Typically, this ignored events during the 1980s at Scottish prisons. Served by a separate criminal justice system, a distinct prison service and a national media, Scotland's penal crisis has been systematically ignored and marginalized in England. Yet the seriousness and regularity of prison protest in Scotland contained within it lessons for all concerned with the provision, management and administration of prisons and their regimes. In 1986 the Gateway Exchange in Edinburgh held public meetings and its directors decided to appoint an independent committee of inquiry into the protests at Peterhead prison. In

November 1987, following a unique survey of prisoners at the prison, the committee published its controversial findings. The Report made 17 specific recommendations and called for the closure of Peterhead. With the crisis extended to other establishments, the Scottish Prison Service embarked on a programme of internal reorganization and change as apparently fundamental as it was unexpected.

This book has been written by the three researchers and co-authors of the independent inquiry's report. It represents a more thorough presentation of the evidence provided to the inquiry by Peterhead's prisoners and a more detailed analysis of the issues raised by prison protest. Further, it considers and evaluates the proclaimed sea change in Scottish penal policy since 1988 which culminated in the publication of the Prison Service's corporate strategy in1990. New senior appointments, reviews of staff training, experimental regimes and widely publicised discussion papers have been offered as hard evidence of the arrival of a new era for prisons. We welcome these changes and statements of intent but, as the analysis shows, they must be placed in the broader and long-term context of the crisis. Throughout the book the voices of those who continue to endure the prison regimes speak as a constant reminder of how far penal reform must go in order to respond to their suffering, brutalization and isolation.

During the development of the research Jimmy Boyle, Sarah Boyle and Ken Murray have helped in providing insights and material. We thank others involved with the independent inquiry, namely Alistair Duff, Sebastian Horsley, Jo McDonald and the staff of the Gateway Exchange. Kathryn Chadwick has been a constant support, particularly during the later fieldwork stages. Rob Dinwoodie provided help on the media chapter. The Director of Scottish Prisons, Peter Mackinlay, and the staff of the Prison Service College have assisted with policy statements and information. Finally, we have benefited considerably from the personal and intellectual support of Anette Ballinger, Kristi Ballinger, Ross Fortune, Deena Haydon, Chris Hughes, Sue Hughes, Karen Lee and Sheila Scraton. Barney Brown typed much of the manuscript and we are grateful to him.

The book, however, would not have been possible had the prisoners at Peterhead not given their time to share their most personal experiences with a wider audience. We recognize that their accounts were written in full knowledge that they would be read by prison staff before being passed to the research team. Within the text their words appear in italics to stress the centrality of their accounts to our work.

Phil Scraton
Joe Sim
Paula Skidmore

CHAPTER 1

Long-term imprisonment in Scotland: the case of Peterhead

THE INDEPENDENT INQUIRY AND THE RESEARCH CONTEXT

Dear Mr. Rifkind,

As a result of a series of public meetings held by us in Glasgow, to bring together concerned parties who feel that something should be done to improve conditions in Scottish Prisons, there was an overwhelming call for an independent public inquiry. I appreciate that you, as Secretary of State, have decided not to opt for this. As a result of our meetings in which members of your party participated, it was felt that the Gateway Exchange should act as a catalyst and bring together the views, experiences and opinions of serving prisoners, ex-prisoners, prisoners' families, lawyers and other outside agencies in this field . . .[1]

This letter, sent by Jimmy Boyle as co-director of the Gateway Exchange in Edinburgh to the Secretary of State for Scotland, announced the establishment of an independent inquiry into the protests of prisoners at Peterhead prison. The Gateway Exchange is a charitable, independent organization with a strong commitment to working in local communities. It provides therapy and counselling, community arts projects, a drug rehabilitation programme and a drop-in centre. The other significant dimension of its work is penal reform, providing support for prisoners inside, advice on release and help to prisoners' families. Apart from the personal experiences of Sarah Boyle and Jimmy Boyle, co-founders and co-directors of the Gateway, there is constant contact between the project and prisoners in all Scottish prisons and their lawyers. The Gateway Exchange has become a substantial research and information resource on life in Scottish prisons, on the conditions and effects of imprisonment and on the human rights violations endured by prisoners. In a climate dominated by security and secrecy, the work of the project has been central in presenting to the public an alternative vision of the Scottish prison system to that actively and persuasively promoted by the selective press releases of the prison department and the Scottish Office.

In November 1986, following a major disturbance and rooftop protest at Peterhead prison, the Gateway held a series of public meetings. The Peterhead disturbance was one of a series of major confrontations. It had been preceded by incidents at Low Moss prison in 1985, a rooftop protest at Barlinnie in July 1986 and at Edinburgh (Saughton) two weeks earlier. It was to be followed by further conflict and hostage-taking at Peterhead, rooftop protests at Peterhead, Perth and Barlinnie and a hunger strike at Barlinnie involving three hundred prisoners. There had been a dirty protest at Inverness in the segregation unit in November 1986. More recently, the conditions at Glenochil became so appalling that prison officers in riot gear were deployed to 'maintain order'. It was in this context that the Gateway launched its independent inquiry. Apart from the two directors of the Gateway, the committee of inquiry included a barrister, a Strathclyde Councillor who formerly was Chief Nursing Officer at the Barlinnie special unit, and the three authors of this book in their capacity as academic criminologists and researchers. Its broad remit was specifically to inquire into the underlying causes of the events at Peterhead and to make recommendations. From the outset it was deemed essential that the personal accounts of prisoners inside and their families outside should form a central dimension of the inquiry. While this was to prove difficult, the access which eventually was achieved provides a unique but harrowing overview of the daily lives of long-term prisoners in a British jail. These accounts form the main case material of this book.

In 1972 Stan Cohen and Laurie Taylor wrote *Psychological Survival*, the first critical account of long-term imprisonment in the United Kingdom.[2] This pioneering and highly accessible study has been followed by a range of significant work including: the analysis of the containment and control of long-term prisoners in England, Wales and Scotland;[3] case studies of the Kafkaesque rules governing the lives of long-termers;[4] the politics of long-term imprisonment in Northern Ireland;[5] the differential impact of long-term imprisonment on women;[6] and the dynamics of life inside from the perspective of the incarcerated.[7] Academics involved in this work have been concerned to give a voice to the confined and to shift the terrain on which the long-term prison debate has been built. It is a terrain dominated by official discourse, with the imprisoned rarely being given the opportunity to articulate their views or express their feelings about life inside the 'electronic coffins'[8] of long-term maximum security institutions. This critical academic work, part of which has been termed 'criminology from below', has been a major and influential strand in the critique and review of British criminology since the late 1960s.[9] It has had a significant impact on prison research and the analysis of the process of incarceration, for example: establishing a platform for prisoners to describe the pains of confinement;[10] challenging official explanations in the contentious area of deaths in custody;[11] and developing alternative accounts and explanations of major prison disturbances over the past two decades.[12]

Between 1969 and 1983 there were ten major prison disturbances in England and Wales alone.[13] Government ministers and official statements explain the underlying cause of such confrontations in straightforward and simplistic terms. They propose that there are a relatively small number of individual prisoners who, either alone or in cliques, manipulate an otherwise quiescent and compliant prison population into riot and violent protest. This 'bad apple' theory of disorder has a long history in common-sense explanations and academic theories. Consequently, it gained a popular and political significance particularly in the state's repertoire of responses following the restructuring of the British prison system which began in the mid-1960s.[14] Since then structural questions, such as the increasing length of sentences, the chilling alienation of long-term prison regimes and the institutionalized use of violence and drugs to maintain order, have been either denied credibility or completely ignored. Rather, an emphasis on psychological irrationality within the long-running theoretical framework of the pathology of the individual has been preferred. Given the connections between the media and the state,[15] these 'academic' focuses and 'official' explanations have been guaranteed immediate and generous press, radio and television coverage. Although they have been challenged, they have reinforced and maintained popular perceptions, fears and fantasies about the 'characters' or 'personalities' of those who contest the authority of the prison regime from within.

One mechanism for generating alternative accounts, in the face of an increasingly corporately owned, authoritarian and centralized media network,[16] has been the independent inquiry. Independent inquiries into the criminal justice process in the United Kingdom have a long, well-established history. In 1922, for example, Stephen Hobhouse and Fenner Brockway published a 728-page report into the prison system in England.[17] In the 1940s the Prison Medical Reform Council conducted a number of independent inquiries into the state of prisons, focusing particularly on prison medicine.[18] More recently, in 1977, the National Prisoners' Movement conducted a four-day inquiry which took evidence from prisoners, ex-prisoners and their families concerning events which followed a major demonstration at Hull maximum security prison during September 1976.[19] Prisoners had alerted campaign groups that systematic brutality had been meted out in the wake of the protest. The Home Office rejected demands for a full inquiry and held, as is usual, an informal inquiry. The schematic report which followed exonerated officers of any acts of brutal treatment, although it did remark on the 'excessive zeal' occasionally employed in quelling the 'riot'. Through the efforts of the National Prisoners' Movement, several MPs and prison reform groups, to say nothing of the courage shown by prisoners in coming forward to provide evidence, eight officers were found guilty of conspiring together and with others to assault and beat prisoners. One of the convictions was overturned on appeal. The officers' 'excessive zeal' had been reconstructed in the courts as criminal offences, and this would not have occurred without the intervention of an independent inquiry.

3

The developing intransigence of the contemporary British state and its obsessive commitment to secrecy concerning the enforcement, application and administration of the law and the criminal justice process inevitably has led to the use of independent inquiries in order to respond to public demands for open investigation of complaints and allegations. In 1978 the Bethnal Green and Stepney Trades Council conducted an inquiry into racial violence.[20] The following year, the killing of Blair Peach, an anti-fascist demonstrator, by an unidentified member of the Metropolitan Police in the aftermath of a permitted and protected National Front march through Southall's black community, led to a National Council for Civil Liberties inquiry.[21] In November 1985 Manchester City Council commissioned an independent inquiry into the Greater Manchester Police operation at a students' demonstration against the visit of Leon Brittan earlier that year.[22] The following year West Midlands County Council published the report of an independent review panel into the disturbances in Handsworth in September 1985.[23] Simultaneously Haringey Council published a comprehensive report on the Broadwater Farm disturbances in 1985.[24] This was the first of three similar inquiries, the others being into the policing of Hackney[25] and race and racism in Liverpool.[26]

This brief, and not fully comprehensive, overview of recent 'unofficial' and independent inquiries demonstrates that they have emerged as a viable alternative to partial, internal and often excessively secret official inquiries. It is rare for independent inquiries to receive recognition from state agencies and the usual response is one of non-cooperation. However, they gain their legitimacy and acknowledgement from grassroots constituents especially as it is the anxieties, fears and motivations of those directly involved which become lost or even neglected in the official construction of events. This point was clearly voiced by Lord Gifford at the opening of the Broadwater Farm Inquiry:

> When there is a conflict in society it is always the powerful institutions which find it easy to put out a version of the events which – even if it is only based on hearsay – is reported by the mass media as if there is no other truth. Those without power have no such voice. Our task is to listen to the powerless as well as the powerful. To listen to the ordinary people of this community and organisations which represent them. And having listened to all of them, to produce recommendations which can be used to bring about change.[27]

There is no equivalent outside the prison to the powerlessness experienced and endured by the prisoner. Symbolically stripped of civilian clothes and clad in the standard ill-fitting issue of the regime, the prisoner loses all access to political status. Without the right to vote, the rights of citizenship, the right to communicate freely, the right of association and the right of access to civilian health care, the prisoner struggles to retain the freedom of intellect and the entitlement to human dignity. Opportunities to speak out about imprisonment, the conditions, the treatment and the regimes are rare. They come in rolled up pieces of paper passed mouth-to-mouth as visitors kiss goodbye and, occasionally, they are draped from prison windows or shouted from the rooftops. This

4

inaccessibility, this submission to the totality of the institution, is demanded by the British prison system. It renders prisoners powerless and it legislates that this should be so. The denial of liberty becomes the confiscation of citizenship.

The main role of the independent inquiry into prisoners' protests at Peterhead, then, was to provide a broader yet more analytical account of the prison regime, its origins and its developments. Given that the deprivation of liberty is the most powerful sanction used by the state in punishing individuals, it is essential that an informed, impartial and wide-ranging debate is stimulated. If this is to reflect the democratic order, of which prisons are established institutions, then it follows that prisoners should be able to make a full and uninhibited contribution. This intention lay at the centre of the independent inquiry and it has become an essential ingredient of this study.

There are several distinct but related points to be made concerning the work of the independent inquiry into Peterhead and the subsequent development of this work. In marked contrast to the obstructive secrecy of all official aspects of the prison service and its operational practices, the project was constructed as an open and public research investigation. The emphasis was on the gathering and distillation of information from the widest possible range of individuals, organizations and other sources, including all relevant documentation and publications. To achieve this objective the project departed from the established practice of internal investigations and attempted to gain first-hand accounts from prisoners who were in Peterhead during the 1986 disturbances. Following an initial approach to the prison department, the independent inquiry team was informed that it could only approach prisoners by name and a list of those men who were in Peterhead in November 1986 would not be made available to the team. Consequently the inquiry had to approach lawyers and campaign groups to gain the names of as many prisoners as possible. A proportion of those involved in the 1986 protest had been moved to other prisons.

In February 1987 prisoners in a number of prisons were surveyed and asked to complete an extensive questionnaire on different aspects of their confinement in Peterhead (see Appendix 1). While some of the questions were constructed to elicit comparative data, others were open-ended. Given the restrictions imposed on independent and critical research in the United Kingdom, it was imperative to enable prisoners to respond as if they were involved in face-to-face unstructured interviews. The open-ended questions encouraged prisoners to write substantial answers and, therefore, provide a rich seam of qualitative data. In approaching prisoners the researchers were well aware that replies would be subjected to thorough vetting over security and prisoners would be warned about making unsubstantiated allegations. The letter which accompanied the questionnaire, signed by Jimmy Boyle, expressed the concern of the Inquiry team:

> I would like to make it clear that if you feel that participating in this project will bring pressure on you then please do not do so. All of us appreciate there can be no confidentiality as your questionnaire will obviously be read by the prison authorities.[28]

While prisoners were encouraged to reply freely to the questions there is evidence from many of the answers to specific questions that individuals were inhibited because they knew that they would be vetted. This ranged from general concern over intimidation and harassment to the possibility of charges being brought for making 'false' or 'malicious' allegations against prison staff. A few examples suffice:

I really can't answer that question because of this security order . . .

No comment . . . I'm keeping out of trouble until my name is cleared.

Excuse my paranoia but THIS IS DANGEROUS GROUND, SORRY.

I would only comment on this to yourself [Jimmy Boyle], *your wife – or someone at the Gateway Exchange.*

While the prisoners reported the threat of intimidation and harassment within the prison, externally the inquiry experienced hostility from the Scottish Office. In April 1987 the Deputy Director of the Scottish prison department, Mr T. J. Kelly, wrote to the inquiry in response to its complaints over the delay in recovering questionnaires from prisoners. It was the inquiry team's opinion that the delay contravened both the European Convention on Human Rights and the Department's rules. Throughout his lengthy letter Mr Kelly referred to the inquiry in inverted commas, clearly indicating doubts over its credibility (see Appendix 2). Further, and this judgement was made before any replies had been returned or before the research phase of the inquiry had begun, he alleged that the inquiry was, 'narrower in scope and less balanced in approach' than the Department's internal inquiry under the Chief Inspector of Prisons.

This strong expression of scepticism was ill-timed although not altogether surprising. His response was in keeping with an inappropriate but inevitable tendency within criminal justice agencies to presume that people will accept the integrity of internal inquiries and to assume that external inquiries or research activity seek to undermine agency policies and practice. This is a closed vision which encourages within the criminal justice profession a 'siege mentality'. In fact the questionnaire issued to prisoners allowed scope to answer specific questions openly and objectively. There was no prescribed or premeditated standpoint. The replies show clearly that most of the prisoners approached the task with care and responsibility. They provided substantive and thoughtful replies, some writing extensively and constructively on the way forward for Scottish prisons.

A total of 76 questionnaires were sent by name to prisoners, 55 to Peterhead and others to Barlinnie (4), Inverness (2), Perth (5), Saughton (7) and one each to Aberdeen, Gateside and Dungavel. Forty-five replies were received, 14 were returned 'not known at this address' and 17 did not elicit a response. It is impossible to know how many of the 17 were not handed on by prison staff. The fact that 14 were returned when the prison staff must have known the 'forwarding' address clearly demonstrates a lack of cooperation. One report was received of a questionnaire being torn up by a prison officer in front of the prisoner. Selection of prisoners was based on those known to the Gateway Exchange or conducted through families or lawyers. The committee of inquiry met with representatives of families, with lawyers and with the Families Outside organization concerning problems of access to Peterhead. The documentary research took place over six months and the committee of inquiry met on 12 occasions. The committee reported on 9 November 1987. Its substantial 140-page report received overnight coverage in the Scottish media, a brief comment in two newspapers in England and a 15-minute slot on BBC 2's *Newsnight*. The research project continued after the report's publication and a certain amount of access was gained to the official documents and debates which have underpinned the 'restructuring' of the Scottish prison system since 1987.

While the primary focus has remained on Peterhead, especially as further disturbances and protests have occurred, it is important to emphasize that conflict in prison is not unique to Peterhead. It is part of a history of discontent within the British prison system as a whole. The questionnaire survey, the interviews and the letters received, together with the official responses to the inquiry report, reflect a persistent and recurrent problem in Peterhead which is inherent within the prison structure. Official and media discourses which construct the 'problem' simply as one of individual pathologies of a minority of trouble-makers actually contribute to the cyclical pattern of disorder, response, harder regimes and more disorder. Professor Roy King, former member of the Home Office Research and Advisory Group on the Long-Term Prison System, concludes:

> Conceptualising the control problem as the product of 'difficult' or 'disturbed' individuals and developing a reactive policy towards them has been both partial and self-defeating. Partial in that it ignores all the structural, environmental and interactive circumstances that generate trouble, reducing it to some inherent notion of individual wilfulness or malfunction. Self-defeating in that the policy itself becomes part of those very circumstances that generate the trouble: it is likely that among those who get defined as troublemakers there are some who are made into troublemakers as a result of the way they are dealt with in prison . . . The probability is that when some are 'dealt with' others take their place. A more rational approach would seek also to obtain a closer bondage of the circumstances which generate disorder, and to develop a proactive stance towards prison conditions generally that would make it less likely that any prisoner should shift from being merely troublesome to being a troublemaker.[29]

The independent inquiry, and the research which serviced it and has continued, sought to be part of such a rational response in contextualizing the circumstances of prisoner protest and presenting the 'view from below' to challenge that 'from above'.

PETERHEAD PRISON:
ITS BACKGROUND AND HISTORY

Peterhead prison, opened in August 1888, is situated approximately 34 miles north of Aberdeen, Scotland's third largest city which is located on the north-east coast. The prison's history can be traced back to 1881, when a Committee on the Employment of Convicts reported that the 'most likely prospect for benefitting the shipping and fishing interest of the country at large and at the same time profitably employing convicts is the construction of a harbour of refuge at Peterhead in Aberdeenshire'.[30] In 1886 the Peterhead Harbour of Refuge Act gave the prison commissioners the authorization necessary to build a prison. When completed the prison was designated a general convict prison which would hold male prisoners sentenced to penal servitude for a minimum of five years. Joy Cameron has described its early days:

> The arrival of the first twenty prisoners caused a great excitement in the town, and for days crowds occupied the railway station avid for the first sight of the convicts. They travelled in a prison van, the only one in use in Scotland for railway purposes, the warders sitting in the middle of the van with ten convicts on either side. They were dressed in rough white sacking with broad arrows and wore smart caps and shoes . . . The convicts quarried the stone for the harbour, travelled daily by train to and from a quarry some miles away, guarded by warders armed with rifles. Cutlass and scabbard were worn by every warder at Peterhead from its opening until 1939. Rifles were carried until 1959 when all weapons were discontinued and batons substituted.[31]

The prison was originally designed to hold 208 prisoners. In the first decade of this century the number of prisoners in Peterhead 'fluctuated around an annual average of 350, reaching a peak figure of 455 in 1911'.[32] In May 1912 convicts, known as 'preventive detainees', were received into the prison but by 1915 the prison ceased to be used exclusively for convicts and began to house what were known as 'ordinary prisoners' serving over 12 months. During the 1939–45 war the prison also contained military prisoners stationed in Scotland who had been court-martialled.[33]

According to the Chief Inspector of Prisons, the main buildings at Peterhead 'reflect prison architectural concepts of the late 19th century and the exterior design of the cell blocks [has] changed little during the past 90 years'.[34] There were additional buildings completed in 1909, 1960 and 1962 which increased the capacity of the prison to 362 and in 1959 some 20 acres were added to the original area of the prison. This was 'developed as an industrial area to provide employment following the completion of the Harbour of Refuge and breakwater project'.[35]

The contemporary role of Peterhead is that of an ordinary prison which takes only those prisoners serving sentences of 18 months or more and for whom

Table 1   Grades of staff at Peterhead prison, 1987

Grade		
Governor I		1
Governor III		1
Governor IV		1
Assistant Governor		2
Chief Officer I		1
Chief Officer II		2
Principal Officer	Discipline	17
Senior Officer		23
Officer		154
Principal Nurse Officer		1
Senior Nurse Officer		1
Nurse Officer		4
Principal Officer		1
Senior Officer	Catering	1
Officer		2
Chief Works Officer I		1
Principal Works Officer		2
Senior Works Officer		3
Works Officer		10
Chief Clerk Officer		1
Principal Clerk Officer		3
Clerk Officer		2
Principal Officer		2
Officer	Instructor	2
Civilian Instructional Officer III		4
Civilian Instructional Officer IV		2
Typists		3
Civilian tradesmen		2
Total		249

allocation to a training prison is considered inappropriate. There are no remand prisoners and no prisoners sent directly from the courts. At the end of 1985 there were 281 single cells in operation and the average daily number of prisoners for the year was 188, with a maximum of 198.[36] Peterhead remains an all-male prison. On 1 January 1987 there were 249 staff in post at the prison. Table 1 provides a statistical breakdown of the grades of staff.[37] The majority of prisoners sent to Peterhead are long-term prisoners in Category A or B security classes. Table 2 indicates the security categorization of prisoners in Peterhead on 30 December 1986.[38] Table 3 provides a statistical breakdown of the average sentence categories at the beginning of 1987. It shows clearly that the overwhelming majority of prisoners were serving sentences of four years or more.

The historical development of the regime at Peterhead has been under-researched. Yet it is clear that if contemporary developments at the prison are to

Table 2 Security categorization of Peterhead prisoners,
30 December 1986

Category A	6
Category B	145
Category C	21

be placed in context it is crucial to consider the historical progression of the regime. However, this is not a straightforward task as there exist few substantial accounts of the prison which are available for public scrutiny or research access. The yearly reports on Scottish prisons which are available are limited in scope and information and, understandably, make little reference to conflict or disturbances at the prison. Despite these limitations it has been possible to trace certain recurring themes in the history of Peterhead over a period of forty years, from the 1920s to the more publicized incidents of the 1960s.

In marked contrast to more recent official reports, the early *Prisons in Scotland Reports*, from the opening of Peterhead in 1888 to the turn of the century, were very much more detailed. They included elaborate breakdowns and tables, for each prison institution in Scotland, on the health of inmates, on offences and punishments, and gave precise details of those who died in custody. This range of information was reduced considerably during the 1950s and, from 1972 tables of offences and punishments for individual prisons, which will be analysed next, were no longer included in reports.

Analysis of the tables headed 'Punishment and Offences for which Inflicted' for the 1920s, and comparatively for the 1950s, shows that Peterhead's prisoners received substantially more punishments per head than in other male prisons in Scotland. On average, in any one year during the 1920s, one in four prisoners received punishment at Peterhead compared to one in 30 at other prisons. The yearly average for the 1950s was one in five at Peterhead, compared to one in 13 at other male prisons. This pattern obtained through the 1960s, when the annual average for other male prisons was one in 13, whereas at Peterhead it was one in nine, rising to one in two by the end of the decade.

Also significant was the different forms that punishments took at Peterhead. From its opening in 1888 until the 1920s, in common with other male prisons, the most common punishment inflicted at Peterhead was 'reduction of diet',

Table 3 Average sentence of Peterhead prisoners, January 1987

More than 18 months but less than 2 years	1
2 years but less than 3 years	8
3 years but less than 4 years	11
4 years but less than 5 years	18
5 years	28
More than 5 years but less than 10 years	41
10 years or more	39
Life	28

followed by 'sleeping on a wooden guard bed'. By the 1950s, however, marked differences began to occur in the punishments, with the most common punishment at Peterhead being 'forfeiture of remission or loss of grade' with 'forfeiture of association or recreation' also featuring significantly. By contrast, the most common punishment inflicted in other male prisons was 'sleeping on a wooden guard bed' followed by 'forfeiture of earnings'.

The actual offences for which such punishments were given were fairly consistent across all male prisons. 'Disobedience and refusal to work' was universally the most common offence. The category 'other offences' featured significantly but details were not provided. This lack of categorization reflects the level of discretion in meting out punishments within the prison system. However, the figures for 'assault' offences in the 1960s show Peterhead to be considerably below the ratio for other male prisons. In 1952, for example, one in 87 offences committed at Peterhead was assault, yet the average for all other male prisons was one in 13. The well-established explanation that prisoners at Peterhead were likely to be more violent and, therefore, a 'danger to warders' is contested by these figures.

What the range of figures up to the 1970s shows is that Peterhead prisoners consistently received more punishments per head of prison population than did prisoners in other Scottish male prisons and that the most common punishment became loss of remission. The significance of loss of remission is discussed in Chapter 4 but clearly this is a punishment which 'hangs over' the prisoner throughout his or her term. The offences committed in Peterhead were comparable to those in other prisons yet historically violence or assault by prisoners was a *less* common offence than in other male prisons in Scotland.

In addition to the above figures, further information is available from other sources to give a more complete picture of the regime at Peterhead. The *Glasgow Herald* recorded very little for the 1920s, but refers to a suicide at Peterhead in 1922. The Scottish Office prison reports referred to four cases of corporal punishment in 1923, the introduction of association and recreation in 1925 and three prisoners making suicide attempts in 1928–9. The *Glasgow Herald* reported various incidents in the 1930s, including two escapes, one of which resulted in the shooting dead of a convict, as well as mentioning an occasion in 1934 when convicts smashed glass at the prison. During the war years there was no mention of Peterhead, and the Scottish Office prison reports were short and insubstantial. Escapes took place in 1944, 1946 and 1949, with prisoners being recaptured. The 1946 prison report also refers to a food riot at the prison. In the 1950s there were escapes every year, with all prisoners recaptured. In addition, the 1955 prison report mentions a hunger strike by prisoners and an officer being assaulted. In 1959 prisoners protested to the Secretary of State for Scotland about a shooting incident, of which there is no previous mention.

Each of these incidents should be placed within the context of the developing regime at Peterhead, a picture of which is further informed by considering specific facts, as well as the conclusions previously reached concerning punishments and offences. Cutlass and scabbard was worn by every warder from the opening of Peterhead until 1939. In 1948 Peterhead was the only Scottish prison where 'the cat', a kind of whip, remained available for use. A maximum of 21 lashes was recommended as a punishment. Rifles were carried by warders until batons were introduced in 1959, which, significantly, is the same year that prisoners complained to the Secretary of State for Scotland about a shooting incident. It is important also to underline the persistence and regularity of attempted and successful escapes, especially throughout the 1950s, which were followed in the 1960s by a security clampdown, as recommended by the Mountbatten Inquiry (1966) into a series of escapes and breaches of security throughout British prisons.

The impression of the Peterhead regime prior to the 1960s is that arbitrary and excessive punishment was commonplace, with loss of remission disproportionately inflicted. Prisoners were recorded as not behaving unusually violently, in fact less so than elsewhere, yet the punitive style of the warder's job was emphasized by the carrying of cutlasses before 1939, the carrying of rifles until the late 1950s, and by the use of the whip well into the 1940s. The intimidatory nature of the warder's job carried over into the 1960s, and became firmly entrenched in the minds of prison officers. The persistent escapes from Peterhead, especially during the 1950s, compounded the issue over the lack of security at the prison.

During the 1960s there were significant changes in the security and control of long-term prisoners. In England, after a number of escapes by long-term prisoners, Lord Mountbatten was asked to inquire into and make recommendations about the treatment of long-term prisoners. He recommended that all top security (Category A) prisoners should be concentrated in one maximum security prison. Mountbatten reported in 1966, but by 1968 the Labour government had rejected this proposal in favour of a recommendation made by a sub-committee of the Advisory Council on the Penal System, chaired by the Cambridge criminologist, Professor Leon Radzinowicz. The committee recommended dispersing top security prisoners in a number of prisons throughout the system where security would be strengthened. The dispersal system became the central plank in the Home Office policy for dealing with long-term high security prisoners in England. It has not stopped the problems in the system where, according to the Home Office and as noted above, there have been at least ten major disturbances in the 14 years between 1969 and 1983.[39]

The case of Scotland has received less attention than England. Again, however, a number of significant changes can be pinpointed from the mid-1960s onwards. As in England, the thread which runs through these changes is the attempt not only to find a regime for long-term maximum security male prisoners in general but also to establish alternative situations for those long-termers labelled as 'violent', 'difficult' or 'subversive'. The key to this lay in classification.

On 1 July 1966, the prison department in Scotland introduced changes into the system of classifying prisoners which had been under review during the year. The Department reasoned that not only was the object of classifying prisoners to give each individual prisoner the 'regime best suited to him' but also that 'those less settled in criminal ways may be kept from the company of more hardened criminals'[40] (female prisoners were not mentioned in this discussion). While classification schemes had been important throughout the nineteenth and twentieth centuries, they took on an added significance from the mid-1960s onwards as the prison department sought to refine the system by presenting an image of prisoners as divided into two main groups: the majority, who recognized the legitimacy of the system; and the deviant, subversive minority, who manipulated the first group to further their own ends.

The prison department in Scotland appears to have had this in mind when constructing its policy in 1966. As the *Prisons in Scotland Report* for that year pointed out, formerly it had been the custom to send a prisoner serving a long sentence to a prison on the basis only of his length of sentence and previous criminal record. Now the Department, through the establishment of a national classification centre at Saughton prison in Edinburgh, took into account 'the man's aptitude for or ability to benefit from a positive form of training'.[41]

Prisoners were to be classified into two groups. Those who showed that they had the willingness and ability to benefit from trade training were sent to either Saughton, if they were first offenders, or to Perth, if they had been previously convicted. Those who had no trade aptitude or who, in the words of the prison department, 'demonstrate their unwillingness to participate in training'[42] were to be sent to the North East of Scotland: to Peterhead if they were 35 years or under; to Aberdeen if they were over 35. Prisoners could be upgraded or downgraded depending on their willingness or otherwise to accept the regime in their allotted prisons. Additionally, in the words of the Department:

> should a prisoner prove to be recalcitrant or subversive or to have a bad influence on other prisoners, he can be transferred to the special Segregation Unit which has been set up in Inverness Prison. The regime in this unit, which has a high degree of security, is strict and privileges are reduced to the minimum.[43]

Prisoners sent to the Inverness unit were not allowed a personal radio and could not watch television. Prisoners were detained there for as long as their behaviour warranted it, their case being reviewed by a special board every two months. This Inverness/Peterhead axis was to become crucial in the developments discussed below. It is important to note that by the end of 1966 the Department was happy to record that despite the fact that all prisons were suffering from a degree of overcrowding, the classification system had been fully introduced and 'was functioning comparatively smoothly'.[44]

From 1966 onwards, therefore, classification operated in Scotland's prisons at a number of different but overlapping levels. First, there was classification into the security categories recommended in the Mountbatten Report: Category A for the highest security prisoner down to Category D for the lowest. Second, as described above, there was the classification of prisoners by age and by what was called 'aptitude for training'. Third, there was the further classification of those who it was felt did not accept the legitimacy of the prison regimes into the solitary confinement unit at Peterhead and the segregation unit at Inverness.

13

From the point of view of the prison department classification appeared to be, in the words of Stan Cohen, 'the key to a successful system'.[45] However, within a short time, it became clear that classification, both in principle and in practice, could not solve the structural problems of long-term imprisonment in Scotland. In fact, by its very nature the procedure and the philosophy underpinning it – coherent though it was – became a contributory factor in the problem that it was designed to solve.

From the point of view of prisoners, classification brought its own contradictions, frustrations and inevitable conflict. Attempting to explain the problems of the long-term prison system as being caused by the behaviour of a hard-core minority did nothing to touch the deeper problems of the philosophy, conditions, lack of accountability and the length of sentences which were being imposed by the courts. This last point is an important variable in the overall picture and will be considered in greater detail below.

In the six years between 1966 and 1972 there was a series of confrontations at both Peterhead and Inverness. Conflict was endemic in both institutions. In making this point, and relating this more recent history to that previously outlined, it is important to raise questions about the structural context of this conflict. This context, as argued above, lay at the root of the conflict. The increasing length of sentences, the repressive segregation techniques, the arbitrary classification system, the psychological and physical brutality each underpinned and provided sustenance to the violent behaviour of individuals. Peterhead itself was regarded as the end of the road for many prisoners, it was Scotland's gulag, a prison of no hope. This position was reflected in the Parole Board reports for the period. The report for 1969 indicated that of the 702 prisoners who were eligible for parole during the year, 152 (21.7 per cent) actually stated that they did not wish to be considered. The Board pointed out that it was 'seriously concerned' that over one-fifth of those eligible did not wish to be considered and that a 'high proportion came from Peterhead and Aberdeen'.[46]

The close relationship between Peterhead and Inverness has been described by Jimmy Boyle in his book, A Sense of Freedom.[47] In the attempt to contain an increasingly volatile situation, the prison department used segregation in each to control the prisoners. Once more, contrary to the historical evidence, the Department emphasized individual 'bad apples' rather than the structural issues which were fundamental to what was happening. In December 1972, this containment strategy failed. At the end of the month there was a serious disturbance at Inverness in which a number of prison officers and prisoners were injured. One prison officer lost an eye and prisoners involved received additional prison sentences of up to six years. This episode marked a turning point in the history of long-term imprisonment in Scotland with the emergence of a new strategy based around the positive philosophy of the special unit at Barlinnie. At the same time Peterhead continued to be central to the question of penal policy for long-term prisoners and a major cause for concern.

14

PETERHEAD: 'THE ROOF COMES OFF'

> There is a wide gulf between staff and prisoners and it is rare for staff to get
> close to prisoners. Violence is endemic. A wall of silence separates staff and
> inmates and punishments are accepted without argument.[48]

This account of the relationships between prison officers and prisoners at
Peterhead was written by a Home Office researcher in 1971. It demonstrated
clearly that by the early 1970s Peterhead institutionally and structurally had
become a prison regime of extreme brutalization and alienation. At one end of
the continuum of institutionalized violence was the daily routine of bullying
and intimidation; at the other was the inhumane, torturous punishment of the
cages. Standing naked before prison officers in a 'cage' 9 feet by 6 feet, the
prisoner underwent a full body search three times a day. The solitary confinement and personal humiliation of the cages represented the ultimate loss of
dignity for any individual receiving this punishment. The prisoner remained
entirely at the mercy of the prison officers and accounts of prisoners who went
through the cages describe how officers regularly exploited their absolute
discretionary powers.

The justification for the introduction and use of 'segregation units', as has
been noted, was well established in the Scottish prison tradition. Peterhead and
its cages were the end of the line for Scotland's 'most violent men'. In other
words, there had to be a place and a form of punishment which in its extremity
responded to those 'few' individuals who were prepared to take violence to
extremes. It was a return to the classical criminological explanations of
individual pathology. As MacDonald and Sim pointed out:

> By individualising the problem attention is distracted from the idea that it
> is the prison system, by its very nature, that generates the 'problems'
> itself. By definition new 'problems' will always arise – it is inherent in the
> repressive, authoritarian structure of the prison system. At an extreme
> level the rhetoric becomes, as it did in Inverness and in the isolation cells in
> Peterhead: 'If you treat a man like an animal, then he'll respond like an
> animal'.[49]

Violence in regimes such as Peterhead is not an irrational response to a
peaceful and calm situation or an aberration in an otherwise smooth-running
system. It is an inevitable and rational reaction to a violent and repressive
regime. In the early 1970s the gradually worsening situation between prison staff
and prisoners and the persistent use of arbitrary and severe forms of punishment for even the mildest of offences led to rooftop demonstrations in August
1972. What the media and government response failed to appreciate, and this
has remained the case, was that the seventy or so men who took to the roof of
their prison did not take this action lightly. For they were aware not only that
they would receive physical punishment when they returned to their cells but
also that they would have their sentences extended. The rooftop protest and the

violent confrontations which followed, leaving several officers and prisoners seriously injured, were a major indication that Peterhead's violent regime was failing badly. Its untrained staff could not cope with the difficulties posed by long-term imprisonment and its regime created and perpetuated relationships within the prison dominated by institutionalized violence.

In 1971 a Scottish Office Working Party report on long-term prisoners recommended that a 'special unit' be set up in Scotland to provide 'treatment' for prisoners known to be violent or potentially violent.[50] The special unit would not simply be an alternative to the cages as the Working Party also recommended the retention of the segregation unit, though with some modifications. In 1973 the special unit opened at Barlinnie prison. Its remit included the provision of 'psychiatric services', the 'treatment of the mentally disordered' and the establishment of 'therapist–patient' relationships. Once again the penal system emphasized where the 'problem' of long-term imprisonment was rooted: those few 'difficult' and violent prisoners unable to respond with obedient compliance to the prison regime. As MacDonald and Sim stated:

> By concentrating on a few 'problem' prisoners the Unit emphasises and reinforces the view that it is the individual that is the problem rather than the prison system itself which generates the 'problems'. Remove the individual prisoner from the situation and you remove the problem. The illusion of order and control is confirmed and restored. This limited logic works for a while until the system throws up more 'problem' individuals . . .[51]

Throughout the 1970s, due to the good work and cooperation of staff and prisoners, the special unit at Barlinnie emerged as a therapeutic community based on personal freedom, self-discipline and collective responsibility. It challenged the oppressive regimes of authoritarianism and petty regulation so long the hallmarks of British penal tradition, and it demonstrated clearly that if structural practices are challenged then the possibilities of developing an environment in which prisoners can retain dignity and develop a spirit of cooperation can be achieved.

The Barlinnie special unit, however, was monitored ruthlessly throughout its early days by the media, which exploited every possible avenue of criticism in a relentless attack on the experimental project. It focused on well-known prisoners who were accommodated at the unit and made claims that 'evil' men who should have been punished were being given privileged and in some cases 'five-star' treatment. This not only served to undermine the difficult work being done at the unit but also reinforced gut-level prejudices that prisons should be places of punishment rather than rehabilitation. Furthermore, it gave the impression that the more violent the man, the more difficult the prisoner, then the better the accommodation. Again, as the focus was put on the unit, attention was distracted from the excesses of the Scottish prison system and the conditions endured by the majority of the prisoners.

Despite the successful development of the special unit little had changed in the primitive, violent and secret world of Peterhead. In 1974 Hugh Brown, Under-Secretary of State at the Scottish Office, called for a complete re-development or closure of Peterhead as tensions again began to mount. In May 1975 five prisoners went on hunger-strike and in 1977 there were two separate incidents involving 87 prisoners refusing food. Each of these protests was against conditions in the prison and the poor response of the staff. In October 1978 seven prisoners lit a fire and barricaded themselves in a cell where they remained for 24 hours. Once again the protest was over conditions within the prison and resulted in loss of remission for each of the prisoners involved. Both the Scottish Prison Officers' Association and the Scottish Office issued statements expressing their satisfaction with staffing levels and conditions at the prison. Clearly, however, the message coming from inside Peterhead was that prisoners were no longer prepared to tolerate the regime.

In April 1979 Robert Love, a prisoner at Peterhead, gave an interview to the Scottish Council for Civil Liberties in which he stated that the conditions at the prison had led to the fire and the disturbance in which he participated.[52] He stated that this was the 'Only way they could draw attention to the fact that they had persistently been refused outside assistance with their complaints about conditions'. Robert Love's account stated that prisoners in the punishment cells were denied all privileges and were often placed on the regime for periods of time in excess of the fixed punishment period.

In May 1979 the *Daily Record* published the contents of a letter smuggled out of Peterhead under the headline 'Zombie Cells Fury'.[53] The article claimed that the 14-cell punishment block at Peterhead was used to keep prisoners in solitary confinement for 22 hours per day for up to a year at a time. In his letter the prisoner wrote:

A festering sore here is the scandal of the punishment block. A week or so in the punishment cells and the inmate is a zombie – yet some are kept there for months on end. The prisoner can only walk up and down or sit on the floor brooding. After 6–12 months of that is it any wonder that the guy is a walking time-bomb?

The letter warned that the prisoners' anger at the conditions at Peterhead would lead inevitably to violent confrontation with prison staff. With John Renton, Secretary of the Scottish Prison Officers' Association, confirming that the punishment cells at Peterhead were worse even than the 'cages' at Inverness, Rear-Admiral Nicholas Polland, Director of the Scottish Association for the Care and Resettlement of Offenders, gave his support to the contents of the letter. The Scottish prisons department confirmed the average time spent in punishment cells to be three months but that some prisoners remained in solitary for 'just under a year'.

In August 1979 the widely expected confrontation at Peterhead took place. Following news that legal aid had been refused to prisoners who wanted to petition the European Court of Human Rights over conditions in the prison, ten prisoners occupied the roof of the observation block. All other prisoners were confined to their cells. The prisoners threw slates at prison officers and shouted to the press: 'This place is the punishment block. They hold guys in here for months. This place is inhuman.'[54] In retaliation prison officers used high-powered hoses against the prisoners, who then barricaded themselves in the attic. Malcolm Rifkind, Minister for Home Affairs in Scotland, held a hastily convened press conference at which he announced a £1 million grant to improve conditions at Peterhead. He stated that he had been 'aware for some time of the unsatisfactory conditions at Peterhead'.[55] The prisoners, however, stated: 'Rifkind is scared to face the allegations made against the prison establishment. He is refusing to negotiate with prisoners.'[56] The Scottish Office responded publicly with characteristic indifference to the incident, stating that it was being treated as 'an internal, prison incident' with 'no clear reason' being apparent for the protest.

After four days the rooftop demonstration ended. While the authorities voiced their concern about how the protesters could escape, stockpile food and harbour makeshift weapons, the real issues over conditions in the prison were restated. A letter smuggled out confirmed that the protest was forced on prisoners, 'because the authorities have never paid any attention to the complaints we made through official channels'. Russell Dobash, a University of Stirling prison researcher whose project included Peterhead, commented:

> I was shocked by the austere environment. I have been in every other Scottish prison and the conditions in Peterhead are exceptional in the negative sense, far beyond what one would have expected. There is an urgent need for change in Peterhead, in fact it should be considered whether it should still operate as a prison in this day and age . . . I don't know if it can be improved without knocking the place down.[57]

From within the prison it was alleged that 42 prisoners had been placed on 24-hour solitary confinement in strip cells under 'strict observation'. They faced charges of assault, malicious damage and fire-raising. On 3 September 1979 Malcolm Rifkind visited the prison and condemned the rooftop demonstration as a 'futile, stupid act'. He gave unqualified support to the prison staff who 'despite massive provocation remained calm and dealt efficiently and courageously with a very difficult situation'.[58] Rifkind also stated that allegations of brutality by prison officers against the demonstrators were unfounded. Two former prisoners wrote to the *Evening Express* after the incident alleging systematic and institutionalized violence by prison staff on prisoners.

A month after the protest the protesters, denied legal representation, were punished within the prison. One prisoner lost three years' remission, 'privileges' were withdrawn and a number of prisoners were placed in solitary confinement. A joint statement made by Radical Alternatives to Prison, the National Prisoners' Movement (PROP) and the Newham Alternatives Project supported those prisoners at Peterhead Prison and elsewhere who take direct action to draw attention to the inhumanity of prison conditions. The solution to the problems of prison does not lie in the spending of money on altering facilities but in a change of attitude towards the whole question of crime and punishment.[59]

At its annual conference the Scottish Prison Officers' Association, however, reviewed the type of riot equipment used in the prison service. This equipment was developed as a direct response to increasing demonstrations, and included helmets, riot-shields, gauntlets, breast plates, back plates, leg guards and long truncheons. The Scottish prison department announced the development of riot training for prison officers, based on paramilitary techniques, to meet head-on situations such as Peterhead. While the debates continued the prisoners responded with an open letter to the *Evening Times* which stated that if conditions in the 'hell hole' were not improved there would be more violent demonstrations.[60]

In June 1980 three prison officers went on trial facing charges of brutality against prisoners in the aftermath of the August demonstration. Prisoners at the trial claimed that they had been beaten, kicked and, in one incident, attempts had been made to push one man over a gallery. Witnesses stated that prison officers were dressed in full riot equipment and 'were running around like madmen swiping at anyone in the way'.[61] After hearing the evidence at the three trials Sheriff Croom reserved judgement for a week, finally returning not guilty verdicts in all three cases. He felt that there had been a 'substantial backing of evidence' that assaults had taken place and that 'despite deficiencies' the prisoners' evidence carried a 'certain ring of truth'. Had he been reaching a decision solely on the 'balance of probabilities' he would have decided that prison officers had struck blows. However, the prison officers were acquitted of all charges and returned to their duties. On the basis of the verdicts the Scottish Prison Officers' Association stated that there was no case to answer. Within a month the Peterhead branch of the association put forward a resolution to the annual Conference which demanded 'a committee of inquiry into a legal implications arising when staff are involved in a riotous situation where a measure of force is required to protect life and property and a set of guidelines to be drawn up'.[62]

Using the three trials as the basis for his statement, John Renton argued that as physical force was necessary to deal with violent offenders in riot situations prison officers were 'open to allegations of wrong doing'. As Peterhead entered the 1980s the issues central to the unrest in the prison remained unresolved, the Scottish Office continued to deny any serious problem and the direction of the regime moved more quickly towards stronger forms of regulation and control – the paramilitary solution – and the need to protect prison officers from the 'violent minority'.

With continuing unrest at Peterhead persisting throughout 1981 the next major incident occurred in May 1982. A letter from a prisoner claimed that a riot on 5 May 'took place after and because of the assaults and beatings meted out by these warders during that week to these prisoners and other prisoners'.[63] This letter was supported by another from the sister of one of the prisoners who claimed the riot resulted from officers' violent attempts to break up a peaceful demonstration over conditions.[64] As a result of the incident four men were transferred to the 'cages' at Inverness. John Renton stated that there had been problems at Peterhead for 'four to five months'. Again the root cause was identified as being the actions of a small group of violent prisoners. By the end of May the Scottish Office confirmed that an unspecified number of prisoners were in punishment cells under mechanical restraint including handcuffs and body belts with the original four still in the Inverness 'cages'. The letters of complaint from within Peterhead led to an informal investigation. In November Philip Barry, Her Majesty's Chief Inspector of Prisons for Scotland, reported that claims that Peterhead was a 'hard, tough and unsympathetic community' no longer applied.[65] He considered the prison to be orderly and well organized but that troubles stemmed from a 'handful' of prisoners prepared to riot and use violence regardless of the consequences to themselves and others. He concluded that these prisoners had long-standing reputations for violence and used relatively minor grievances as justification for creating major confrontations.

Early in 1983 it was reported that 'disruptive' prisoners in Scottish prisons were to be selected for transfer to the newly completed ten-cell segregation block at Peterhead. A letter from a prisoner at Barlinnie claimed that the new unit was the start of a 'new hard-line policy geared to break the resistance of those refusing to accept the present system'.[66] The fear from within the prison was that the electronic gates, cameras, maximum security conditions and periods of solitary confinement would combine to produce a regime of 'sensory deprivation' and 'total surveillance'.

In October 1983, following a serious confrontation at Peterhead, 15 officers were injured and three prisoners were transferred to the 'cages'. This was the prelude to a major protest in January 1984. The 18-hour protest involved a rooftop demonstration by 12 prisoners which was ended when riot-equipped prison officers stormed the barricades. Following calls for a public inquiry into Peterhead the Scottish Home Affairs Minister, Michael Ancram, reassured the House of Commons that he would await the prison governor's report on the incident.[67] In February he decided not to publish the report in the 'interests of security'. A Scottish Conservative MP, Albert McQuarrie, warned of the need to publish the details of such serious situations especially because the situation at Peterhead was deteriorating.[68] By March letters were being sent from the prison which indicated that the punishment block was overflowing and that the 'dirty protest' had spread. One letter, published in *The Scotsman*, pleaded for notice to be taken of the plight of the prisoners in Peterhead.[69]

On 1 July a letter, signed by five men on the dirty protest, warned of 'trouble and tragedy' as other prisoners had been moved to the segregation block so that cells could be cleared. The letter argued for a 'humane existence', claiming confinement 'like animals' with two 30-minute exercise periods in every 24 hours. Prisoners were without newspapers, radios, earnings, tobacco or writing

20

paper and were forced to sleep on concrete floors because of their protest. They stated:

> It would seem that rather than give us basic human needs the authorities would let this protest go on for ten years, would rather have a disgruntled staff and a permanent focal point of dissent within the prison system.[70]

In June, at the trial of 13 prisoners on charges of mobbing and rioting during the previous January, prisoners alleged that they had been stripped and beaten in the aftermath of the disturbances. At the end of the trial a prisoner's spokesman, Frank McPhie, was acquitted amidst allegations that the authorities had attempted to 'frame' him. The other 12 were convicted, receiving sentences totalling 45 years for their part in the riot. Frank McPhie predicted that the situation in the prison would worsen as long-term prisoners faced injustice and little hope of change in a situation of prisoner-baiting by the staff. He concluded:

> I believe the position would be improved if some of them [prison officers] were cleared out and replaced by people who were more concerned and more experienced in penology. Over the years we have sought change but the only way of bringing the state of life in Peterhead to the public's attention is by means of protest . . . They should see this latest protest and demonstration as just a warning of what could happen if the prisoners used the power they have shown that they possess to make their point by violence. The regime should be relaxed.[71]

By December 1984, with the tensions of the earlier part of the year still unresolved, Renée Short raised questions in the House of Commons concerning assaults by prison officers on prisoners and the destruction of their property. The Secretary of State denied knowledge of such allegations and reiterated his commitment to the necessity of the ten-cell unit at the prison.[72] There followed a series of incidents in 1985 including the taking of hostages by prisoners during a break-out attempt, a refusal to work by 20 prisoners protesting over the treatment of one of their colleagues and another hostage-taking incident later in the year. In November 1985 a prison officer was charged with striking a prisoner repeatedly with handcuffs. The prisoner told the court: 'Brutality goes on at Peterhead all the time. There is a guy lying in Aberdeen Royal Infirmary now over brutality.'[73] This was a reference to a prisoner, Thomas Campbell, admitted to hospital following a separate incident at the prison. In June 1986 Campbell, charged with assault on a prison officer during that incident, claimed before the court that a squad of officers had come to his cell in retaliation for the previous disturbance. He claimed that they had carried riot batons, and kicked and beaten him, grabbing him by the testicles and stamping on his stomach. An internal injury sustained during this assault led to a stomach operation in Aberdeen Royal Infirmary. By mid-1986 further reports consistently claimed that tensions at Peterhead were 'unbearable'.[74]

In October 1986 the Scottish Office Industry and Home Affairs Minister, Ian Lang, toured Peterhead and claimed that conditions at the prison were 'extremely good'.[75] He concluded:

Peterhead has always had difficult prisoners and there is always the potential for unrest. I think the professionalism of the staff in managing the prison so well is highly commendable. I have been very impressed with the atmosphere. It is quite plain that the prison officers take their role very seriously and are making every effort to ensure that the atmosphere is kept low key rather than highly charged.

Within a month several Scottish prisons erupted in scenes of unprecedented anger and frustration. James Freeman, Home Affairs correspondent of the *Glasgow Herald*, wrote that 'the last reaction anyone should display to the Peterhead hostage-taking is surprise'.[76] The demonstration lasted 93 hours and in March 1987 three men received ten years for mobbing, rioting and hostage-taking. One of the prisoners, John Smith, submitted a written plea in mitigation. It stated:

Can anyone ever understand the horrors of prison life even by visiting prison? Of course not. No one can understand this without being part of it, feeling the anxieties, knowing the helplessness, living in desolation. Prison life does not provide the creative correction and training needed for a man to be able to make a new beginning on the outside. Instead it is geared to use the men as labour, punish them if necessary and disregard their inner spirits as of no consequence. Physical and mental brutality does exist in Peterhead. This matter can only be resolved with the introduction of rehabilitation. If the prison authorities insist on treating prisoners like animals, then prisoners will naturally continue to act like animals. Prisoners, including myself, have been described as incurable psychopaths, subversive and hell-bent on destruction. This can only be described as an excuse rather than a truth. I ask you, have prisoners been given the chance to express themselves in any other way?[77]

Against this position the Advocate-Depute argued that sufficient and adequate formal channels existed through which prisoners could air grievances and make complaints. These included 'going to an officer, writing to people including solicitors and MPs, requesting to see the governor or official from the prison department, or the prison visiting committee'.[78] In passing sentence, Lord Murray stated that he 'took fully into account the pleas in mitigation' but set them against the 'menace and threat which the situation contained'. Given that all three received ten-year sentences it is difficult to estimate the length of sentences had he not accepted the pleas. Throughout the trial prison officers agreed that tension had been high in Peterhead for months prior to the November disturbances but repeatedly denied knowledge of any use of violence by prison officers against prisoners.[79]

At the High Court in Edinburgh four men coincidentally received sentences, including one of seven years and one of six years, for their part in the 1986

22

Saughton siege. During these two trials it became clear that the prison authorities had developed new strategies of inter-agency cooperation in responding to sieges and hostage-taking. Throughout the Saughton siege special cameras and listening devices were inserted in the walls of B Hall, providing security specialists with full observation at all times. Their role was to relay information to assault teams on stand-by which were equipped to deal with a riot. The 'front line' was supported by advisers from SAS headquarters in Hereford and by psychologists who advised senior prison officers on 'how to handle the increasingly desperate and unstable leaders of the riot'.[80] Specialized observational equipment, including fibre-optic cables, was provided by MI5.

The range of inter-agency cooperation and commitment of resources at Saughton, and at Peterhead, where the SAS was widely thought to have ended the siege, marked the consolidation of a new direction in the regulation of prison disturbances. The connection between the civil and military authorities, together with the development of hard-line responses, has become the most significant change in the prison authorities' handling of disorders. It has been justified on the basis of escalating disorder, the intensity and regularity of 'riot' and the new dimension of hostage-taking including serious 'threat to life'. The series of events, however, has resulted in a model for dealing with prison disturbances based on a civil–military connection which resembles closely that which has prevailed, with disastrous consequences, in the United States.[81]

Revelations of the extent of inter-agency involvement in settling the sieges at Peterhead and Saughton, together with the severe sentences handed down, did little to deter the protests in Scotland's prisons. In May 1987 prisoners held a prison officer hostage at Shotts prison, releasing him after 25 hours. The disturbances at this new prison were used by the authorities and the media as evidence that the riots were caused by a minority group of violent and disruptive prisoners rather than by a complex relationship of factors such as rights, parole, punishments and inflexible regimes. In early June at Peterhead two prison officers were taken hostage, one was released within a day, but the other was held for five days and freed only after prison officers stormed the cell block. Within 48 hours of the end of the Peterhead siege prisoners at Perth prison took a prison officer hostage. Throughout 1987 Perth had been the scene of fires and prisoner protest. In April there was a rooftop protest and the hostage-taking was the inevitable consequence of a series of unresolved disputes within the prison.

In late September there was a further incident at Shotts which preceded the two most serious incidents at Peterhead and Perth. On 28 September at 8.30 p.m. a siege started in Peterhead's D Hall. There were 46 prisoners in the hall and two prison officers were taken hostage. By the weekend 43 prisoners and one of the prison officers had left the hall. Jackie Stuart, a 56-year-old prison officer, was held by the three remaining prisoners who occasionally brought him on to the roof to be displayed before an eagerly waiting press corps. Discussion of the background to the siege and explanations for its apparent severity were lost in the headlines and media accounts which turned the hostage-taking into an hourly drama. Alongside a photograph of a prisoner holding a hammer high above Jackie Stuart's head the *Daily Record* ran the headline '"HAMMER OF HATE": "HE'LL GET IT" THREAT TO BRAVE HOSTAGE'.[82] The account continued:

> Three times he swung at Mr. Stuart's head – holding back only at the last second. Mr. Stuart appeared to be shaking and numb with fear. Onlookers gasped in horror and many looked away – because they thought the middle-aged prison officer had lost his two-day battle for life. It was the dramatic flashpoint of a 35 minute humiliation of Mr. Stuart, a softly-spoken grandfather, in which the prisoners had flaunted their power over their helpless hostage.[83]

This one incident, more than any other over the previous five years, penetrated the consciousness of public opinion. For the first time and in front of the world's media, a prison officer appeared about to lose his life. The impact of the sensationalist reporting was dramatic and removed all attention from the prisoners' demands. On 3 October, 105 hours into the siege, Jackie Stuart was freed. It was widely reported that the siege was ended by an SAS team using CS gas and stun grenades. Following the previous commitment to inter-agency cooperation the 'inevitable' had happened: 'Prison chiefs decided to call in the snatch squad – made up of an A-team of special [prison] officers and led by top SAS officers.'[84] Jean Stead, in *The Guardian*, noted the significance of this development:

> The SAS's rescue on Saturday of the prison officer held hostage at Peterhead gaol was the authorities' first use of armed force in the recent series of disturbances in Scottish prisons. In the previous incidents, the most serious of which were at Peterhead last year and at Barlinnie in Glasgow, negotiations and offers of investigation into complaints had proved sufficient . . . The siege operation was under the general control of Grampian police. But it is understood that a squad from the SAS headquarters in Hereford was brought to RAF Buchan, a mile from the prison, several days before the rescue.[85]

No sooner had the Peterhead siege ended, with Jackie Stuart publicly reunited with his family and, presumably, the SAS officers returned to their barracks, than four prisoners at Perth prison took a prison officer hostage. A statement issued by the Scottish Council for Civil Liberties gave a warning concerning the use of the SAS: 'It could lead to prisoners attempting to emulate these tactics. We are getting extremely frustrated because no one seems to understand what the problem . . . is at the root of the whole Scottish prison system.'[86] Predictably, the *Daily Record* lost no time in publishing its 'colour exclusive'. Under the banner headline 'KNIFE-EDGE' it proclaimed 'terror for hostage as tension explodes into naked violence'.[87] The prison officer, George Jolly, was held in C Hall, used for remand prisoners. The Perth siege ended after two and a half days and was negotiated on the basis of the publication of the prisoners' demands. In the climate of violence and hostility which surrounded the Peterhead and Perth sieges the demands of hostage-takers had been lost. At Peterhead the main demand was simple – a full public inquiry into the regime at that prison. At Perth the prisoners demanded the closure of Peterhead prison, greater opportunities for parole and an end to brutality in the prison. The escalation of violence at Perth, however, was clear from a further demand that 'the names of Robert Raiker and Gary Skellet should be publicised and that the media should be made aware that they had stabbed and slashed three inmates in the hall'.[88] This unusual self-proclamation by two of the hostage-takers was compounded when three men appeared at the windows of C Hall, one brandishing a knife. He drew the knife several times across the throat of another man and slashed open a pillow. They unfurled banners which read 'Siege Will End in Deaths' and 'Rob Raiker and Gary Skellet Will Murder'.

The escalation in violence had produced a new level of concern. It was now possible to consider that a hostage might be killed and the tabloids lost no time in fuelling such a fear. John Renton returned to the well-worn theme of isolating the trouble-makers in small control units and an end to free association among prisoners: 'We have lost control of the prisons because we have been too soft. Now is the time to regain control and run them as they should be run.'[89] Renton's comments were echoed by Andrew Coyle, Chair of the Scottish Prison Governors' Committee. In commenting on the imposition of an immediate clampdown in all 'closed' prisons, which included the closure of workshops, reduction in recreation time, the serving of meals in prisoners' cells and restrictions on visits, he stated:

> We recognise that in the short-term this action was necessary. I hope that in the near future we will move to the second and more important phase which is identifying and controlling that small group of prisoners which abuse the normal freedoms.[90]

Malcolm Rifkind confirmed this position, stating that the prison modernization programme in Scotland would not be inhibited or delayed by a 'small number of vicious animals'. He concluded: 'We intend to keep those [incidents] to an absolute minimum and to deal ruthlessly if necessary with those who might be responsible'.[91] Graham Fenwick, Branch Secretary of the Prison Officers' Association in Leeds, was in no doubt as to the extent of that ruthlessness. According to him, the violent and desperate men with no release date had nothing to lose: 'the next time prisoners get on the roof they should be shot'.[92]

Prison reformers and campaigners once again attempted to reply to the hard-line response. Dr Russell Dobash stated: 'Frustration, angry feelings of hopelessness, a deep sense of deprivation and deep-rooted claims of injustice can trigger off unrest. The prisoners are not acting irrationally. For they are trying to highlight and make public their grievances.'[93] Dobash's position was taken further by John Carroll, a Glasgow solicitor, in an extensive interview with Angus MacLeod of the *Sunday Mail*. He commented:

> All this has to do with bad attitudes on the part of management. I believe some prison officers go out of their way to upset inmates. What they don't realise is that they are dealing with prisoners who are intelligent and know their rights . . . If a prison officer tries to buck the system by stopping a

colleague from doing something to a prisoner he knows he'll get nowhere within the system. The people who percolate to the top of the prison management simply do not want change . . . It's not true that a lifer has nothing to lose when he makes a roof-top protest. He knows he's facing at least six to ten years on the normal life sentence . . .[94]

Professor J. E. Thomas, a former assistant prison governor and Dean of Education at the University of Nottingham, argued:

Some of the causes of stress in the Scottish prison system are incontrovertible. They include the fact that prisoners are getting longer sentences which they often have to serve in Victorian prisons designed for short-term prisoners . . . The appalling conditions, *still*, of most of our prisons are regularly reported by that most restrained body, the Prisons Inspectorate. Prison staff know from experience that long-term prisoners faced with such conditions simply will not tolerate them. The prospect of 10 years under such conditions is *not* tolerable.[95]

While the media ran its 'exclusives', complete with specially designed mastheads such as 'Siege Prison: Scotland's Crisis', the words of Ken Murray, written for a *Scotsman* investigation earlier in the year, appeared to have been forgotten. In responding to the January sieges, Murray reflected on his 28 years in the Prison Service. His insight and first-hand experiences provided a rare but critical appraisal:

Prisons are not natural habitats, they can't be. But they need not be the unnatural places that they are with an atmosphere in which fear and anger thrive. Prisons are hostile places, prisoners are abused and debased in a variety of ways yet they are not deterred from re-offending. What is wrong with the system? What is it about the human spirit which tolerates the intolerable? . . . Prisoners most of the time are scared and they concentrate on the one major imperative in their life – survival . . . It should be understood that fear [of the staff and of the peer group] is the all-prevailing influence in the prison culture.[96]

Murray listed the full range of circumstances which contribute to the 'intolerable' conditions in Scotland's prisons: decrepit buildings; overcrowding; inadequate sanitation; mutual distrust and suspicion between officers and prisoners; insensitivity and cruelty on the part of the officers; brutality; an ineffective complaints system; frustration over visits and parole.

After the October events, however, the Scottish Council for Civil Liberties' spokesperson, Dr Carol Jones, was adamant about the next move in attending to the crisis: 'Nothing less than a Royal Commission and a total overhaul of the system can put an end to the disturbances'.[97] This call was taken up by some newspapers. The *Glasgow Herald's* editorial argued that the call for a commission of inquiry had become 'irresistible and its implementation should be treated as a matter of urgency'.[98] Such a commission would examine 'our whole prison philosophy'. *The Scotsman* demanded 'much more research' focusing on the 'administration of the Scottish system' which would challenge the 'anonymous and far-reaching power' of the Scottish prison department. It concluded:

> the last thing that an authoritarian, hierarchical establishment will admit is a mistake and the last thing it will wish upon itself is a searching independent inquiry. It believes that it is right in all circumstances . . . The case for one [an inquiry], for even a Royal Commission, is formidable and grows more so with each outburst of turbulence at a Scottish prison. [99]

The Independent challenged Malcolm Rifkind's assertion that 'most prisoners merely want to serve out their terms in peace unless intimidated by their fellows'. It continued:

> He brushed aside calls by the Scottish Council for Civil Liberties for a Royal Commission into the prison system rather than circumscribed inquiries into particular outbreaks of violence. Mr. Rifkind was wrong to do so. It is not necessary to take at face value all the complaints against the Scottish penal service made by some of the toughest and most unscrupulous prisoners in the country to accept that the disturbances are now so routine and accusations so sustained as to merit full and public investigation. [100]

Finally, *The Guardian* also was highly critical of the Secretary of State for Scotland, commenting that his response to a most serious crisis was to offer 'tired explanations and no remedies'. It emphasized the need to consider a reduction in the prison population, remission for good behaviour and the development of small units, such as the Barlinnie special unit, with programmes geared to rehabilitation. It stated:

> While Mr. Rifkind dismisses talk of a Royal Commission to look into the crisis by saying it would take too long, others on the ground refer to the Working Party on Alternative Regimes, set up in 1982 and containing senior figures in prison administration, which produced a report a year ago – findings neither published or acted upon. [101]

While most of the popular newspapers opted for the sensational aspects of the hostage-taking, devoting considerable coverage to the harrowing ordeal of the hostages and the reactions of their families and colleagues, the considered opinion of sections of the media was that only a full, independent and public government-backed inquiry could explore the deep-seated ills of Scotland's prisons. Such an inquiry necessarily would have a broad remit to examine the context of escalation in prisoner protest. It would take evidence openly from prisoners, their families and their representatives as well as from official sources. The inquiry would consider penal philosophy, sentencing policy and the administration of regimes rather than limit itself to questions of social disorder and individual pathology. Campaign organizations, reform groups and academic researchers were united in the call for such an inquiry.

Mr Rifkind, however, was not to be persuaded. His response was predictable, reasserting the position taken by his Department and the Scottish prison department throughout the earlier disputes. At a press conference, also attended by Mr W. Reid, the civil servant with overall responsibility for the Scottish Home and Health Department, Mr A. Thomson, Director of the Scottish Prison Service, and Lord James Douglas-Hamilton, the Minister for Home Affairs, he made it clear that his main concern was the existence of a conspiracy between a hard core of violent prisoners incarcerated in different Scottish prisons. He concluded:

> The vast majority of the prisons and the prisoners are under control. What we have here are the actions of a very small minority of evil men. The incident at Peterhead and . . . at Perth involved a tiny number of prisoners. A large number of the prisoners in the incident at Perth wish to leave the block. There are those who seek to explain these incidents as the basis of claims made by the perpetrators. They ignore the extent to which staff and other inmates who want no part suffer in these incidents. [102]

On the basis of an argument founded on the existence of a silent compliant majority and ultimate faith in the accountability and administration of the prison authorities, he opted for internal reports and recommendations. If the storm was to be survived by the prison department it would be achieved within the existing organizational structures, using the very mechanism which had been found wanting. Effectively the door was closed on public debate and unofficial participation.

THE SCOTTISH PRISON SERVICE RESPONSE: 1988 ONWARDS

In March 1988 the Scottish Office produced its 'more detailed statement of the corporate philosophy and plans for the Scottish Prison Service'. [103] The paper, entitled 'Custody and Care', had been commissioned by the Secretary of State for Scotland two months earlier[104] and was constructed to 'initiate a period of sustained and intensive development in the Scottish Prison Service'. [105] In October the 'Custody and Care' paper was taken further by the publication of a second paper entitled Assessment and Control which sought to explain the 'approach of the Scottish Prison Service towards the particular problems of violent and disruptive prisoners'. [106] The paper was based on the premise that 'assessment' and 'control' are the essential constructs in the management of 'difficult prisoners':

> assessment means identifying early those inmates who may be prone to violent or disruptive behaviour and ensuring the appropriate resources are directed towards resolving the problem which may lead them to engage in such behaviour. Control means ensuring that we have adequate procedures and facilities to minimise the effect of such behaviour, when it does occur, on other inmates and on staff. Assessment and control are not ends in themselves, however, but must be supported by an appropriate system of opportunities and sanction. [107]

In introducing its policy and plans for Scottish penal establishments 'Custody and Care' stated the need for a 'coherent corporate philosophy . . . to guide the regimes and management of individual penal establishments'.[108] Central to this policy would be the objectives of 'a better quality of life for inmates' and 'better professional standards for staff at all levels'.[109] The paper was divided into four sections: the task and responsibilities of the Scottish Prison Service (including imprisonment and penal policy, the legal framework, and its updating, account-ability, the use of accommodation and 'local' overcrowding); policy and priori-ties for prisoners (including allocation, principles on the opportunities and restrictions for those in custody, 'sentence planning' and preparation for release); planning for individual establishments (including establishing regime plans for each prison and for categories of prisoner, the implications for management of individual prisons, and closer cooperation between prison establishments); training and development of staff (including the organization and content of training, the developing role of governors, prison officers and other staff).

The Secretary of State had laid down the main aims of penal policy in commissioning the paper: appropriate punishment; protection of the public; deterrence; and rehabilitation. He stated:

> The balance between deterrence, punishment and protection of the public on one side and attempts to rehabilitate the offender on the other is always difficult. It is vital, however, that the balance should be carefully assessed by the courts at the time of sentence and constantly kept in mind by the agencies which enforce sentences including, of course, the prison service.[110]

The tasks of the Prison Service were specified thus: keeping in custody untried or unsentenced prisoners and presenting them to the courts; keeping in secure custody those prisoners sentenced; providing prisoners with 'as full a life as is consistent with the facts of custody'; promoting and preserving prisoners' self-respect; enabling prisoners to maintain links with family and community; and encouraging prisoners to contribute positively to society on discharge. While this statement emphasized a commitment to the 'custody and care' of prisoners, the priorities for its realization clearly demonstrate that 'care' would be realized within the context of 'control'. The first two priorities provided the determining context for all others and effectively subordinated care to control:

> The duty of lawful *secure custody* is paramount. The first priority must be SECURITY to ensure that inmates do not abscond before their appropriate date of liberation or release.[111]

And:

> It is crucial to ensure that Governors assisted by staff retain CONTROL of penal establishments. Disciplinary measures, including restrictions of location or association of some inmates, may be necessary to protect the

29

safety or welfare of others and to preserve the fabric of the establishment.[112]

Once again a major 'new' initiative had been constructed from within the prison department and the Scottish Office, the main emphasis of which were security, good order and control. Despite four of its six objectives showing a commitment to the needs of the prisoner, those needs were bounded by a primary emphasis on security and regulation. Accepting implicitly that prison regimes had failed at a range of levels to provide adequate or appropriate experiences for prisoners the 'Custody and Care' document prioritized the promotion and presentation of self-respect for prisoners. Yet the lens through which such widely acceptable objectives were viewed was that of segregation and control.

This theme was taken up by Assessment and Control, which aimed specifically at the 'violent' and 'disruptive' minority of prisoners in the Scottish system. The Scottish Prison Service position on the causes of 'major' incidents since mid-1986 was made clear in the introduction: the incidents

> have served as the focus of considerable public attention and interest in conditions within the Prison Service in general and in the particular problems of managing violent and disruptive prisoners. The incidents suggest that previous assumptions about security and control of establishments have not stood the test of time and that new approaches are needed to reduce the continuing threat to the safety of staff and other inmates and the risk of further damage to prison property.[113]

On this basis the paper was concerned specifically with dealing with 'inmates who present violent and disruptive behaviour'. Chapter 2 of the paper considered the 'pattern' and 'causes' of the 'incidents', arguing that 'new features' had emerged since 1986. These were: longer duration; hostage-taking; premeditation and planning; involvement of 'others' through intimidation; unprecedented media interest; and fire-raising. The paper went on to consider the reasons put forward by prisoners and other commentators. On the basis of Her Majesty's Chief Inspector's report (March 1987) it 'found no basis for the allegations which had been made of brutality by prison officers at Peterhead' and warned that 'inmates also have a responsibility not to make frivolous allegations of brutality in an effort to discountenance and intimidate staff'.[114] Arguing that 'capacity in the Scottish Prison Service is adequate to meet needs', it rejected claims that overcrowding or poor conditions were major factors in the disturbances.[115] It denied the relevance of changes in the parole policy, arguing: 'it is puzzling that inmates allegedly protesting about their release prospects take part in action which is likely to have the effect of extending the period they spend in custody'.[116] Using the same argument, that protest leads to a greater restriction, it rejected all complaints raised over the quality of life or the granting of privileges within the regimes. In establishing the principal cause the Scottish Prison Service accepted that specific incidents be evaluated in terms of a 'different combination of factors and circumstances' but, predictably, it concluded:

rather than looking to changes in the way in which the Prison Service as a whole goes about its task . . . a more productive approach may be to concentrate on the individual personality and the 'repertoire' of particularly disruptive and violent inmates.[117]

To this end the paper constructed a 'profile of violent and disruptive individuals' which used the classic models of individual pathology and undersocialization so deeply entrenched in the criminological tradition. 'Violent and disruptive persons tend to display': hostile attitudes towards authority; imagined grievances towards authority figures; inability to come to terms with offences or length of sentences; poor perception of social values; outbursts of violence triggered by domestic problems; peer pressure from the criminal community, including being steeped in the behaviour patterns of gang culture; inability to live to order in a structured and regulated environment; oversensitivity to false rumour (for example, ill-treatment of another prisoner); drugs; and personality disorder manifesting itself in low tolerance levels and low thresholds to violence.[118] The root or 'true' causes of the incidents were identified within this range of behaviour problems. Consequently:

> If it is accepted that it is the response of the individual to the pressures inherent in the prison environment which lies at the root of violent and disruptive behaviour, then the importance of identifying those individuals who may be particularly prone to violent and disruptive behaviour becomes apparent.[119]

Founded on this claim, popular within the Prison Service and challenged by prisoners, campaign groups, lawyers and academics, the Scottish Prison Service discussion paper embarked on its analysis of disorder and, accordingly, presented a series of proposals: to conduct further research work to quantify the numbers and location of violent and disruptive prisoners; to refine the principles for selection of control risks; to improve procedures for identifying potential trouble-makers in advance; to review security categorization procedures; to develop a new system of profiling for individuals assessed as potential control risks; to give further consideration to staff training specific to violent and disruptive prisoners; to develop the concept of small units for persistently difficult inmates; to proceed with a maximum security unit of 60 places to test and assess new concepts of design, layout and regime (at Shotts); to develop the 'role' of Peterhead with improved opportunities and regime for prisoners; to continue the Inverness unit for short-term segregation and to construct a similar unit at Perth; to monitor the operation of small units; and to improve the screening of long-term prisoners on initial allocation, identifying those who 'require exceptional measures of security and control'.

The restricted publication of both papers was accompanied by a widely publicized and major reshuffle of senior positions within the Scottish Prison Service. In the two years following the 1986 protests over 40 prison governors (approximately half of the Prison Service hierarchy) were moved.[120] Younger governors and deputies gained accelerated promotion, some moving through grades, and those in post were moved sideways or retired early. Starting with the appointment, in 1986, of a new Prison Service head of operations, most prisons which had experienced major disturbances gained new governors: Barlinnie, Glenochil, Saughton, Perth, Inverness and Peterhead. Not all the moves were received as 'progressive' steps. Gordon Jackson, Chairman of the Association of Scottish Prison Governors and seconded to the Operations Division, was appointed to the conflict-ridden Glenochil Prison in May 1988. The media were invited to Glenochil and the revelation came as a shock:

> Here were officers clad like Martians, their features masked by riot visors. Here were filthy, unshaven men living among their own urine and excrement. Even those familiar with prison disturbances and dirty protests were profoundly shocked at the extent to which communications had broken down . . . Many senior officials within the prison department see the formation of riot control squads and the locking up of disruptive prisoners over lengthy periods as a new hard-line policy – a way of demonstrating who is in control.[121]

Such a policy, however, was sustained by the two discussion papers in their emphasis on security, control and isolation of violent offenders. In that sense the reactive and severe regime epitomized by Glenochil was the sharp end of such a policy. This was no surprise to Ken Murray, previously Chief Nursing Officer at the Barlinnie special unit. Gordon Jackson, he said,

> is a man who is attracted to military-style strategies as we learned when he was in the Special Unit. He used to glamorise his own military service. I cannot imagine that he could bring stability to any explosive situation. On the contrary, the kind of solutions he favours are known to create unrest.[122]

In 1989 Gordon Jackson was charged with unauthorized possession of ammunition in the prison at Glenochil, including seven RIP 12-bore cartridges containing CS gas and 23 Hatton 12-bore cartridges.[123] Following protracted discussions on the case, he pleaded guilty to the charges. Eventually he was dismissed from the Prison Service and lost a court battle to secure his pension rights. Although he was portrayed as a maverick who had single-handedly attempted to develop military-style options, according to The Scotsman the Glenochil affair raises crucial issues concerning the role of the Scottish Office, the Prison Service and government ministers.[124]

Of major significance in the reorganization of senior positions in the Prison Service was the appointment of a governor or principal at the Prison Service College. As expected, this new appointment, together with the development of new initiatives for training, produced a revamped training course for prison staff. In July 1988 the initial training course was replaced by 'initial recruit training', with the first year in the Prison Service referred to as 'the training year'. The training year is divided into eight stages with eight 'core' training weeks at the College and three development training weeks at a prison. 'Core' training is defined as that 'required by all prison officers' while 'development' training is that which enables 'the recruit to operate effectively at his/her establishment'.[125] The emphasis of the new training programme is on 'interpersonal skills' with 'physical training' also given a high profile. Having initially been issued as a discussion paper, 'Custody and Care' was adopted as the 'basic source book' for initial recruit training.

Also in April 1988 the management development programme was set up in line with the needs identified in 'Custody and Care'. The College Annual Report for 1988–9 revealed the paucity of management training in the Prison Service: 'There had in fact been little or no management training for Governors in the last 5 years and virtually none at all for the ex-chief officer and principal officer grades apart from induction courses.'[126] The Annual Report commented that the most successful package delivered on the management programme was 'Action Centred Leadership and Team Briefing' which had been developed from early military training and provided by the Industrial Society. It is a package used also by Scottish police. With a one-week intensive training programme focusing on management skills and technical operations training, 600 staff 'were trained' between September 1988 and May 1989. Despite the speed of its introduction and the brevity of the course the Annual Report stated confidently that:

This quantum of training represents a significant input and all indications are that the programme is generating improved performance at all levels. It is rare that an organisation of our size has the opportunity to train all of its management staff in such a short space of time and improved communications (sic).[127]

In October 1988 a new nine-month Scottish Grade V course was introduced as a replacement for the two-year assistant governor course. Its 'new strategies' included: modularization; the Open University Business School course, The Effective Manager; an association with the University of Edinburgh (not specified); inter-agency attachment electives; outdoor development; and functional development. Finally a Higher National Certificate in prison studies was validated and introduced in 1990 with the following course structure: background to developments in Scottish penal establishments; managing penal establishments; current issues in the Scottish Prison Service; establishment communications; criminology; functional management; organizational psychology. The contract for the two-week course for training the Prison Service College staff went to Jordanhill College of Education, with 52 staff members having attended between mid-1988 and mid-1989. Reflecting the emphasis on control of disorder, the Annual Report noted that 'additional' control and restraint training was given to 140 prison staff to 'bring them up to tutor standard' and that 60 staff had attended 'management of aggression' courses, the content or details of which were not specified.

Evaluating the current initial training programme is not straightforward, but an examination of the six-week programme which represents the main bulk of core training is instructive. Training takes place over eight sessions a day five days a week; each day begins with drill and inspection. The programme opens with two sessions on the structure of the Scottish Prison Service and two sessions on its philosophy. All aspects of work in the Prison Service are given one or two sessions, with the 'new' elements (interpersonal skills, judging others, non-verbal communication, and listening) presented early in the course. The overwhelming weight of the programme, however, remains geared to regulation and control. There are a minimum four sessions per week on control and restraint and extensive sessions on: search; cell strip searches; rumour; segregation units; mechanical restraint; incident response (including hostages).

In discussing the emphasis on regulation and control the former principal of the Prison Service College reflected the dominant thinking in the Scottish Prison Service in focusing on the 'disproportionate' effect of difficult prisoners on the smooth running of prisons. He questioned whether 'psychopaths are treatable' and maintained that paramilitarism within the prison is inevitable 'otherwise prison officers eventually will be killed'.[128] He rejected the proposition that hard-line regimes or the growth of paramilitarism contributed to an intimidatory climate in which brutality occurred. This extended to prisoners' complaints of harsh treatment:

> Every prisoner could have seen the Inspector's inquiry but at the end of the day all that it came down to was that officers were wearing heavy boots on the landing or whistling on the night shift . . . the prisoners weren't able to specify what they are complaining about and if they can they can't quantify them.[129]

It is difficult to assess the impact of changes in training in the Scottish Prison Service. The 'training year' remains little more than an eight-week college-based course with the remainder of the year taken up with 'on-the-job' training under an officer-trainer. This was not what the Scottish Council for Civil Liberties had in mind when it recommended a minimum of one full year's professional training.[130] Further, the claim to have provided appropriate training for all management staff within a year of the initiative appears overstated when it is revealed that such training is restricted to a one-week course, however intensive the course might be. Ken Murray remained sceptical:

> According to the new Director 50% of the staff are made up of new men and women and this influx will bring change. But I heard all this 30 years ago. The Director considers that in ten years it will be different but the style will be fixed by then. It is not a training college but a blight on training. 'Interpersonal relations' might be the new rhetoric in training but the primary relationship is on rules and regulations taught top-down by established prison officers. Interpersonal relations says treat the person as an ordinary human being . . . but what's an ordinary human being? The prison system is largely unprofessional in terms of dealing with the real complexity of human problems. People off the street are taken on the basis of being able to read and write, then after 8 weeks they are expected to be able to deal with the most complex set of people you are ever likely to meet. This is what I mean by amateurism.[131]

34

In May 1990 the Scottish Prison Service presented its definitive document on 'new approaches' to the management of the long-term prison population.[132] Entitled *Opportunity and Responsibility*, the document opened with the 'mission statement' of the Scottish Prison Service:

> To keep in *custody* those committed to the courts;
> To maintain *good order* in each prison;
> To *care* for inmates with humanity;
> To provide all possible *opportunities* to help prisoners lead law-abiding and useful lives after release.[133]

In his Foreword to the document the Secretary of State for Scotland proclaimed a commitment to a new approach within the Scottish Prison Service rooted in the priorities established by the previous two discussion papers. He stated:

> The present document . . . addresses the specific issues of how the Scottish Prison Service should respond to the needs of the long term prisoner. A new approach is required which will recognise the mutual responsibilities of the prisoner and the prison authorities and ensure the long-term prisoner is encouraged to address his offending behaviour and offered an appropriate range of opportunities to use his time in prison responsibly for personal development . . . The key words are opportunity and responsibility. If we do not treat prisoners as responsible people, and if they are not given opportunities whilst in prison to exercise more responsible choice over their daily life, then we can hardly claim to be preparing them to live responsibly on return to society.[134]

Clearly the development of a vocabulary of liberal reformism which combines concepts such as care, opportunity and responsibility gives the broad appearance of significant forces of change within the penal system. The 'rehabilitative' ideal, however, is not new and much of the history of imprisonment has been presented within official discourses as seeking to realize the objectives of caring, therapeutic communities reforming wayward individuals and preparing them for a 'good' and 'useful' life. As has been argued, this rhetoric has been used to mask the reality of punitive, hostile and brutal regimes more concerned with control and enforced discipline than with the notions of care or opportunity.

The Scottish Prison Service, under its recently appointed Director, Peter Mackinlay, has set out its stall with an undeniable commitment to major change. While there has been some disquiet voiced by governor grades that the wind of change has blown too forcefully, too quickly, the impact of the consultation/discussion papers, the business plan, the development of training, the document *Opportunity and Responsibility* and the overhaul of managerial posts together have led to the establishment of the present corporate strategy.[135] Within this broad order of priorities the issue of long-term imprisonment has been focal. *Opportunity and Responsibility* aimed to consolidate the work on long-termers and develop ideas voiced in *Assessment and Control*. The underlying ethos is that long-term prisoners are 'responsible' individuals and require a range of opportunities for personal development.

What the document accepted was that a range of external and internal factors contributed to the crisis of the 1980s. It acknowledged that overcrowding, arbitrary policy decisions, differential application of more liberal initiatives, deterrent sentences especially for drug-related offences and changes in parole policy each have contributed to a universal tension. Further, it accepted the criticism that Peterhead contained a 'very mixed group of prisoners, including maximum security prisoners, prisoners who presented management problems, and a wider group of inadequate, often disturbed prisoners'.[136] Yet again, however, the document made claims for 'considerable improvement' in the fabric of the prison and its regimes since 1984 and made no mention of the deep grievances expressed by prisoners concerning the regime and its operation since that date.

Following the last serious phase of protest at Peterhead it was agreed that 60 prisoners who were considered to pose the most serious management problem for the Prison Service should be held at Peterhead. By 1989, 125 prisoners were held in Scottish prisons under Rule 36, thereby removed from normal circulation. Forty-seven of these were at Peterhead. The estimated figure of the most 'disruptive' category for 1990 was forty. The following passage illustrates well the 'new approach' of the Scottish Prison Service:

The message gradually got through to most of these prisoners that whilst the prison authorities did not wish to impose such conditions longer than was necessary, we were prepared to do so until such time as good order was restored. Given this structure, the vast majority of prisoners have shown a willingness to respond positively. The remainder are constantly encouraged to behave. For the small number who are actively disruptive the option of Peterhead remains available.[137]

With other prisons encouraged to manage 'disruptive' prisoners within their own walls, often in purpose-converted small units, Peterhead's role as the sole regime dealing with those prisoners so categorized was reduced. Yet it is still offered as the 'end of the line' for those who *choose* its regime as an *option*. Again the assumption remains that 'disruptive' prisoners are a minority given every opportunity to benefit from enlightened regimes but who, presumably pathologically, opt for Peterhead.

While the document committed the Scottish prison system to the development of initiatives based on small-scale regimes for long-termers including Peterhead, it also welcomed the use of Peterhead for prisoners who 'have to be kept apart from other prisoners for their own safety'. A separate hall, with a capacity of 60 cells, was assigned to such prisoners, mainly sex offenders. As with the presentation of the 'disruptive' so then also with the presentation of the 'inadequate':

All are in open association and enjoy a normal prison regime which includes work, education, physical education and recreation. One consequence of dealing with groups of prisoners in a discrete way is that direct attention can now be given to the development of courses and regimes, both for individuals and groups of prisoners, which address the various problems which they may have in relation to their various offences and their personalities.[138]

The withdrawal of prisoners from mainstream prison life for their protection accepts the reality that because of their offences or because of the sexuality ascribed to them they are vulnerable to often vicious attacks. Given the constitution of prisons at present, it is clear that open association would place these prisoners at considerable risk. Scotland's approach, however, is in danger of developing an allocation policy which legitimates and reinforces their marginalization. Clearly this is an important debate in itself. The choice of Peterhead, with its history of ghettoization and its physical as well as symbolic isolation, appears to be wholly inappropriate. There is less than subtle irony in a prison which functions to house those prisoners labelled the 'most violent', the 'serious disruptives' alongside, but separate from, those identified as being the most in need of protection. First indications are that those allocated to Peterhead for protection are relieved to escape the tension and pressure of the main prison system. Criticisms over the fabric and location of the prison, however, remain.

Opportunity and Responsibility developed a new commitment to smaller regimes now fundamental to the corporate strategy of the Scottish Prison Service. This strategy withdrew support for the 60-place maximum security unit at Shotts prison proposed in the earlier discussion paper and asserted the case for small-scale specialist regimes as follows:

> The move towards smaller regimes within the mainstream will have a number of advantages including: greater flexibility to accommodate the needs of the Service at any point in time; greater flexibility to accommodate the changing needs of smaller groups of prisoners with similar problems; greater opportunity for inter-personal relationships between prisoners (it is clearly very difficult for staff to develop relationships of trust and support when they are handling large groups of prisoners); greater opportunity for prisoners to feel that the system has given personal recognition to them and to their problems.[139]

With new small units opened at Perth (August 1989) and Shotts (April 1990) in addition to the Barlinnie special unit and the renamed Peterhead E Hall (1988) five objectives were adopted to establish a 'common thread' for the two distinct traditions of 'segregation' and 'community-based' units. These were:

1 To provide an additional option for the location of prisoners who present management problems, or the potential for management problems, within the mainstream prison system;
2 To hold such prisoners securely;
3 To provide a range of additional opportunities geared to the personal development of such prisoners within a small, supportive environment;
4 To return prisoners to the mainstream better able to cope and to make progress towards release;

5 To provide settings within which it is possible to test the relationship between prisoners and prison officers, from which lessons may be drawn for the mainstream of the prison system. [140]

Despite the liberal, progressive vocabulary of the new strategy, there remained the problem within the long historical tradition of imprisonment concerning the dichotomy between control/restraint and treatment/rehabilitation, as well as questions concerning prisoners' rights and institutional accountability.

Just — CONCLUSION
mention here

This extensive introduction to the Peterhead case study has sought to locate prisoner protest and the persistent disturbances at the prison within the broader social, historical and political contexts of imprisonment in Scotland. While it is clear that prison protests take on a range of manifestations, involve varying degrees of 'violence' and occur for quite diverse reasons, there has been a consistency and gradual escalation in the Scottish protests. Essentially much of the aggravation has arisen from prisoners' collective responses to harsh regimes and an inflexible occupational culture which prevail in the operational policies and practices of the Scottish prison system. Inevitably considerable pressure has come from long-term prisoners whose frustrations and anger over petty and serious matters build up and eventually come to a head around a specific incident or grievance. The incidents of 1986–7 were the worst and most violent confrontations in recent penal history. They reflect the deep feelings of brutalization and alienation endured by long-term prisoners in institutions universally condemned for their conditions and staff–prisoner relations. Yet, as has been shown, the Scottish prison department appears to be unmoved by this recent catalogue of human misery, personal despair and violent reaction.

It is clear from the preceding discussion that the optimism of 1973, when the 'cages' were closed and the Barlinnie special unit was opened, was short-lived. Here, at least, was a major initiative with the potential to shift penal philosophy away from its punitive and authoritarian legacy. The analysis presented traces the historical roots of that legacy and reveals the long-term emergence of the disciplinary regime at Peterhead. The special unit turned that tradition on its head. It is some measure of its direct contrast to the Scottish penal legacy that its heaviest criticism and resistance came from within the occupational culture of prison officers. This underpinned the continual political and media criticism of the special unit and it was direct pressure from the Scottish Prison Officers' Association which brought the reopening of the 'cages' in 1978. [141] Consequently the Scottish prison department's commitment to traditional, punitive methods of containment and regulation was reaffirmed.

In its *General Assessment* of Peterhead in 1981 Her Majesty's Inspectorate of Prisons for Scotland returned to well-worn themes:

Despite its considerable problems, Peterhead is an orderly and well-organised prison in which staff and inmates have apparently established a *modus vivendi* which is acceptable to both and appropriate to the long-term population . . . Peterhead has an ethos all of its own which finds favour with the majority of staff and inmates who respectively assured the Inspectors that they wished to serve and complete their sentences at this establishment. There is however a small number of inmates who are prepared to create serious trouble . . . and who are not deterred from aggressive, disruptive and violent behaviour.[142]

Overall the Inspectorate found the prison to be satisfactory and argued that there was no overcrowding in the prison, stating that it was 'understandable' why so many long-termers 'prefer' to serve their sentences at Peterhead. The 1985 inspection, in the wake of the 'first round' of major disturbances, affirmed the assessments of the 1981 inspection particularly with regard to 'the attitude of the inmates and the conduct of the staff'.[143] Again the conclusion was that 'attacks on the staff' were indications of a 'certain minority of inmates, some of whom are encouraged by the attention of the media and the support and interests of external agencies'.[144]

The 'official version' of events has never wavered from its dominant theme that a small group of violent men, unable to handle their long-term sentences, reach the 'end of the road'. Peterhead became the end of the road and so the pathological violence of embittered individuals was pitted against the system and turned against its officers and its fabric. Other prisoners became involved either as opportunists or as weaker individuals intimidated by the core of hard men. According to this version the regime was essentially fair, just and acceptable to the majority of prisoners. The protesters were the violent minority which would have caused trouble in *any* system and as the language of protest is that of violence the response had to be punitive. In 1985 the Inspectorate added two further dimensions to this well-worn 'analysis': the influence of a critical press and the existence of unspecified groups intent on pursuing their 'own' interests. The Chief Inspector's 1988 report reflected the official position:

> The rapid changes in the population that followed, coupled with commend-able efforts to establish open/liberal regimes – which were sadly subjected to abuse – led to some loss of control, with a small number of the most anti-authority prisoners then able to exert undue influence. . . .
>
> The discussion paper 'Assessment and Control' also reviews the main reason for disruptive behaviour, putting most emphasis on the activities of individuals as a prime cause.[145]

While the 1988 report declined to involve itself in any discussion of 'root causes' of unrest and attempted to concern itself with practical suggestions to improve conditions, the two 1988 discussion papers confirmed a commitment to the identification and management of the 'disruptive and violent' minority. These initiatives have become the primary guidelines in establishing policy priorities via the corporate strategy plan for the 1990s. In meeting the growing criticism of the ineffective management of establishments and the inadequate training of prison staff, the revamped training programme and the commitment to small-scale regimes represent, at first sight, a new departure. The discussion above, however, demonstrates the real inadequacy of management training programmes which run for one week and the paucity of effective training for newly recruited officers. The occupational culture, so firmly entrenched in the Scottish Prison Service tradition, adopts and incorporates the language of 'self-realization' and 'awareness training' but there is little evidence that it is anything more than rhetoric.

Against the recurrent and well-worn themes contained in internal reports and inquiries, discussion papers and statements from Scotland's Secretary of State, there has been a mass of evidence from Scottish Prison Officers' Association members, home affairs correspondents of the quality press, independent researchers and penologists, campaign groups (especially the Scottish Council for Civil Liberties) and even successive government ministers that there were serious institutional problems with the Peterhead regime and, more broadly, with Scottish sentencing and penal policy. In addition, there are the voices of the prisoners who in significant numbers have condemned the poor living and working conditions, the brutality of certain staff, the excessive use of punishment and the secrecy and non-accountability of the regime. The level of political pressure from *within* Peterhead's walls involving letters and statements, as well as protests, served warning on the authorities that they are dealing with large numbers of prisoners who refused to be marginalized as a 'violent minority'. As with all other evidence, it was a warning the authorities chose to ignore.

NOTES

1. Letter from Jimmy Boyle, co-director of the Gateway Exchange, to Malcolm Rifkind, Secretary of State for Scotland, 23 February 1987.
2. S. Cohen and L. Taylor, *Psychological Survival*, Harmondsworth, Penguin, 1972.
3. M. Fitzgerald, *Prisoners in Revolt*, Harmondsworth, Penguin, 1977; D. Mac-Donald and J. Sim, *Scottish Prisons and the Special Unit*, Glasgow, Scottish Council for Civil Liberties, 1978; M. Fitzgerald and J. Sim, *British Prisons*, Oxford, Blackwell, 1982.
4. I. Cameron, 'Life in the Balance: The Case of Frank Marritt' in P. Scraton and P. Gordon (eds), *Causes for Concern*, Harmondsworth, Penguin, 1984.
5. B. Rolston and M. Tomlinson, 'Long-term Imprisonment in Northern Ireland: Psychological or Political Survival?' in B. Rolston and M. Tomlinson (eds), *The Expansion of European Prison Systems*, Working Papers in European Criminology, no. 7 (1986).
6. See various editions of *The Abolitionist: The Journal of Radical Alternatives to Prison*; A. Mandaraka-Sheppard, *The Dynamics of Aggression in Women's Prisons in England*, Aldershot, Gower, 1986.
7. J. Boyle, *A Sense of Freedom*, Edinburgh, Canongate, 1977; B. Sands, *One Day in My Life*, London, Pluto, 1983; P. Adams and S. Cooklin, *Knockback*, 1984; P. Carlen *et al. Criminal Women*, Cambridge, Polity, 1985; Ain and Eibhlin Nic Giolla Easpaig, *Sister in Cells*, Westport, F.N.T., 1987.

8. R. King and K. Elliot, *Albany: Birth of a Prison: End of an Era*, London, Routledge and Kegan Paul, 1977, p. 3.
9. For a more fully developed discussion of this work see: J. Sim, P. Scraton and P. Gordon, 'Crime, the State and Critical Analysis' in P. Scraton (ed.), *Law, Order and the Authoritarian State*, Milton Keynes, Open University Press, 1987.
10. Fitzgerald, *Prisoners in Revolt*.
11. P. Scraton and K. Chadwick, *In the Arms of the Law: Coroners' Inquests and Deaths in Custody*, London, Pluto, 1987.
12. Fitzgerald and Sim, *British Prisons*, ch. 4; J. Sim, 'The Fire from Below: Prisons in Scotland', *The Abolitionist*, no. 23 (1987), pp. 28–30.
13. Home Office, *Managing the Long-term Prison System: The Report of the Control Review Committee*, HMSO, 1984.
14. Fitzgerald and Sim, *British Prisons*. It should be noted that this is the explanation for disturbances in *men's* prisons. Women prisoners react very differently to the pain of confinement. It is an area in which far more research needs to be conducted. See Carlen *et al.*, *Criminal Women*.
15. S. Chibnall, *Law and Order News*, London, Tavistock, 1977; M. Hollingsworth, *The Press and Political Dissent*, London, Pluto, 1987. See Chapter 5 of this book.
16. See Hollingsworth, *The Press*; J. Pilger, *Heroes*, London, Pan, 1987, ch. 11.
17. S. Hobhouse and A. F. Brockway, *English Prisons Today*, London, Frank Cass, 1922.
18. Prison Medical Reform Council, *Prisoners' Circle*, London, PMRC, 1943; Prison Medical Reform Council, *The Case of Prisoner Alpha*, London, PMRC, 1945.
19. National Prisoners' Movement, *Don't Mark His Face*, London, NPM, 1979.
20. Bethnal Green and Stepney Trades Council, *Blood on the Streets*, London, BGSTC, 1978.
21. National Council for Civil Liberties, *Southall: 23 April 1979: The Report of the Unofficial Committee of Inquiry*, London, NCCL, 1980.
22. Manchester City Council, *Leon Brittan's Visit to Manchester University Students' Union, 1st March 1985: Report of the Independent Inquiry Panel*, Manchester City Council, 1985.
23. West Midlands County Council, *A Different Reality: Report of the Review Panel*, Birmingham, West Midlands County Council, 1986.
24. Haringey Council, *The Broadwater Farm Inquiry*, London, Haringey Council, 1986; Haringey Council, *Broadwater Farm Revisited*, London, Karia Press, 1989.
25. Roach Family Support Committee, *Policing in Hackney 1945–1984*, London, Karia Press/RFSC, 1989.
26. Lord Gifford QC, Brown, W. and Bundy, R., *Loosen the Shackles: First Report of the Liverpool 8 Inquiry into Race Relations in Liverpool*, London, Karia Press, 1989.
27. Ibid., p. 5.
28. Letter from Jimmy Boyle which accompanied the issue of questionnaires to prisoners, 5 February 1987.
29. R. King, 'Control in Prisons' in M. Maguire, J. Vagg and R. Morgan (eds), *Accountability and Prisons*, London, Tavistock, 1987, p. 184 (emphasis in original).
30. Cited in J. Cameron, *Prisons and Punishment in Scotland: From the Middle Ages to the Present*, Edinburgh, Canongate Press, 1983, pp. 153–4.
31. Ibid., p. 154.
32. Ibid., p. 155.
33. HM Inspectorate of Prisons (Scotland), *Report on HM Prison, Peterhead*, Scottish Home and Health Department, 1981, p. 5.

34. Ibid., p. 5.
35. Ibid.
36. Scottish Home and Health Department, *Prisons in Scotland Report for 1985*, HMSO, 1986, p. 22.
37. Written reply from Lord James Douglas-Hamilton, Scottish Office, to House of Commons Request by Robert Maclennan MP, 22 July 1987.
38. HM Inspectorate of Prisons (Scotland), *Peterhead*, p. 8.
39. Home Office, *Managing the Long-Term Prison System*, pp. 63–8.
40. Scottish Home and Health Department, *Prisons in Scotland Report for 1966*, Cmnd 3319, HMSO, 1966, p. 5.
41. Ibid., p. 6.
42. Ibid.
43. Ibid.
44. Ibid., p. 7
45. S. Cohen, *Visions of Social Control*, Cambridge, Polity, 1985, p. 194.
46. Scottish Office, *Report for 1969 – Parole Board for Scotland*, HMSO, pp. 7–17.
47. Boyle, *A Sense of Freedom*.
48. J. McMillan, 'Some Notes and Observations on the Prison Subculture', unpublished, 1971, p. 2.
49. MacDonald and Sim, *Scottish Prisons and the Special Unit*, p. 11.
50. Scottish Office Working Party, *Treatment of Certain Male Long-term Prisoners and Potentially Violent Prisoners*, Scottish Office, 1971.
51. MacDonald and Sim, *Scottish Prisons and the Special Unit*, p. 10.
52. SCCL interview held at HM Prison, Peterhead, 4 April 1979.
53. *Daily Record*, 11 May 1979.
54. *Glasgow Herald*, 22 August 1979.
55. *The Scotsman*, 23 August 1979.
56. *Glasgow Herald*, 22 August 1979.
57. *Daily Record*, 22 August 1979.
58. *The Scotsman*, 4 September 1979; *Glasgow Herald*, 4 September 1979.
59. *The Abolitionist*, no. 4 (1979).
60. Letter from W. S. Ellis in *Evening Times*, 27 September 1979.
61. Statement by Francis Mullen reported in *The Scotsman*, 6 June 1980.
62. Resolution published in the *Glasgow Herald*, 30 June 1980.
63. Letter from Alan Wardlow, *Newsline*, 25 May 1982.
64. Letter from Sarah Bryan, *The Scotsman*, 22 May 1982.
65. *The Guardian*, 6 November 1982.
66. Letter to the *Glasgow Herald*, 17 January 1983.
67. Written answer from Mr Michael Ancram, *Hansard*, 19 January 1984.
68. Reply to Michael Ancram's statement in *The Scotsman*, 9 February 1984.
69. *The Scotsman*, 5 March 1984.
70. *The Scotsman*, 19 July 1984.
71. *Glasgow Herald*, 9 July 1984.
72. Statement by Mr Michael Ancram, *Hansard*, 10 December 1984.
73. Statement by Gary McMenamin, reported in *The Scotsman*, 9 December 1985.
74. *Glasgow Herald*, 7 May 1986.
75. Statement reported in the *Glasgow Herald*, 15 October 1986.
76. 'Battle to Keep Lid on Simmering Prison', *Glasgow Herald*, 15 October 1986.
77. Submission by John Smith read by Mr Donald Robertson QC, Defence Counsel, High Court, Peterhead, 4 March 1987.

78. Statement to the Court by Mr Colin MacAuley, Advocate-Depute, reported in *The Scotsman*, 5 March 1987.
79. *The Scotsman*, 27 February 1987.
80. *The Scotsman*, 3 March 1987.
81. See T. Wicker, *A Time to Die: The Attica Prison Revolt*, New York, Bodley Head, 1975.
82. *Daily Record*, 1 October 1987.
83. Ibid.
84. *Daily Record*, 4 October 1987.
85. *The Guardian*, 5 October 1987.
86. Ibid.
87. *Daily Record*, 6 October 1987.
88. *The Guardian*, 6 October 1987.
89. *Glasgow Herald*, 5 October 1987.
90. *The Independent*, 7 October 1987.
91. Malcolm Rifkind, interviewed on BBC Radio Scotland, 6 October 1987.
92. Reported in *Daily Record*, 6 October 1987.
93. *Daily Record*, 6 October 1987.
94. Quoted in *Sunday Mail*, 4 October 1987.
95. J. E. Thomas, 'Prisons: A System under Siege', *The Independent*, 6 October 1987.
96. K. Murray, 'Fear and Loathing in Our Prisons', *The Scotsman*, 12 January 1987.
97. Quoted in *The Guardian*, 5 October 1987.
98. 'Reform Vital' (editorial), *Glasgow Herald*, 5 October 1987.
99. 'Prison Inquiry is Unavoidable' (editorial), *The Scotsman*, 1 October 1987.
100. 'Need to Look into Prisons' (editorial), *The Independent*, 6 October 1987.
101. 'Scotland's Prison System' (editorial), *The Guardian*, 6 October 1987.
102. Malcolm Rifkind, Secretary of State for Scotland, reported in the *Glasgow Herald*, 6 October 1987.
103. Scottish Office, *'Custody and Care': Policy and Planning for the Scottish Prison Service*, Scottish Office, March 1988.
104. Speech to representatives of the Scottish Prison Service, 25 January 1988, Circular No. 20/88 (Miscellaneous).
105. Lord James Douglas-Hamilton, Minister for Home Affairs and the Environment, in the Foreword to Scottish Office, *'Custody and Care'*.
106. Scottish Prison Service, *Assessment and Control: The Management of Violent and Disruptive Prisoners*, a Discussion Paper, Scottish Office, October 1988.
107. Lord James Douglas-Hamilton, in the Foreword to ibid.
108. Scottish Office, *'Custody and Care'*, para. 1.1.
109. Ibid., para. 1.4.
110. Ibid., para. 2.3.
111. Ibid., para. 2.6.
112. Ibid., para. 2.7.
113. Scottish Prison Service, *Assessment and Control*, para. 1.2.
114. Ibid., para. 2.5.1.
115. Ibid., para. 2.5.2.
116. Ibid., para. 2.5.3.
117. Ibid., para. 2.11.
118. Ibid., para. 2.12.
119. Ibid., para. 2.13.
120. *The Scotsman*, 26 August 1988.

121. R. Wishart, 'Struggle to Contain the Hardmen', *The Scotsman*, 12 August 1988, pp. 12–13.
122. Ibid., p. 12.
123. *The Scotsman*, 10 January 1989.
124. See A. Hutchinson, Exclusive Report, 'How a war was won and a career lost', *The Scotsman*, 2 December 1989.
125. Scottish Prison Service College, *Annual Report 1988–89*, p. 10.
126. Ibid., p. 13.
127. Ibid., p. 14.
128. Interview with Mr M. J. Milne, Principal, Prison Service College, June 1989.
129. Ibid.
130. Scottish Council for Civil Liberties, *Facing Reality: The Scottish Prisons Crisis in the 1980s*, Glasgow, SCCL, 1987.
131. Ken Murray, personal interview, June 1989.
132. Scottish Prison Service, *Opportunity and Responsibility: Developing new approaches to the Management of the Long Term Prison System in Scotland*, Scottish Prison Service/HMSO, May 1990.
133. Ibid. p. 2.
134. Rt Hon. Malcolm Rifkind MP, in the Foreword to ibid., p. 4.
135. Scottish Prison Service, *Corporate Strategy for the Scottish Prison Service*, Scottish Prison Service/HMSO, November 1990.
136. Scottish Prison Service, *Opportunity and Responsibility*, p. 21.
137. Ibid. p. 24.
138. Ibid. p. 52.
139. Ibid., pp. 50–1.
140. Ibid., p. 59.
141. See M. Fitzgerald and J. Sim, *British Prisons*, 2nd edn, Oxford, Blackwell, 1982.
142. HM Inspectorate of Prisons (Scotland), *Report on HM Prison Peterhead 1981*, paras 2.2–2.3, p. 3.
143. HM Inspectorate of Prisons (Scotland), *Report on HM Prison Peterhead 1985*, para. 2.6, p. 3.
144. Ibid. para. 6.4, pp. 7–8.
145. HM Inspector of Prisons (Scotland), *Report for 1988*, HMSO, September 1989, paras 3.1 and 7.1.

CHAPTER 2

Inside the machine

Prison in Scotland is like living in a place time forgot.

... the High Court Judge sentenced me to life imprisonment. I don't recall him saying anything about being kept in abject poverty in a filthy, condemned slum.[1]

The previous chapter indicated how official explanations of disorder in prisons have ignored the centrality and influence of the material context in which disturbances occur. These reductionist explanations are located within parameters which describe the determinants of social action in relation to physiological or psychological factors which propel some of the confined into confronting the system. Much of the research conducted within state (and other) institutions in the United Kingdom has been built around these parameters, closely associated with the search for the Holy Grail of criminological endeavour: *the* cause of crime.

This chapter provides an alternative analysis to such managerial reductionism. It focuses on the environment and culture within which the disturbances in Peterhead took place. In particular, it analyses the quality of life within the institution and illustrates how the meaning of protest was structured by the prisoners' experience of Peterhead's environment. There are three dimensions to this experience which are central to the analysis: the physical condition of the prison; personal autonomy and privacy; and the relationship between prisoners and prison officers. For the purpose of the argument each dimension has been separated out. From the perspective of the confined they are not mutually exclusive but are inextricably woven into a disciplinary web which has a profound and deleterious effect on their consciousness.

THE DISCIPLINARY ENVIRONMENT

Peterhead is unique among the institutions for male long-term prisoners in the United Kingdom. This uniqueness is embodied in the abject nature of its architecture and environment. While there has been widespread and vociferous condemnation of the appalling conditions inflicted on those in the remand and local prisons[2] it is often forgotten that the confined in Peterhead live, work, eat, sleep and, on occasion, die in conditions that are comparable to the worst in the short-term system. Prisoners, therefore, are confronted not only with the psychological impact of serving long sentences but also with the added pain of enduring confinement in circumstances that are both primitive and humiliating.

In addition, the institution operates within a set of ideologies, policies and practices which were established and consolidated in the first three decades of the nineteenth century.[3] Central to these practices was the concept of 'less eligibility' which maintained that the criminal and the destitute should be subject to institutional regimes which were punitive, harsh and humiliating. Comfort, safety and satisfaction were to have no place within the daily programmes that operated in prisons and workhouses. In the words of Sir Walter Scott, 'they should be a place of punishment and that can hardly be if men are lodged better and fed better than when they are at large'.[4]

This ideology has endured into the twentieth century. It underpins official and managerial discourses while simultaneously permeating popular attitudes in the wider society. It ensures that prison regimes continue to be built on the twin pillars of discipline and regulation. Punishment for the confined therefore extends beyond the deprivation of liberty. Physical degradation and psychological fragmentation are central and inescapable features of their lives. For those imprisoned in Peterhead in 1986 the daily routine provides a clear illustration of the degrading nature of the regime.

HYGIENE AND SANITATION

The day in Peterhead began at 6.00 a.m. when the cells were unlocked. As there was no fixed sanitation the first task of the prisoners was to slop out the urine and faeces from the small, plastic pots which served as toilets. The unhygienic nature of this operation, and the smell and stench which accompanied it, was compounded by the lack of facilities for personal ablutions. Up to 40 prisoners shared two wash-hand basins and two showers. They were restricted to one shower each week.

Through pressure and age the drains were often blocked. In the words of one prisoner they tended 'to overflow and stink'. Ventilation was equally poor. The air vents contained dead pigeons. When alive they 'fly about the hall and their droppings tend to fall everywhere, sometimes in the food'. As another prisoner pointed out, 'Peterhead prison stinks (literally) – you always have the feeling of being dirty'.

The physical degradation was reinforced by the uniforms, which were ill-fitting and uncomfortable. The lighting and heating facilities turned the disciplinary screw still further. Lighting in the cells was poor. This caused headaches and eye problems. Prisoners had no control of the lights as the switches were located outside the cell doors. As with children, having a light on or off was left to the discretion of others. The heating system was similarly regressive. In winter, because of the severe cold, the prisoners slept in their uniforms:

> *The cell block – cold filthy blankets, cell ventilation shafts – lack of fresh air, windowless – steel plates with drilled holes to allow for daylight poor lighting.*

> *I have, on occasions, been so cold in the cell block, I wouldn't even write a letter without my hand turning blue. I have to keep moving at all times.*

The bleak winter weather also ensured that they had no respite from the cells and landings of the dingy prison halls. The Chief Inspector of Scottish Prisons noted in his report on the disturbances that because of 'security reasons prisoners do not go to the remote workshops in darkness, nor in conditions of poor visibility'.[5] This situation was compounded by the prison timetable. They were locked up at 9.00 p.m. on weekdays and 5.00 p.m. on weekends. Enforced boredom and withering isolation were therefore central to their everyday lives.

The solitude and isolation was particularly intense for those in segregation. They were confined in the punishment cells for 23 hours a day, the only physical movement being slopping out, washing and exercise. No association was permitted. Heavy steel plates were fitted across the window spaces in five of the 16 punishment cells. They were ventilated by holes which had been drilled in the plates but, as the Chief Inspector indicated, 'natural light is very restricted. Artificial light is provided by a recessed light above the door but is barely adequate to allow serious reading'.[6] For one prisoner the time in segregation was spent *'wall climbing, pacing, brooding, reading, writing and radio'*.

This is the material context in which the majority of Peterhead prisoners served their sentences. Dirt, stench and squalor were embedded in the prison's architecture, uniforms and hygienic rituals. It was also the context in which the prisoners demonstrated. As one commented:

> *There will always be trouble at Peterhead and other prisons unless the Government radically changes its policy of wanting to give out 'American-type' sentences but only wants to pay for 'Russian-type conditions'.*

AUTONOMY, PRIVACY AND REGULATION

The appalling conditions were not the only legacy of the nineteenth century. The prison timetable also reflected wider concerns with order, regularity and discipline. Nineteenth-century prison managers saw the timetable as an important mechanism for instilling discipline into a population whose criminality indicated that they lacked the moral fibre to live respectable lives. The contemporary prison timetable in Peterhead was still built around regularity and order with a set routine of counting and movement between wings and workshops. It operated as follows.[7]

6.00 a.m.	Cells unlocked, prisoners slop out, make their requests to see the doctor, social worker or governor. Breakfast.
9.00–9.15 a.m.	Prisoners counted and escorted to workshops (weather permitting).
11.30 a.m.	Lunch locked in their cells (except for C Hall who dine in association).
1.00–2.00 p.m.	Exercise (weather permitting).
2.00–2.15 p.m.	Gather in prison yard, counted and escorted to workshops.
4.30 p.m.	Return from workshops, eat alone in cells.
5.00–6.15 p.m.	Locked in cells.
6.15–8.45 p.m.	Recreation on each weekday evening except for one night when prisoners have a shower or a bath.
8.45–9.00 p.m.	Tea, which consists of a mug of tea and a bun.
9.00 p.m.	Lock-up.
10.15–10.45 p.m.	Lights out.

While the general routine applied to the majority of prisoners there are several important qualifications. First, there were groups of prisoners to whom the routine did not apply. Prisoners in segregation, as noted above, were locked up for 23 hours. They were allowed one hour's exercise which could be abandoned if the weather was bad. Second, those in the hospital wing also followed a different routine because of illness. Finally, the general timetable only applied during the week. At weekends the prisoners were locked up at 5.00 p.m. This left them to endure long hours alone at precisely the time when those on the outside (and they themselves when free) engaged in collective socializing. For many in Peterhead these hours, built on both memories and yearning, could be the most painful of all.

The fixed rigidity of the timetable was designed to have a psychological effect on the prisoners. Through the sentence of the courts they had relinquished the power to determine the direction of their lives. They were no longer autonomous individuals exercising personal responsibility, with decision-making reduced to the barest minimum. They had become the property of the state.

One of the most profound psychological dimensions in this process related to the issue of privacy. Living and working in a highly regulated, closely monitored world left little scope for personal privacy or intimate moments. Rather, as the accounts below make clear, it reinforced a brooding introspection further alienating individuals who had already been damaged by their previous institutional experiences.

The nature of the regime ensured that they were kept under constant surveillance both by prison officers and high security cameras, which were connected to a central control room. This was legitimated by the concern for security and meant that privacy was minimal. Every activity from defecation and urination to family visits and letter-writing was scrutinized by the state.

48

Through these techniques information was collected, personal files constructed, prisoners were atomized and the power of the institution reinforced:

(Illegal) prolonged periods of solitary confinement (years) regular cell searches without my presence, sensitive confidential legal files searched, seized, disrupted and confused. Strip searches, perverts peeking in every half hour reading my mail, reading my wife's mail, my solicitor's mail, watching me have my weekly shower, having a crap . . . refusing private interviews with my solicitor, searching his baggage and person, rifling documents etc. etc. etc. etc. etc. etc.

I was very ill last year and spent 5 days in bed. There was no privacy as staff continuously opened my door. I really ought to have been in hospital for a few days but it wouldn't have made much difference because there is not much privacy over there either. I don't think there is such a thing as privacy in Peterhead — not even in the toilet! Privacy is from 9.00 p.m. until 6.00 a.m. only, when I am locked up for the night and the staff go off duty.

There are too many people living in too small a space and screws have the right to enter your cell and search through personal property, all in the name of security . . . The only privacy I have is when I am locked up behind my door at night. You can't even have privacy when using the toilet or having a shower or a visit.

There is a camera on us twenty-four hours a day. Everywhere we go, there is always a member of staff watching us. We have to undergo searches nearly every day, strip searches and rub-downs.

Solitude was therefore at a premium. Prisoners were unable to withdraw to places where they could either be alone or anonymous. They were scrutinized continually by the technological and human gaze of the state and by their fellow prisoners. This, in turn, left no room for intimacy and the development of what Stan Cohen and Laurie Taylor have called the 'maximum personal affinity' between two or more people:[8]

At times when things get on top of me, I could be doing with some place quiet to go to by myself to get my head squared up. Quietness is hard to find in prison.

When you really need time on your own, you can never be alone at all, anywhere.

All WC doors, shower doors are of the half-cut type, with a two foot gap at the bottom and are so low anybody walking by can see right over the top.

Lack of privacy causes stress . . . There's the deep-down feeling that it's all deliberate.

The state's intrusion was particularly intense for those on Category A, the highest security classification. They were subjected to a rigorous regime which included: the strict regulation of every movement by prison officers; the use of a log-book to enter, date and time these movements; the vetting of visitors by the police; the denial of education classes, trade training courses and recreation facilities; the removal of uniforms for the night; and the use of cells in which the light burned throughout the night. Finally, they could not be released without being reclassified:

> For the past three years, four months, I have had my light on in the cell twenty-four hours and have a prison officer specifically assigned to monitor my movements and restrict my movements at his discretion.

> Cell searches – different staff each week, going through my personal belongings. Embarrassment! And every hour the warden checks my cell, with me being an escapee, also my light is left on all night.

> Searches sometimes nine times a day. They just barge into your cell or look through the spy-hole. I suffer more because, for some reason known to no-one, I am a security prisoner.

The psychological balance of the prisoners was also affected by violence and intimidation. This is discussed more fully in the next chapter. For the moment it is important to recognize how fear for their own safety led to continuous stress and tension and diminished the quality of their everyday lives. This fear could be generated by the behaviour of prison staff:

> At any time you can be dragged to the cells and placed on Rule 39 . . . They could do anything to you without anyone knowing. You feel totally helpless.

Personal threats and actual assaults from other inmates compounded their insecurity. The prisoners were clear, however, that the roots of the violence lay in the mistrust and paranoia generated by the institution:

> One is always wary of other prisoners, even friends. They can snap under the pressure any time. You have to tread softly with staff as they can, and do, what they like with no come-backs. An assault here or a report there. When there is the first sign of trouble, they run out of the hall, lock you in, refuse to let you out.

> No-one gives a damn about anyone else, so how can one feel safe?

> Due to the last riot, prison officers ran from 'A' Hall and left us to be subjected to threats of violence from other prisoners. How can you feel safe with so much tension and paranoia about you?

> There is an atmosphere of stress so strong . . . that one can almost feel it physically . . . trouble is likely to flare up spontaneously as prisoners are under constant mental pressure.

The combination of squalor, boredom, lack of privacy and fear thus ensured that the everyday experience of the confined in Peterhead was both physically uncomfortable and psychologically damaging. Life in the prison wings was built around this disturbing and detrimental combination. In other parts of the prison, the same processes also operated. Those who left the wings to labour in the workshops were confronted by an equally regressive regime built on discipline and subservient to the wider demands of security and control.

WORK

Prisoners in Scotland are compelled to work. Individuals are excused work only on medical grounds approved by the prison doctor. If they refuse to labour or are idle, careless or negligent at work, they are punished. In 1987, 2357 women and men in Scottish prisons were punished for disobedience and refusing to work.[9] Just under one-third of the respondents to the Peterhead survey were not engaged in work.

When transferred to Peterhead prisoners were placed in a work party by the Induction Board. Changes in the work parties were considered by the Labour Allocation Board at its weekly meeting. The main industries in the prison were woodwork, ropework and tailoring/textile work and some work in the small laundry. Prisoners' responses, however, presented the reality of these 'industrial' vocations when asked what they did (for example, *'tearing foam for soft toys'*). Other work included 'passmen' (cleaning), various jobs in the cookhouse, painting and basic joinery. A vocational training course was running at the prison and one prisoner in the survey had taken it and commented that it was *'interesting'*. Another prisoner stated: *'there is a vocational training course but it is limited to a very few. It is finishing at the end of the year'*. When the Chief Inspector of Prisons visited the prison in 1986 he found that the industries were working below capacity. This was due to the 'reduced prisoner population and the high demand for service work elsewhere in the prison'. There was also 'a serious shortage of instructors'.[10] Prisoners overwhelmingly condemned Peterhead's work and wage structure. The work was restricted to boring, unchallenging and alienating tasks which allowed no potential for personal development and made no contribution to securing a reasonably paid job on release. The boring nature of the work contributed strongly to the perception that prisoners were vegetating in an atmosphere which encouraged neither initiative nor creativity:

> *My first 3½ years were spent bored to near insanity in a workshop that had no work to offer.*

> *I sew hems on jackets . . . it's really soul destroying to look at blank faces all day.*

Cohen and Taylor have suggested that long-term prisoners face a double burden in relation to work in prison. Not only are the tasks uncreative and unchallenging but even if the jobs were interesting,

> work for a life prisoner has a very peculiar status indeed, if factory workers

have to desperately invest jobs with meanings and time markers, then prisoners without clear meanings or time markers have to find them in the work they are given.[11]

For Cohen and Taylor the absurdity of work on their security wing was 'perhaps most neatly illustrated by the fact that what is a "job" in one wing – making soft toys – is offered as a hobby in another'.[12] The jobs on offer at Peterhead were equally absurd. They bore no relation to the conditions and expectations with which the men would be confronted in the wider labour market. Many spent the time sweeping floors, cleaning, painting the cells and halls, and cooking. In the tailor's shop they sewed buttons, stitched pockets onto jackets and made buttonholes. The overall response was summed up by the comment that all work on offer was no more than *demeaning slave labour'*.

In winter the working day was restricted to three or four hours. The wage structure reinforced prisoners' despair about the working environment. Wages averaged £3 per week, a sum they felt was both exploitative and humiliating. It gave them little opportunity either to save for their release, send money to relatives or buy goods within the prison. None of the prisoners considered the wages paid to be 'excellent' or 'good'. The replies were divided beween 'poor' (44 per cent) and 'awful' (56 per cent). Several prisoners considered the derisory pay to be *'humiliating'*. Their views are supported by official figures which reveal the low priority accorded by the Scottish Office to providing adequate and humane remuneration for physical labour. In 1987, the prison department spent £370,000 on prisoners' earnings – this amounted to 0.7 per cent of the department's budget. It compared with £56.5 million spent on general staff costs, which was around 77 per cent of the expenditure on penal institutions in Scotland for the year.[13] As one prisoner commented:

> the conditions are inhumane and barbaric, dehumanising . . . geared simply towards the cheapest possible confinement and maintenance and maximum industry, i.e. slave labour camps.

The prisoners were asked their opinion on the provision of work in the prison. The categories were: interesting; useful on release; helps pass the time; boring; useless. Only one prisoner suggested that the job he had been allocated might be useful on release. None considered the work to be interesting. Fifty-eight per cent considered prison work 'useless', 28 per cent said that it was 'boring' (although a considerable number stated that it was both useless and boring), and 14 per cent thought that it helped pass the time. However, there was a clear correlation between the latter category and those jobs which enabled association and movement (for instance, working in the cookhouse or laundry, or painting). The need, which was stated repeatedly, was to *'encourage enterprise and interesting, constructive work'*. The desolation and alienation experienced collectively is well illustrated in the following statement:

> The system does not cater for a person with 'bad eyesight' and I cannot work with tools. Because I carry in my blood Hepatitis B I sit on a chair all day and have done for 6½ years.

FOOD

Rule 101 of the Prison (Scotland) Rules 1952 states that the diet for prisoners 'shall at all times be wholesome and appetizing, reasonably varied and adequate for the maintenance of health'. In 1987, the Scottish Office fulfilled this requirement by spending £3,650 each day on food for prisoners. This amounted to 81p for each prisoner.[14] In Peterhead, as the Chief Inspector of Prisons noted, there is a discretionary payment which allows catering staff to buy extras to season and garnish food. In 1986, the staff were allowed to spend 34p per prisoner, per week, or just under 5p a day.[15] The Chief Inspector made a number of critical observations regarding the preparation and serving of food. He was particularly concerned about the 13 distribution points scattered around the prison and the deterioration in the temperature and texture of meals because of the gap between packing and serving them to the men. This could take 45 minutes. Finally, he noted that the dietary scale did not take account of 'current tastes, availability of goods, new products on the market or the variety of products which can be made from these items (e.g. dried vegetables are introduced when the price of fresh rises above a certain level)'.[16] On the staff side, the Inspector found that prison officers who wished to improve their craft training had to do so at their own expense and in their own time. They were given no additional training. The only specialist advice available was from a catering adviser who also had responsibility for prisons in England and 'whose attendance at Peterhead is normally restricted to an annual visit lasting half a day. Our view is that this is totally inadequate.'[17]

The prisoners were highly critical of the food and its preparation:

Let us purchase fruit from our PPC . . . We can smoke ourselves to death even though the Government knows the dangers of smoking, yet we cannot purchase vitamin pills, etc. . . .

Most of us supply our own vitamins bought from our own wages as the food is all wrong in preparation and very odd, ever had spaghetti hoops for breakfast, or a salad when it's below freezing point outside?

The food is a big problem – lacking in essential vitamins and minerals.

They made these criticisms against a background of possible disciplinary action. In the mid-1970s the prison department issued an *Abstract of the Rules and Regulations* to prisoners. This document warned them that 'repeated groundless complaints made with the evident purpose of giving trouble will be regarded as breaches of prison discipline'.[18]

RECREATION AND EDUCATION

Recreation is not a right but a privilege. As with other privileges in the prison system it can be withdrawn as a punishment. The Scottish Office made this clear to prisoners in the *Abstract of the Rules and Regulations* issued to them in January 1976:

Prisoners under sentence of imprisonment for not less than six months whose conduct and industry are considered by the Governor to have been satisfactory may be granted the privilege of associated recreation . . . This privilege may be forfeited or postponed by the Governor for a period not exceeding 28 days or by the Visiting Committee or the Secretary of State as a punishment for misconduct . . .[19]

In Peterhead, the recreation period occurred between 6.15 p.m. and 8.45 p.m. on weekday evenings and on Saturday and Sunday afternoons. Cell doors were unlocked and prisoners moved around the hall, participated in evening classes, used the gymnasium and in summer played football outside.[20]

They were scathing about the facilities in relation both to their quality and to the lack of privacy for pursuing individual interests. In A and D Halls there was a pool table, colour television, video cassette recorder, table tennis table, dartboard and some board games. They were shared by 40–50 men:

Recreation for me is walking about my gallery or sitting in a cell. There's one pool table for 50 men. One T.V. which 10 can view clearly, gym; due to staff shortages only 3 can be taken from each hall. But yet, 13 officers sit about bored on the galleries.

Mostly I sit in my cell talking to other prisoners (friends). Now and again I watch a programme on T.V. or play pool or write a letter, read a book or listen to an L.P. record. Walk up and down in the hall or round the gallery to pass the time and [get] rid of the boredom.

I stay in my cell and try to read despite the noise and the headaches I get because I can't get glasses. The lighting is poor and artificial only . . . At times I go for a walk around the landings like many others. You have to make your own recreation such as hobbies, but the restrictions on how and where to purchase them make even that impossible in this prison. In others, family can hand them in. Not here.

T.V. and pool table are only yards apart and there's always people being shouted on from T.V. to play pool. The rec. is all in the hall, record players are going, people shouting – total lack of facilities.

Long-term prisoners in other parts of the United Kingdom have higher standards of recreational facilities, a fact recognized by the Chief Inspector of Prisons in his report on the regime in Peterhead.[21] Furthermore, unlike long-termers in England, Peterhead prisoners were required to wear the prison uniform at recreation rather than more informal dress such as T-shirts and denims.

As with food and wages, expenditure on recreation and leisure was also a low priority for prison managers. In the financial year up to March 1987, the prison department spent £119,000 on what was termed 'educational, sport and recreational materials and equipment' – 0.2 per cent of the £56 million allocated for prison expenditure during the year.[22]

Educational provision was also limited. The institution lacked materials for use in the classroom, subject choice was narrow and classes were few:

Education is poor – not because of the teachers, but the lack of basic equipment, pencils, paper, etc. In Art, you make a model, the teacher takes [it] to the kiln and you don't see it again. It is put in your property – security!!

Due to cutbacks in the budget, the education facilities are diabolical – example – whereas the remedial, 'O' level and 'A' level English classes were separate, they are now all in the one class which naturally causes problems for teacher and pupils alike – also less subjects.

Education is limited to two days per week per prisoner despite the fact prisoners sit twiddling their thumbs in worksheds the other three. And it is on a cost-effective basis – that is, paper passes are required to justify the cost which is off-putting to most prisoners intitially, so classes are cut as attendance falls due to the prospect of exams.

The prisoners' experience of 'doing time', therefore, was influenced profoundly not only by the conditions but also by the timetable. Regularity and order were deeply embedded in the day's routine. This routine left little scope for individual development because of both the ideological reluctance within state institutions to provide humane facilities and, more fundamentally, the drive to contain such development within the vice of discipline. Consequently, the everyday lives of the confined were deeply paradoxical. While the institution insisted on uniformity and consistency in the routine and treated them as a group, through constant surveillance it also defined them as atomized individuals whose only bond with their fellow men was in their status as convicts and their need for individual discipline. It was in this contradictory space that they encountered the third force that determined the quality of their everyday lives, the prison officers.

STAFFING THE MACHINE

Since the mid-1970s prison officers have been a central focus of attention in the debates around penal policy. Through their professional organization, the Scottish Prison Officers' Association (SPOA) they have been highly influential in directing the minds of senior state servants and politicians to policies and practices which they feel not only are in the material interests of their members but also do not contradict the ideologies of discipline, punishment, security and control which lie at the heart of their occupational culture. The SPOA is neither a progressive nor a reformist organization. While it recognizes, as do prison governors, that there are individuals in prison who should not be there (people with mental health and drink problems, the homeless, and so on) it tends towards supporting long sentences and severe regimes for the incarcerated. The SPOA's hard line and successful demand for the reopening of the Inverness 'cages' in 1978, despite being based on contentious statistics for assaults on prison officers, provides a good example of the organization's influence. It retained this influence in the 1980s both in public through its access to the media and in private through its connection with senior state servants and politicians.

Within the invisible world of the prison, officers have substantial power and influence in the direction of the regime. While the prison governor has immense discretion in deciding an individual prison's managerial style, s/he will be transferred after a set number of years in post. This leaves ultimate control in the hands of senior line managers – the principal officers – many of whom spend years at a particular prison. It is this group, supported by the rank-and-file officers, which sets the often rigid and intimidating parameters for everyday life on the landings and in the workshops. While new recruits participate in a rudimentary six-week training programme at the Prison Service College, the most influential period of development in an officer's life is that spent at her/his designated prison under the tutorship of more senior officers and in the environment of the occupational culture. The nature of the job, the anti-social hours and the social isolation experienced by prison officers outside their workplaces reinforce the strengthened camaraderie of the occupational culture and encourage a reliance on the regime and its routines. Thus the professional dominance of the SPOA operates at two levels. Outwardly it is manifested in its image as a professional body, conference delegate and lobbyist. Inwardly it is rooted in the control of the job, the knowledge of the daily routine and the sharing of ideas and traditions within tight and restricted occupational bound-aries. It is at this level, serviced by the existence of lawful discretion and guarded by the parameters of recruitment and training, that professional relations of power are founded, nurtured and reproduced. Alongside military establish-ments, mental hospitals and the police, the modern prison maintains a level of obscurity in terms of operational practices which effectively denies outside scrutiny and accountability. This autonomy enables regimes to be developed at the discretion of prison governors but crucially to be interpreted and operationalized at the discretion of prison officers.

The role of the prison officers in Peterhead in 1986 provides a good illustra-tion of these points. Their role was primarily custodial: locking, unlocking, counting, guarding and punishing were the key elements in their day's work. Each day was highly routinized and was built around the containment and control of the confined. In practice, officers ensured that prisoners did not escape and that 'good order and discipline' was maintained in the institution. Their collective will was enforced through the discretionary and selective interpreta-tion of the scores of rules, regulations and standing orders which had been developed to ensure the conformity of the confined. As Chapter 4 makes clear, this discretion raises significant questions not only about the everyday practices of prison officers but also about the policies implemented by the state and the accountability of both.

As with other areas of Peterhead's regime, prisoners were clear and consistent in their criticisms of the staff. There were a number of dimensions to these criticisms. The most common related to casual but persistent inhumane treatment:

> When I first came to Peterhead I spoke to staff with respect and civility. Now after 15 months of mental suffering and dehumanising treatment I do not look upon them as men. They do not care about the effect that this awful regime is having on me or other prisoners.

> The majority of prison staff are indifferent to prisoners whom they think of as 'bodies'. I am a human being not a body.

> I'd be willing to co-operate with staff if they treated me like a human being.

> I don't trust them because they are always trying to find out my weak points so as to use them against me. If a screw treats me like a human being then I will treat him the same.

> Older members of staff have the wrong attitude, they think we are all 'no hopers' and the 'scum of the earth'.

In addition, prisoners consistently criticized the unpredictability and variation in treatment coupled with direct provocation:

> Some are O.K. but some are right bastards and treat you like shit.

> They do their utmost to antagonise me to get a reaction to justify locking me up.

> Nothing can be said to staff in confidence because at the end of the day it would be noted and relayed back no matter how insignificant.

> It's a question of degrees. Some staff may ignore petty rules, others may be zealous in applying them, if there's a personality clash between you and a member of staff then treatment can vary wildly.

> How can you have a good relationship with a member of the staff when you know that he will be right in there kicking the shit out of you if that's what the other staff were doing.

> You have a good squad and a dog squad that go out of their way to annoy you deliberately.

> Some are just pure dogs.

In the prisoners' accounts most prison officers, but not all, were concerned only with locking them away, drawing their wages and picking up overtime. There was no sense in these accounts of an atmosphere of care and responsibility often stressed by prison officers in their public statements. The following comments were typical:

> They are not interested in the problems here unless it involves their wage packets. Warders are here only for the wages and are not interested in the

job. Like most people in menial jobs they hate everything about their jobs.

Their attitude is terrible. If they could they would lock you up permanent. All their interests are centred around double shifts and money and this reflects on the way I treat them. I treat contempt with contempt.

Staff in general have no time for prisoners and can't wait to lock them up. They are no help whatsoever. To be fair, their hands are tied and about 10% of them are human and do see what is going on and show sympathy. Most enjoy the silly games they play or watching you strip – humiliating you. They are all too quick to say 'I go home at night' or 'I get £500 a week' or 'you are my overtime this weekend' (security). The staff could bring about changes but the conditions, petty rules, etc., keep the temperature up so that means more overtime. None of them would hesitate to put you on report, false or factual. If you show signs of being intelligent they really don't like you. There are few that are O.K.

This led to a situation in which meaningful contact between staff and prisoners was impossible:

I regard warders as they do me, each tries to hide the contempt for the sake of peace. Sometimes I feel like a prisoner of war.

They play with psychology with the worst possible results. I am sympathetic towards them because I cannot understand why they create regimes that prove a heavy burden to them and cause tensions and stress to them.

As virtually all of them are not in the least bit interested in the way I am feeling or thinking about any subject including ways we (us and them!!!) can improve the day to day (year to year!!!) running of prison life and the system in general tends to make me reluctant to try and form a relationship with people who have such dogmatic and lethargic attitudes, it is also off-putting that as a body of men they have recently voted unanimously for the re-introduction of the death penalty.

I stay away from them, they stay away from me.

Also they recognized that the concentration of power and its discretionary application provided them with minimal opportunities for effective redress or accountability. In the words of one, prisoners learned *'to live with this vulnerability'*:

As prison walls are built not to keep prisoners in but prying eyes out, they can literally do as they wish – after all, who believes a prisoner, or wants to?

The issues identified by the prisoners, and the feelings articulated, can be explained in terms of what Erving Goffman called 'the mortification of the self'.[23] Institutional regimes and those who staff them attack, undermine and attempt to replace the self-images that prisoners have and which have been constructed outside the walls of the prison. This attack is mounted on a number of fronts. From the denial of autonomy to the enforced control of every movement, from the invasion of privacy to the use of degrading and ill-fitting uniforms, prisoners are told that their previous identity and patterns of behaviour are no longer acceptable and should be abandoned. The state, both literally and figuratively, silences the confined and creates a conforming individual and through this claims victory in the 'war against crime'. For prisoners, this experience of material and psychological deprivation can be profoundly painful. At the same time, the institution rarely, if ever, achieves their consent. Indeed, the mortification of prisoners can create its own contradictions in which the brittle and fragile order of the regime is challenged. As Ken Smith has pointed out, 'repressive regimes create rebellion and defiance . . . boredom makes people desperate . . . reform does not follow from reaction and squalor'.[24]

This is the material context in which the disturbances in Peterhead took place. Viewing them from this perspective provides a more analytical starting point for understanding the complexities of prisoner protest. It is this complexity which the majority of media, official and professional commentators have ignored in the rush to identify and label the small group of malcontents thought to be responsible for defying the legitimate authority of the institution and its managers.

There is one further, and highly significant, omission in traditional accounts. This relates to the question of violence. While the activities of prisoners have been a central and well-publicized focus of attention, the violence of institutions has been marginalized in the majority of accounts about prison life. And yet this is also a key element in the generation and escalation of conflict. The next chapter is concerned with the dynamics of institutional violence in Peterhead and the contribution it has made to prisoner protest during the last two decades.

NOTES

1. These quotes are taken from the questionnaire. All such quotes in this chapter appear in italics.
2. The studies are too numerous to list. They come from academics, politicians, prison reform groups and the media. They have dominated debates about short-term and remand prisoners in the 1970s and 1980s. For an overview of the 1970s, see M. Fitzgerald, and J. Sim, *British Prisons*, 2nd edn, Oxford, Blackwell, 1982; for an overview of the 1980s, see V. Stern, *Bricks of Shame*, 2nd edn, Harmondsworth, Penguin, 1989.
3. See M. Fitzgerald, G. McLennan and J. Sim, 'Intervention, Regulation and Surveillance' in M. Fitzgerald, S. Hall, G. McLennan and J. Sim, *Law and Disorder: Histories of Crime and Justice (1–3)*, Block 2 of Open University course D310, *Crime, Justice and Society*, Milton Keynes, Open University Press, 1986.
4. Cited in S. McConville, *A History of Prison Administration*, London, Routledge and Kegan Paul, 1981, p. 239.
5. HM Chief Inspector of Prisons (Scotland), *Report of an Inquiry By HM Chief Inspector of Prisons (Scotland) into Prisoner Grievances at HM Prison, Peterhead*, Scottish Home and Health Department, 1987, p. 24.

6. Ibid., p. 16.
7. Details taken from ibid., pp. 18–19.
8. S. Cohen and L. Taylor, *Psychological Survival*, Harmondsworth, Penguin, 1981, p. 90.
9. Scottish Home and Health Department, *Prisons in Scotland Report for 1987*, Cm 551, HMSO, 1989, p. 23.
10. HM Chief Inspector of Prisons, *Grievances at Peterhead*, p. 24.
11. Cohen and Taylor, *Psychological Survival*, p. 111.
12. Ibid., p. 112.
13. Scottish Home and Health Department, *Prisons in Scotland 1987*, pp. 26–7.
14. Ibid., p. 26.
15. HM Chief Inspector of Prisons, *Grievances at Peterhead*, p. 50.
16. Ibid., pp. 49–50.
17. Ibid., p. 51.
18. *Abstract of the Rules and Regulations for Convicted Prisoners*, January 1976, p. 2.
19. Ibid., p. 4.
20. HM Chief Inspector of Prisons, *Grievances at Peterhead*, p. 29.
21. Ibid., p. 28.
22. Scottish Home and Health Department, *Prisons in Scotland 1987*, pp. 26–7.
23. E. Goffman, *Asylums*, Harmondsworth, Pelican, 1968.
24. K. Smith, *Inside Time*, London, Harrap, 1989, p. 228.

CHAPTER 3

The violent institution

VIOLENCE IN PRISON

All forms of incarceration imply the use of force. Regardless of the outward appearance of compliance few people taken into custody would accept their loss of liberty so willingly if the full potential of state coercion was not handcuffed to their wrists. The 'moment' of imprisonment is captured clearly in the following account by Trevor Hercules as he reflected on the routine losses outside:

> I remember the van feeling cold as I hunched myself up against the window, one hand in my pocket while the other was in the middle of the seat cuffed to some white guy . . . It was cold, yet I would have given anything to be outside in that cold, chilly night, that wonderful fresh, chilly night . . . I was desperate to get out of this van. I even thought about escape, but that was not on. The door was secured by several locks with one screw sitting at the front of the van carrying the keys while several more sat at the back and the sides of the van. Besides, where was I going to go, me a black man with a white man attached to him, like some kind of monkey . . . We had now arrived at the Scrubs. The driver bibbed his horn and the gates of hell swung open.[1]

The authority imposed by the prison is not a consensual authority. It is not derived in consultation and agreement, nor is it legitimated by any process of representation and accountability. The 'totality' of the institution, in terms of its political and professional autonomy, is underwritten by a degree of 'totality' or absolutism in power relations which virtually strip the prisoner of civil rights. The Scottish Office, the prison authorities and the prison officers' organizations strongly deny their access to 'absolute power', pointing to the official channels of appeal, complaint and petition and are adamant that no

61

prison officer or prison governor is 'above the law'. On paper the procedures exist and in theory all prisoners have equal recourse to the law. In practice the hurdles are often insurmountable as the inaccessible world of the prison, the closed ranks of its professionals and the climate of fear and intimidation stand in the path of even the most persistent complainant.

Life in most British prisons is an unrelenting imposition of authority. Any attempt by prisoners to negotiate or modify the regime is identified as a challenge to authority and, specifically, an affront to the authority of a particular prison officer. A range of factors influence direct responses by prison officers to 'awkward' or 'difficult' prisoners but they know, as the prisoners know, that their range of official sanctions – from loss of remission to the punishment cell – and their potential use of unofficial sanctions – from harassment to beatings – are permissive, non-negotiable and unaccountable. It is in this sense that the authority imposed within the institution is 'total'. This does not mean that it results in a total determination of the lives of prisoners. Occasionally, and usually only because of the involvement of outside agencies, the abuses of power within prisons and state mental hospitals are revealed and the perpetrators prosecuted. What these few cases demonstrate is that allegations of inhuman and degrading treatment and brutality in the British state's interrogation centres, mental hospitals and prisons, are well founded.[2] Successful prosecutions, however, are a rare exception, especially given the high level of allegations made by prisoners and ex-prisoners. Prisoners argue that the 'official channels' are impotent and, if anything, lead to further harassment and victimization.[3]

Inevitably, then, the choices available to prisoners to voice their complaints are seriously limited. Faced with harsh regimes, threats, intimidation and violence, prisoners respond in different ways. Despite these differences official discourse relies on fundamental assumptions about the 'natures' and 'backgrounds' of prisoners. Labelled as 'inadequates' or 'weak' by their 'guardians', it is their personalities which are scrutinized for any sign which might suggest defectiveness. In the Scottish Office inquiry into the spate of suicides at Glenochil Youth Detention Complex the team's assumptions were clear. Rather than considering the broader institutional contexts in which the deaths occurred, the inquiry addressed the issue solely in terms of the 'personal and situational' definitions of 'inmates at risk'. Even 'situational' definitions were restricted to those specific to the individual rather than those present in the regime. Personal factors were listed as: 'changes within the inmate . . . alterations in mood or energy . . . loss of interest, statements that the inmate feels miserable or casual remarks indicating a degree of anxiety or despair'. Situational factors included, 'crisis at home . . . bereavement, anxiety prior to release, uncertainty about the date of release'.[4] Prisoners' problems with Glenochil, then, were redefined as Glenochil's problem with particular prisoners whose personal inadequacies and psychiatric condition put them 'at risk'. This emphasis was shared by the Sheriff who inquired into the deaths and it suggested that the regimes which operated at Glenochil were above question and that the problem lay with certain individuals who, because of limited intelligence, physical disability, serious social or domestic problems, could not cope and presented 'major problems for the management'.[5]

Suicide, self-mutilation and the debilitating consequences of chronic depression are each explained in the official and medical discourses on imprisonment as psychological conditions connected directly, if not exclusively, to individual pathology. Such professional opinion, readily supported by generous research awards, sets out to explain suicide attempts, head-banging and persistent crying in terms of personality 'disorders'. The underlying assumption of this influential work is that of irrationality in the face of rational regimes. This assumption, however, might be reversed. Given the anti-social, hostile, inhuman, degrading and intimidatory reality of many British prisons,[6] why is it that so *few* prisoners are broken to the point of self-inflicted injury or death? What sustains the strength and will of many women and men locked away in overcrowded, isolated, insanitary, brutal and depersonalizing conditions?

In marked contrast to the depths of introversion and breakdown is the force and collective potential of rebellion. This is the opposite end of the spectrum of prisoners' responses to prison regimes. The refusal to recognize official authority and the organization of 'resistance' against the absolute power of the regime also guarantees the labelling and victimization of prisoners. To them is ascribed the status of 'awkward', 'difficult' or 'violent'. They become the frequent visitors to the punishment block and the proscribed target of psychotropic drugs under the ironic misnomer of 'treatment'.

Occasionally the full potential of rebellion is unleashed as accumulated frustration or specific injustices provoke a major demonstration of collective anger. Rebellion in prison, however, is not readily associated by the authorities, politicians or the media with meaningful behaviour. It is easily dismissed as 'mindless', 'drug-induced' or 'hysterical', thus negating any possibility that a prison 'riot' could be an expression of reason or a demonstration of desperate resistance. By stripping prisoners' actions of meaning and by criminalizing their acts the authorities depoliticize and pathologize their resistance. Punishment is extended and intensified, thus emphasizing the absolute authority of the regime and protecting its established order and practices.

In their detailed discussion of the 1976 demonstration at Hull, its causes and the various inquiries into them, Thomas and Pooley stated that

> long-term prisoners in modern times are less amenable than their forebears. They are infected, like the rest of society, with the experience that blind submission to authority encourages that authority to be complacent, lazy and rigid. If you take a number of strong, active men holding such beliefs, which are by no means unusual in modern society, and put them into a Victorian prison, then there is a good chance that trouble will result . . . The prisoner is not a committed left wing radical. He is simply a modern man who is likely to resist any imposition on his freedom which is unnecessarily restrictive . . . the gradual restriction of the regime in the years leading up to the riot annoyed prisoners who, year by year, observed their freedom within this secure perimeter being eroded.[7]

Their conclusion was clear: that the imposition of a harsh regime which was dedicated to the pursuit of trivial, petty rules created a 'potentially explosive' climate. The denial of access to prisoners removed from association and placed on Rule 43 as a punishment emphasized the absolute authority vested in the regime. Finally, 'incompetence', 'neglect' and 'misbehaviour' on the part of the staff not only typified the regime's reluctance to negotiate but also affirmed the authoritarianism implicit both in the role of the prison officer and the permissiveness of discretion.

Similar events took place at Wormwood Scrubs in August 1979. Prisoners complained about increasingly restrictive conditions and the curtailment of privileges and the Governor gave reassurances that he would reply to the complaints within two weeks. Nearly three weeks later, and following the withdrawal of further cell 'privileges', the prisoners refused to return to the landings and staged a peaceful sit-in demonstration. A National Prisoners' Movement [PROP] special report described the subsequent events:

> At 10pm two squads of 50 helmeted prison officers flung open the end gates of the wing and stormed in lashing out with staves at prisoners who were sitting peaceably . . . Clearly the authorities had learned a lot since Hull. Not only were most of the riot squad drawn from other prisons but many of them wore masks around their faces, cowboy fashion . . . On the landing, prisoners were forced to run the gauntlet as they ran to and fro to find an unlocked cell. Those in cells were dragged out to be beaten and senior officers were among those who selected which prisoners to haul out . . . the beating in D Wing was accompanied by jeering prison officers shouting 'that's for Hull'.[8]

Following the deployment of the Minimum Use of Force Tactical Intervention Squad (MUFTI) at Wormwood Scrubs the Home Office announced that order had been restored and that there were no injuries sustained by prisoners. Ten days later it was announced that five prisoners had received 'very minor injuries'.[9] This was extended four days later to 'a few who had bruising, minor cuts and other injuries', sustained during, but not following, the incident. On 27 September the Home Office reassured concerned campaigners and prisoners' rights organizations that 'there is no special anti-riot force'. Yet the announcement revised the number of prisoners injured to 53 explaining that the original number of five referred to those who needed hospital treatment. In October the Home Secretary announced that the number of injured was 54.[10] In November he replied that officers in 73 establishments were trained and equipped for 'minimum use of force, tactical intervention'.[11] This was the first formal recognition that MUFTI squads were available to respond to demonstrations in British prisons.

What the Wormwood Scrubs incident provided was an important, but still rare, insight into the close and closed collaboration between the prison system and the Home Office. The early denials of a riot squad and extensive injuries were exposed as information eventually leaked out to the media and campaign groups. Ten years earlier the then Home Secretary, James Callaghan, had refused to act on the findings of an inquiry set up by the Home Office into the beatings of prisoners at Parkhurst.[12] The report, by Michael Gale, an assistant prison director, was suppressed. Brian Stratton considered that the responsibility for the disturbances which followed could be laid at the door of the Home Secretary, James Callaghan:

> If . . . the . . . screws had been prosecuted, the cons would have thought something had at least been achieved and the brutality would have stopped, thus easing the atmosphere in the prison tremendously as early as by 1969. There would have been no riot, of this I am sure.[13]

The events of the 1970s consolidated a climate in British prisons in which prison officers appeared to be secure in their broad use of discretion and exempt from prosecution for their worst abuses of power. While it has been argued by the authorities that the successful Hull prosecutions demonstrated the effectiveness of accountability, they owed nothing to Home Office intervention or internal inquiries. In fact, it could be argued with some justification that the prosecutions succeeded *despite* the Home Office and the prison department.[14] Consequently the prevailing belief among the prisoners, confirmed by the work of prison reform groups, is that incidents of harassment and brutality by prison officers will persist unchecked.

Prisoners, their families and their solicitors receive repeated reassurances that their allegations will be taken seriously if they make an official complaint to the prison governor. Complaints against the behaviour of prison staff, however, are difficult to substantiate. Witnesses often refuse to come forward for fear of reprisals or victimization. If it comes down to a prisoner's word against that of a prison officer, and the latter has no problem in finding supporting witnesses from her/his colleagues, the governor is unlikely to decide in favour of the complainant. Finally, unsubstantiated allegations usually lead to a counter-charge against the prisoner and, inevitably, punishment. The internal processing of 'justice' in prison has little in common with the courts outside. The prisoner has no legal representation, no access to an 'independent' judiciary and, if the case is lost, faces conviction for making the complaint in the first place.

The complaints system in prison reflects the long tradition of state institutions in which accused professionals 'close ranks' and successfully deflect independent appraisal or effective accountability.[15] It reinforces the officially held position, which regularly appears in the media, that there exists in every prison a handful of subversive prisoners who are disruptive and disorderly. It is this core group of men and women who, it is claimed, attack each other, assault officers, wreck the prison, cause riots and make unfounded allegations. Having successfully pathologized their actions, denied them any meaningful context and criminalized the behaviour of this 'disruptive element', the prison authorities have established justification and support for the use of segregation, punishment cells and various forms of control units.[16] The lesson of the last twenty years is that those who rebel will suffer the informal sanction of arbitrary victimization and brutality and the formal sanction of a lengthy extension to their sentence. It is a double jeopardy which does make many think again but has not eroded completely the spirit of resistance in prisons.

Clearly not all violence, in the day-to-day routine of prison life, can be explained in terms of conscious struggles against oppressive regimes. All male prisons house men who settle their arguments through fear, intimidation and fighting. Many are convicted for violent assault and present a no-compromise, hard-man image. They gather around them a network of support based on their coercive influence within the prison. Protection rackets, dealing, settling scores and victimization are ingredients of the institutionalization of male violence. The culture of masculinity which pervades male prisons is all-inclusive and reinforces hierarchies based on physical dominance. Jimmy Boyle provides a chilling account of bullying in Peterhead and the dominance of a particularly violent prisoner:

> He was doing 15 years for offences concerning rape and prostitution, but while serving this sentence he was found guilty of murdering another prisoner and received a life sentence. This left him a hopeless case. The way he coped with his sentence was to prey on weaker guys and there were instances where some younger prisoners, or young-looking, were raped by his group. It became widely known . . . and screws in their uncouth way would pass remarks to the younger guys on the transfer bus that he would get them when they arrived in the prison. They would be terrified when they arrived, and some of them would ask for 'protection'. The screws thought this all very funny, but personally I felt deeply humiliated that another prisoner would allow himself to be used in this way . . . he was policing the prison for them, causing conflict amongst the prisoners and pressure was taken off the screws.[17]

Accounts by prisoners reveal a daily routine of violence and bullying which feeds an atmosphere of fear and intimidation. As Jimmy Boyle's account indicates, however, it is a routine virtually unpoliced by prison staff and often openly reinforced. While the prison authorities denounce publicly the activities of a hard core of pathologically violent prisoners, their officers utilize privately the full potential of control which is rooted in their violence. This quite different expression of violence, which dominates interpersonal relations within prison, is also implicitly condoned, if not actively supported and exploited. A clear example of this is the brutal treatment suffered by sex offenders. Their institutionalized brutalization reinforces their damaged personalities and does nothing to alleviate the oppression of women. Yet it consumes the energies and reinforces the aggressive masculinity of many prisoners.

This discussion of violence in prison, then, challenges the official discourses based solely on traditional criminological constructions of the pathological individual. It moves beyond the stereotypes of the 'inadequate' personality, ascribed to those who cannot cope, and of the 'violent' personality, ascribed to those who use violence in any context. Essential to a critical analysis of violence in institutions is the drawing of distinctions between situations which, taken together, comprise a violent institution. Harsh regimes damage the minds and bodies of some people more than others but the oppressive climate which they establish and reproduce and the neglect or brutality experienced by certain prisoners contribute to depression, illness and death. The acts of violent men in prison, sustained by a culture of masculinity which idealizes and equates personal power with physical dominance, reflect the world outside. Inside, the dominance can be total, with nowhere to hide from the bullying of other prisoners. It is concentrated within a totality of masculinity, the ground-rules heavily underlined by official male authority. Prisoners' violence is often part of the symbol, ritual and reality of a hostile male environment. However, it can also be of a quite different order – the individual or collective expression of anger, fear and frustration bottled up for months, even years, and fed by personal anxieties and institutional injustices. The prison 'riot' is manifestly an expression of violence, usually directed towards the fabric of the prison, but it carries a rational and conscious dimension. It is intended as a vehicle of change.

VIOLENCE IN PETERHEAD

Peterhead, with a prison population made up of a disproportionately high number of prisoners with violent histories and convicted of very serious crimes of violence, has developed and perpetuated a regime based on the spectrum of institutionalized violence discussed above. The prisoners' accounts leave no doubt as to the climate of violence and its debilitating consequences. Two Peterhead prisoners described the mental anguish and isolation of daily life in a harsh regime which condoned interpersonal violence between the prisoners:

I was a walking time bomb with no-one or place to turn to. I slashed the veins in my wrist and took an overdose of sleepers which I had been prescribed . . . The guard noticed a pool of blood coming from under my door and put up the alert. I woke three days later lying on a slab of concrete in a bare cell within a heavy canvas bag. [18]

My own mind has become tortured. I cannot escape from the madness I feel. I know that I am suffering and need help. I have asked for it to no avail as they think I am a hard man. I have tried to communicate but have failed as they just do not want to know. I can only communicate if I use the language of violence which is their language. If I don't communicate in that manner I am left to rot, until I react in the way in which they want me to. In all my time at Peterhead I have watched men who have resorted to violence. I can tell you that they have never had any choice because of the mental torture they are put through here. If you remain here you are not in the end capable of rational thought. You are no longer responsible. [19]

Both these accounts provide vivid pictures of a system in which prisoners are imploring the staff for help and support yet are denied even basic consideration for their state of mind. Both resort to violence, the first internalized and the second externalized. Both result in isolation and the punishment block, the

67

first for observation, self-protection and 'treatment', the second for punishment.

In considering the prisoners' responses to the questionnaire survey it is clear that Peterhead instils fear in most prisoners. Asked if they 'felt safe' in Peterhead, 86 per cent of the sample stated categorically they did not and 62 per cent stated that fear was a 'predominant factor' in their daily lives. Some prisoners talked of threats of violence from other prisoners:[20]

> At any time a prisoner can snap and go crazy. The screws don't give a damn as long it isn't their heads on the chopping block.

> I have been threatened on numerous occasions, and my life is in danger, especially at Peterhead. So when no-one seems interested I have to resort to demonstrations and protests to bring attention to my plight in prison.

> You can cross someone at anytime not even realising you've done it, an incident could flare up and you could find yourself in the wrong place at the wrong time and end up involved unwittingly.

> I feel safe most times but paranoia creeps upon you, so you know others can be paranoid also.

> I have been assaulted four times by other prisoners two of which left me with large, visible scars for life. All of which made it necessary for me to be housed in the annexe at Peterhead.

Many prisoners argued that it was the tense atmosphere at Peterhead which created much of the hostility between prisoners and allowed the bullies to be predators on others:

> Due to the tense atmosphere that is almost constant, one feels on the edge of what could end up an explosive situation.

> Peterhead is a dangerous place to be in for a great many reasons. It is not easy to avoid trouble when there is constant unrest on either side.

> It is almost impossible to live at peace with each other due to our situation and tempers can flare quite easily over the least little thing.

> No one feels safe in prison. I for one don't. That's why I end up in so much trouble . . . I fear dying, loneliness, going insane, solitary confinement.

The fear of solitary confinement, particularly the silent cell, pervades the experiences of all prisoners. Only one of the respondents stated that he had not been in solitary and one other did not answer the question. The average stretch of solitary confinement was three months but several had been in solitary for over 12 months.[21] The effect of solitary confinement and the silent cell can be grasped from the following account:

> My head aches from morning until night. To put another human being into that silent cell you would have to be pure barbarous. The effects are

severe! The thought of returning to Peterhead is very frightening. I've been locked up in the silent cell for 8 days . . . When you step into the cell you see a box. That's the silent cell. Around this is all their strip lights and big heaters. The inside is about 3 square yards. There are two spy holes and two small air vents. Its a human furnace. I've had headaches all week. Sitting there in this cell is like having a band clasped around your throat.

The most serious aspect of the violent institution, however, is the unlawful or unreasonable use of force by prison staff. In Peterhead brutality within the regime appeared to be endemic. Prisoners were asked to comment on their experiences of brutality directed towards themselves and directed towards other prisoners. Perhaps understandably in the circumstances, a number of prisoners declined to answer these questions for 'security' reasons. Despite this inhibition on the survey, 71 per cent stated that they had suffered assaults by staff and 62 per cent stated they had witnessed assaults by staff on other prisoners. This second figure cannot represent the full picture as many prisoners commented that assaults usually took place 'behind closed doors', in the absence of other prisoners.

You hear it going on, the fighting and kicking, you hear your mates screaming but you're powerless. Either you protest and shout, knowing you're next or you put your pillow over your head and block it out.

Recently and following strong denials by prison authorities, prisoners have made complaints about the level of brutality at Peterhead. Undoubtedly the support given by outside agencies and lawyers has added substantial weight to their grievances. Following repeated publication of these grievances the issue was taken up as part of the internal inquiry conducted by Mr T. Buyers, Her Majesty's Inspector of Prisons (Scotland). This was his conclusion:

In line with legal advice given, we cautioned the inmate at the outset of each personal interview that it was not within our remit to investigate allegations of criminal conduct. It was explained to him that it is the statutory duty of the police and Procurator Fiscal to investigate such matters and he should direct any such remarks to either body or request an interview with the police if he wanted to make a formal complaint . . .

Other comments from the inmates included reference to the much publicized allegations of staff brutality. It has been well documented in the press, of course, that these allegations were *later retracted* in favour of 'mental brutality'. Many of the inmates who spoke with us *volunteered the information that allegations of physical brutality were untrue . . .*

We enquired into these remarks and made discreet observations of the prison routines at various times and we must state that we found *no evidence whatsoever of physical maltreatment* of prisoners. Records show that in the last five years only one officer has faced charges of assault against an inmate and he was subsequently found not guilty by the Court. At this point we feel it must be said that implicit in the regularly reported comments in the media of former Peterhead inmates is collusion between prison staff, medical officers, the local police and the Procurator Fiscal to conceal evidence pertaining to alleged criminal offences. Despite a thorough examination we found nothing to substantiate or lend credence to any such remarks.[22] *have looked a other evidence*

What the report did not state was that a number of allegations of brutality had been put to him both written and in conversation. A serious case was that of a prisoner who alleged that he came close to death following a beating by prison officers. The prisoner wrote to Mr Buyers as follows:

Dear Sir,
I have been fortunate enough to have acquired your name, position and duty from a copy of a letter sent to my solicitor in reply to my petition to the Secretary of State . . . I would like to complain about the censorship of that information from prisoners. Prisoners are not being made aware of whom and where to complain to, nor how to go about it, nor that they may request a letter of petition form to go about it . . . I would like to complain about the suffering and physical and mental torture I have endured in prison and in particular at Peterhead prison. This would include a brutal assault to the danger of my life and permanent disfigurement . . .

Mr Buyers replied:

My brief, as Chief Inspector, does not include the investigation of individual complaints. However, I am concerned with procedures for handling complaints and I have passed on your letter to Prison Management, asking them to check that procedures are being followed correctly and without due delay in your case.[23]

On the publication of his report, Mr Buyers stated during a radio interview that prison officers at Peterhead were men of integrity and it was inconceivable that they should commit acts of brutality. Yet at this time, March 1987, Lord Cowie gave a judgement in favour of a former Peterhead prisoner who alleged that he had been stoned as he tried to escape. He was left with a serious disability as a result of the alleged assault and was awarded £35,608 compensation. Lord Cowie concluded:

The other factor which might have made me wary of the Pursuer's credibility and reliability would have been strong, acceptable evidence from the Prison Officers who were called as Witnesses. I regret to say, however, that their evidence did not impress me and in some respects I found it evasive.[24] *only*

The Buyers Report gives the clear impression that all allegations of physical brutality made by prisoners against prison staff were retracted, that interviews with prisoners indicated such allegations were false and that prison officers were men of integrity and fairness. As the Report was being discussed prisoners at Peterhead were writing their replies to the questionnaire survey, in full knowledge of the prison procedure concerning the 'vetting' of correspondence

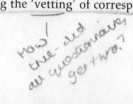

with the possibility of prosecution for making unsubstantiated or malicious allegations. Whereas Mr Buyers found 'no prisoners' willing to give evidence of brutality, the survey found otherwise.

The prisoners were asked a series of questions concerning brutality by staff. It was clear from the replies that a number of prisoners chose not to answer these questions for fear of victimization. Others stated that they had been assaulted or had witnessed assaults but they would not give details because 'the questionnaire is subject to censorship', 'my lib. date is imminent, and I want it to stay that way' and 'I'm allowed to fill in this questionnaire as long as I stick to standing order (M)'. When asked about making complaints through 'official channels' the prisoners' collective disdain for the procedures was clear. Many did make official complaints and pursued them outside the prison but there was no illusion as to the effectiveness of the complaints procedure. Intimidation and victimization were significant deterrents, especially the likelihood of being 'put on report for making false allegations' and the fear of a beating: 'if they get away with it once, they'll do you'. Drawing attention to oneself, gaining a 'name' as a trouble-maker, and the consequences of harassment featured highly in the response to questions about pursuing complaints. Apart from this, there was a deep sense of futility concerning the complaints system with 'What's the point?' and 'it's a waste of time' being the most frequent responses.

Finally, the entire discussion revealed a total lack of faith and trust in what prisoners identified as a broad-based system which 'fabricates' and 'rewrites' evidence, denies legal representation, always 'takes their word over ours' and places prisoners in a position of double jeopardy 'for making false allegations'. More than any other issue it is this implicit lack of trust which negates the effectiveness of accountability concerning the violence of staff and feeds the climate of paranoia and fear:

> Such is the atmosphere in Peterhead that you learn not to trust anyone. In my opinion, a situation created by staff. My motto: 'On guard'.

> I have experienced staff telling other prisoners that I have been grassing other prisoners for no apparent reason other than to put con against con and not con against screw . . . When things are tense in here you can't help being afraid.

Prisoners stated that this climate of tension feeds into specific moments or flashpoints which occur over the most petty issues and lead to direct confrontation:

> There's a total breakdown in communication between prisoners and staff. At any time trouble can flare. If you're singled out you are beaten or simply restrained even though you haven't struggled. Restraining technique is virtual strangulation.

> During any incident or argument staff are liable to lash out first, due to fear, and this is frightening as it usually involves anything up to 6 of them. Six lashing out with sticks can cause some damage to a person.

71

You have to tread softly with staff as they can, and do, do what they like with no comebacks. An assault here, or a report there. When there is the first sign of trouble they run out of the hall, lock you in and refuse to let you out. I was stabbed in the prison. Even after warning the authorities, they just don't care and they won't get involved. [Is fear a predominant factor in your daily life?] *Yes, very much so.*

It was the question concerning personal experiences of brutality and the witnessing of acts of brutality directed towards others which presented the most serious indictment of the regime. Many of the written answers provided substantial descriptions of specific situations:

One evening, while going to my cell at lock up time an officer started shouting at me for no apparent reason. Then he pushed me into a cell and started punching me about the head. As I wasn't in any fit state to defend myself, I put my hands through the windows to make him stop because it would attract attention. It resulted in another officer pulling the screw off me. I was then dragged down to the cells. The next day I was put in front of the Governor and charged with assault. The officer said I had assaulted him . . . The Governor didn't believe my side of the story. He said his staff don't go around beating up prisoners. I was sent to see the psychiatrist.

I have been quite lucky, one assault only. Punched, kicked, wrists bent, neck bent, ankles twisted, this was me being 'restrained' after an incident protesting the way another inmate had been treated.

They forced an internal search on me without a doctor and an officer jumped on my arm in the cell-block in Peterhead.

Christmas Day '86 they set about me with riot sticks for throwing a cup of tea out my door. They charged me with assaulting them with a knife & gun. I was found not guilty of these charges.

I have been very badly assaulted in the past by some staff. I have had my leg broken, my head bust open, and my face very badly marked.

I've had too many assaults to mention in various penal establishments. In PH only once – assault involved batons, feet, hands.

Several times the most serious being in the yard leading to the silent cell, 4 staff beat me up which led to me being taken to an outside hospital for X-rays on my head plus bruising on my body and legs and face.

Clearly the informal 'punishment' can be related to quite serious charges against prisoners for which they will receive the formal sanction of loss of remission, solitary confinement or further prosecution. Yet, it would seem, prison officers feel entitled to 'teach the cons a lesson' as described in a letter from a prisoner:

They accused me of escaping down a tunnel and I was put in front of the VC. They took 60 days remission and locked me up for 28 days in the punishment block. They kicked me unconscious for protesting and when they came back it was the same old brutality all over again, beaten, stripped, handcuffed and thrown into an empty cell.

The initial incident need not be as dramatic as an escape attempt. One prisoner catalogued three other *'typical instances'*:

I refused to go to a 'separate cell-block' so I got punched, kicked, and dragged; Lit a fire in cell in solitary confinement to keep warm so I got a black eye off the staff; Fingers fractured while being escorted to cell block after attempted escape; Nose broken after taking hot water for tea after being refused permission.

Major prison disturbances, as evidenced at Albany, Hull, Parkhurst, and Wormwood Scrubs, often are followed immediately with systematic and sustained attacks on prisoners.[25] While no one is left in any doubt that prisoners who are named and prosecuted will be punished severely in the courts the use of calculated violence towards the prisoners by baton-wielding 'riot squads' is more than a symbolic gesture indicating the regaining of control.

After the roof riot in '79 I was beaten unconscious for my assaults on staff, when my brother threatened the staff's families with revenge. I had my head split open with a baton in the silent cells.

The last time officers, clad in semi riot-gear, riot sticks like baseball bats, further officers outside my door: (date provided). Struck by baton, used like bayonet, kidney, left leg gave way, jumped all over me, mainly booted, handcuffed arms up my back, squeezed testicles, etc. (usual) internal life endangering injury, 10 inch scar, med. reports max. 24 hour life expectancy without emergency op. 16 hours left on floor, no doctor unless a deal that I fell.

How safe I feel depends on the situation at a given time, especially when the MUFTI squad are operating; then no one is safe.

1984; A Hall was destroyed; I was put into a windowless cell, with nothing apart from a mattress, 18 solid weeks. A 'pneumatic consolidated drill' with a jack hammer attachment pounded the floor of the above cell. One night I lit a fire in the hope that I would be taken from A Hall. The officers came in force dragged me from the cell, hit me with fists, sticks and kicked me all over the place, tried to break my arms and choke me.

The level and extent of violence reported by prisoners in the survey is emphasized by the range of assaults on other prisoners by staff. The survey provided evidence of what appear to be 'routine' assaults:

I saw my friend, T.P., being beat up in the exercise yard; my friend J.B. beat up on the corridor, another man in the hall.

Saw a member of the staff punch a guy then they grabbed him and forced an internal examination on him.

I saw an inmate assaulted on exercise at PH by 3 members of the staff. Witnessed this from my cell window.

I saw a prisoner punched in the face for refusing to drop his underpants without an M.O. present. I have heard prisoners getting beaten up but everyone is locked up before this takes place.

I have seen prisoners being put on report in the past for next to nothing and dragged to the cells and hit with sticks . . . I have seen it all.

Over many years, in many prisons, the instances I have personally witnessed of prisoners being assaulted by prison staff are too numerous to enumerate.

This final comment is typical of what many prisoners feel – that routine, small-scale assault is so commonplace that it is barely worth a mention. The responses suggested that anyone who did not accept that the prison regime was based on fear, intimidation, bullying and the threat of assault by staff was naive. It was the more serious cases, however, which formed the main concern of the prisoners.

The most recent was a man being kicked near to death and being left in a cell for 5½ hours before the Authorities would call a doctor. The man was badly injured and had to undergo an emergency operation to save his life. I was a witness.

Of all the liberties I witnessed among them was an assault on a young cripple. This particular day his sticks were at surgery being adjusted. He intervened in a slanging match on behalf of another prisoner, the officer seized him by the throat and punched him 3 times or so in the face, officer later said that he had hit him with a stick. [The prisoner] got 14 days for assault.

I saw him [a prison officer] whack a man over the head with several sets of steel handcuffs, bursting his head open which was later stitched up. I was only 4 yards away, as were 5 other prisoners . . . At the time the warder hit the man on the head, five warders were holding on to the man; they all denied the warder hit the man with the cuffs.

Once I saw a man almost beaten to death by about 15 screws . . . Only extensive surgery saved this man's life. The screws used 'riot-sticks' as well as the 'black aspirin' [their boots].

I heard an inmate being assaulted on Xmas night, battered with sticks. Heard the screams, he was taken to hospital. I saw him next day with his arm all bandaged up and in a sling plus a bruise on cheek.

[My] bruises were witnessed by a few prisoners one of which was placed on report and lost 14 days remission because he vented his anger at the state I was in. Only verbally I might add. The assault had taken place in the separate cells area.

74

These accounts are a brief selection of the range of responses by prisoners on the use of brutality at Peterhead. In the often lengthy replies the prisoners identify strongly with the problems of violence at both ends of the spectrum. They are poignant accounts of suffering in which the most hardened man identifies with the anguish of another but remains frustrated and angry at the indifference of the institution and its officers.

> *The guy has slashed his own face twice in the past couple of weeks. What state of mind is the poor guy in? Not one person has lifted a finger to help him.*

At the other end of the spectrum is the statement of intent, the response which suggests that, regardless of the consequences, violence will be resisted by violence.

> *My views on violence are simple enough: if they have a license to inflict brutal beatings – then you must do likewise at the earliest opportunity as a defensive act to show them you're prepared to stand none of it. I don't believe in abusing or assaulting warders just because they are locking me up. I treat them as they do me.*

> *The only way I can communicate with these people is in a cell block. By tension, abuse, violence, hatred and excrement. They won't allow for a man to change, so fuck them. No way will they be able to talk to me because when I talked they didn't listen. Fuck them.*

The allegations of brutality at Peterhead are not new. For over twenty-five years, through celebrated cases, Peterhead prison officers have been accused of systematic assault, the 'pound of flesh' taken before the prisoner is charged formally. Such allegations are not unique to Peterhead. Brutality by staff, denied by the prison department, the Scottish Office, the Scottish Prison Officers' Association and by some prisoners, has to be considered in the broader context of the prison regime. The well-established, some would say entrenched, dynamics of each identifiable group in the prison leads inevitably to physical assaults by prisoners on prisoners, prisoners on staff and staff on prisoners. Prisoners live by values which fundamentally, and not without justification, distrust authority within the criminal justice process. The face of authority is the prison officer. Prison staff, however, are similarly rigid in their rejection of prisoners. The harmony and tolerance which seems to be in evidence is no more than a surface illusion. The tension, mistrust and frustration underpin the illusion.

Ken Murray, the senior officer behind the establishment of the Barlinnie special unit, a Strathclyde Councillor and penal reformer, considers the problem here to be the 'cultural gap' or the 'them and us mentality' which exists between prisoners and prison officers. He states:

> The main instruction to prison officers was not to become too familiar with the prisoners. Getting close to a prisoner created problems, because when it comes to a collective proposition there's no doubt where the loyalty must

75

lie as ranks are closed. As an industrial situation they live with each other and establish a good first name relationship but in a moment of trouble he will have no compunction in taking a stick to him . . . 'Interpersonal relationships' is the new rhetoric in training, I heard this 30 years ago. The Director [of Prisons] argues that all will change in ten years but the *style* will be fixed by then. The Prison Training College is a blight on training, the primary relationship is on Rules and Regulations taught 'downwards' by established prison officers . . . The point is, prison officers can't stand the client and employing people who hate the client is equivalent to employing fire officers who are allergic to smoke. It is a complete lack of professionalism we are dealing with here.[26]

The arbitrary use of force by the prison staff, and the rejection of evidence of its institutionalization by the prison authorities, is the most divisive function within the prison system. Acts of violence between prison officers and prisoners at Peterhead produced a climate both tense and volatile. The downward spiral is evident from the survey. Tension mounts, there is confrontation over the most trivial of issues, a prisoner lashes out at an officer, he is taken to the punishment cell and 'taught a lesson'. If the prisoner is marked as a result of such an assault the prison staff have to justify their actions. They cannot lay themselves open to a criminal prosecution so they conspire to reconstruct events in which the prisoner was injured through control and restraint methods which were 'reasonable in the circumstances'. Other prisoners sometimes will support the prisoner's story although they may not have seen the events but will have heard the struggle.

In such cases prison officers have the opportunity to put together a well constructed version of events, whereas prisoners will be kept apart, probably in isolation and not allowed to consult. When such cases are heard before the court, despite people giving testimony on oath, two quite different stories regularly emerge. Clearly one version of events must be false and it is rare indeed for the prisoners' story to be believed. Meanwhile in the prison proper, other prisoners are aware of the incident. They see themselves in prison for committing the same acts of violence and experience themselves being locked up by people they believe to be as bad or worse than they are. In the follow-up to such instances they have read in newspapers that prison officers are living in fear of these violent men. They see the propaganda war waged against them simply because the Prison Department, the Governors' Association and the Scottish Prison Officers' Association will not concede that some prison staff . . . have been involved in perpetrating serious assaults on a number of prisoners over the years.[27]

The build-up of frustration, resentment and anger at Peterhead ultimately led to violent disorder in which hostages were taken. Other than murder this constituted the most serious crime which could have been committed against the person in the prison. The stakes were heightened yet again. Previously it was an

76

assault on the bricks and mortar of the prison's fabric but hostage-taking was a public exhibition of the threat to kill.

Whatever the underlying tensions, the institutionalized use of unreasonable force and the endemic presence of violence at Peterhead, the extreme use of aggression by prisoners in taking hostages cannot be condoned. Apart from the inevitable escalation of alienation between prison staff and prisoners the political gains made by the prisoners, their lawyers and penal reform groups were lost on the prison rooftops. The public were treated to masked violent men threatening the life of a helpless prison officer. Expecting that media publicity would pay the dividend of public support the prisoners accepted 'mediation' by a journalist from the popular press. Jimmy Boyle spelt out the problem thus:

> What this did was to confirm the reputation of violence which the Prison Department had made central to their case . . . The newspapers had a field day exploiting the 'callousness' and 'violence' of the hostage-takers . . . In the prison the response was inevitable. The lid was screwed down with a 23 or 24 hour bang up. Men were cracking up inside. This leads to men coming out as embittered, violent guys when they went in with a drug problem. [28]

Jimmy Boyle's position is that if prisoners are to gain ground in the struggle to reform harsh regimes they must 'take responsibility for their actions'. This includes accepting that the use of violence will bring an escalation in the state's response both in the ending of sieges and in the consequences for all inside. Together with the diminution in public support, these factors undermine the possibilities of beneficial reforms and divide the prison population. Finally, they become the living proof of the assumption that the troubles in British prisons are derived in and orchestrated by the words and deeds of a handful of pathologically violent men. This enables the authorities to affirm their commitment to the traditional criminological classifications of inadequate and violent personalities and to reject the charge of institutionalized violence within harsh regimes. The very celebration of masculinity, then, reduces its most violent manifestations to the level of opportunism and restricts its analysis to the psychologies of a few men. The culture and cult of masculinity which permeates all aspects of life in male prisons, so evident in this chapter, remains dominant and reinforced.

NOTES

1. T. Hercules, *Labelled a Black Villain*, London, Fourth Estate, 1989, pp. 24–30.
2. On Castlereagh, see P. Taylor, *Beating the Terrorists*, Harmondsworth, Penguin, 1980. On Broadmoor, see D. Cohen, *Broadmoor*, London, Psychology News Press, undated. On prisons, see National Prisoners' Movement (PROP), *Don't Mark His Face*, PROP, undated.
3. See J. Boyle, *A Sense of Freedom*, Edinburgh, Canongate, 1977; W. Probyn, *Angel Face: The Making of a Criminal*, London, Allen & Unwin, 1977.
4. Scottish Home and Health Department, *Report of the Review of Suicide Precautions*

at HM Detention Centre and HM Young Offenders' Institution, Glenochil (Chiswick Report), HMSO, 1985, paras, 7.3.4–5.

5. Ibid., para. 9.8.2.

6. For a good example of this issue, see the Report of the Chief Inspector of Prisons, Judge S. Tumin, on *Risley*, HMSO, 30 June 1988.

7. J. E. Thomas and R. Pooley, *The Exploding Prison*, London, Junction Books, 1980, pp. 81–2.

8. PROP, *Wormwood Scrubs: Special Report*, London, PROP, 1979.

9. *The Guardian*, 11 September, 1979.

10. Reply to written question 201, *Hansard*, 22 October 1979.

11. *The Guardian*, 2 November 1979.

12. See B. Stratton, *Who Guards the Guards?*, London, PROP, 1973.

13. Quoted in M. Fitzgerald, *Prisoners in Revolt*, Harmondsworth, Penguin, 1977, p. 133.

14. For further discussion of this point, see M. Fitzgerald and J. Sim, *British Prisons*, 2nd edn, Oxford, Blackwell, 1982. The authors show that the original Home Office inquiry 'completely exonerated prison staff' but over two years later eight officers were found guilty of 'conspiring together and with others to assault and beat prisoners'. One of the officers had his sentence overturned on appeal.

15. Recent work on the police has highlighted this tendency. See R. Reiner, *The Politics of the Police*, Brighton, Wheatsheaf, 1985; P. Scraton, *The State of the Police*, London, Pluto, 1985; S. Spencer, *Called to Account*, London, The Cobden Trust, 1985; L. Lustgarten, *The Governance of the Police*, London, Sweet and Maxwell, 1987. D. Leigh, *Frontiers of Secrecy*, London, Junction Books, 1980, discusses the issue specifically with regard to prisons. See also J. Sim, 'Book Reviews', *International Journal of the Sociology of Law*, vol. 15, 1987, pp. 225–9.

16. See Fitzgerald and Sim, *British Prisons*, ch. 4.

17. Boyle, *A Sense of Freedom*, p. 196.

18. Letter to the Gateway Exchange from a Peterhead prisoner.

19. Letter to the Gateway Exchange also from a Peterhead prisoner.

20. These quotes and others throughout the chapter are taken from the questionnaire survey and are italicized.

21. These figures are based on information given in the questionnaire survey.

22. HM Chief Inspector of Prisons (Scotland), *Grievances at Peterhead*, pp. 2–20.

23. This correspondence is held on file at the Gateway Exchange, Edinburgh.

24. The Gateway Exchange, *The Roof Comes Off: The Report of the Independent Committee of Inquiry into the Protest at Peterhead Prison*, Edinburgh, Gateway Exchange, 1987, p. 90.

25. See R. D. King and K. W. Elliott, *Albany: Birth of a Prison – End of an Era*, London, Routledge and Kegan Paul, 1977; PROP, *Don't Mark His Face*; Fitzgerald, *Prisoners in Revolt*; Thomas and Pooley, *The Exploding Prison*.

26. Personal interview, Glasgow, June 1989.

27. Gateway Exchange, *The Roof Comes Off*, pp. 87–8.

28. Personal interview, Edinburgh, June 1989.

CHAPTER 4

Discipline, punishment and the maintenance of order

The crux of the problem with this prison is that there is not even a pretext of rehabilitation – it is made quite clear that they have the methods to 'cow' prisoners into submission by use of the separate cells, 'B' Hall and the ten-cell unit. Calling it an 'alternative regime' does not detract from the fact that they are isolation cum punishment units for non-conformists.[1]

One member of the Visiting Committee who I knew told me, with a laugh, 'I don't know why I was appointed to this Committee. I don't know what's going on but the Governor keeps us right'.[2]

The central and overriding tenet of the British prison system is the maintenance of what prison managers call 'good order and discipline'. Both individually and collectively, the daily lives of prisoners are dominated by a secret maze of rules, regulations, Standing Orders and Circular Instructions. Access to many of these rules is strictly controlled. For example, prisoners have no right to see the Standing Orders and Circular Instructions generated at prison department headquarters and circulated to prison governors. In addition, they may not be allowed to possess a complete copy of the Prison (Scotland) Rules 1952. They may be given a brief guide to 'those parts of the prison rules and regulations which the prison authorities have decided prisoners should know about'.[3] As the Scottish Council for Civil Liberties (SCCL) has pointed out, while the rules can be consulted by the general public in local libraries, the confined

> have no such access. Every prison cell is supposed to have a copy of an extract of the rules. In practice this is very selective, containing some of the rules and the standing orders – which have no status in law. . . . Prisons cannot become actively accountable until prisoners have easy access to all the rules.[4]

The formal rules and regulations are underpinned by a series of informal rules which develop within a particular prison's sub-culture and which are as potent in controlling prisoners as official sanctions. Basic grade prison officers working on the landings, wings and workshops often operate their own system of reward and punishment. Conformity is demanded and rule-breaking chastised – for example, by moving prisoners from single cells to sharing with known 'difficult' prisoners or moving individuals from 'good' prison jobs to 'bad' more discipline-orientated tasks. This informal network of control interlinks with the formal mechanism of discipline and regulation to produce an all-embracing and highly discretionary system of penal policing. Strip searching is a clear example of this interlocking network of power. Rule 14 of the Prison (Scotland) Rules allows for the search of every prisoner on admission and, crucially, at any other time if the authorities decide that security or order is threatened. The process is discretionary and can range from 'frisking', through 'skin searches' through to 'an intimate body search i.e. search of the body's orifices, including the anus and vagina regardless of menstruation'.[5] The SCCL has indicated that these searches are used disproportionately against imprisoned women in Scotland and in 1984 the incidence of searches in Armagh prison, Northern Ireland, was 'less than a quarter, pro rata, of what it [was] in Scotland'.[6] In 1985, there were 4219 strip searches in Cornton Vale women's prison. The prison had an average population of 172 women during the year. Writing in May 1987, the Council concluded that 'there are strong grounds for believing that intrusive searches may be significantly on the increase and that they can be used to humiliate and oppress and as a form of sexual bullying'.[7]

For many men in Peterhead the formal and informal disciplinary system and the lack of an adequate complaints procedure was, in its own way, equally oppressive, built on and compounded by subjective and non-accountable decisions made by the prison's managers. It was a vital link in the chain of events which led to the disturbance in November 1986.

THE DISCIPLINARY SYSTEM

The formal system of discipline which operated in Peterhead in 1986 derived from the Prison (Scotland) Rules 1952 and, in particular, Rule 42 which listed the offences for which prisoners could be punished. Rule 42 stated:

A prisoner shall be guilty of an offence against prison discipline if he:
1 Disobeys any lawful order, or refuses or neglects to conform to these rules.
2 Treats with disrespect any officer or any person visiting the prison.
3 Is idle, careless, or negligent at work, or refuses to work.
4 Uses any abusive, insolent, threatening or other improper language.
5 Is indecent in language, act, or gesture.
6 Commits any assault.
7 Communicates with another prisoner without authority.
8 Leaves without permission any place in which he is required to be.
9 Loses by neglect prison property.

10 Wilfully disfigures or damages any part of the prison or any property which is not his own.

11 Commits any nuisance.

12 Takes improperly, or is in unauthorized possession, of, any article.

13 Gives to or receives from any person or has in his cell or possession any prohibited article.

14 Escapes from prison or from legal custody.

15 Mutinies or incites other prisoners to mutiny.

16 Makes repeated and groundless complaints.

17 In any way offends against good order and discipline.

18 Attempts to do any of the foregoing things.[8]

Many of these rules were based on subjective and discretionary decisions made by individual prison officers. The notion of committing 'any nuisance' or making 'repeated and groundless complaints' gave officers the ability 'to term anything and everything which irks and irritates, an offence against good order. It is not simply that the rules invite *abuse* but that *use* gives wider and arbitrary powers to staff whether they wish it or not'.[9] As Table 4 below makes clear, the offences committed in Scotland's male prisons in 1986 reflected the discretionary nature of prison officer power. Offences against good order and discipline (31.5 per cent), disobedience and refusal to work (22.2 per cent), disrespect, improper and indecent language (13 per cent) and committing a nuisance (11.5 per cent) were the major categories within which prisoners were grouped. As the table indicates, serious offences against discipline, such as assaults on officers, assaults on inmates and damaging property, were in the minority. Official and popular discourses built around the image of prisoners violently

Table 4 Types of Offence Committed in Scottish Prisons, 1986[10]

	Male	(%)	Female	(%)
Disobedience and refusal to work	2215	22.2	50	7.5
Disrespect, improper or indecent language	1298	13.0	67	10.0
Assault on officer	145	1.5	9	1.3
Assault on inmate	163	1.6	7	1.0
Damaging etc property	608	6.1	51	7.6
Committing a nuisance	1149	11.5	86	12.8
Taking etc unauthorized or prohibited articles	583	5.8	36	5.4
Escape, absconding or attempted escape	39	0.4	—	—
Breach of parole or licence	31	0.3	—	—
Making repeated and groundless complaints or false allegations	51	0.5	12	1.8
Offending against good order and discipline	3143	31.5	265	39.6
Other offences	562	5.6	87	13.0
Total	9987		670	

[handwritten: might seem petty but its the rules.]

assaulting staff and state property is seriously challenged by the Scottish Office's own figures. On the contrary, the figures illustrate the petty nature of most offences in male and female prisons during 1986.

For those in Peterhead the continual enforcement of the rules and regulations for often petty and trivial offences added a significant dimension to the corrosive and smouldering resentment they already felt about the conditions and the philosophy of the regime, discussed earlier:

[handwritten: what though]

> The 'against good order and discipline' rule is too open and gives them scope to put you on report for what is most of the time virtually nothing more than a slip of the tongue, or merely a reaction to what has been said to you or the manner in which it was said . . . also there are no fixed guidelines when the punishment is being meted out, it depends on who [it is] and what kind of mood they are in.

> I went to trial and was found not guilty of mobbing and rioting and taking hostage, but in the eyes of the screws and governors, they still have me guilty, so what chance have I, or any others in my position? I will be dug out all the time for that, set up, locked up for the least thing (probably writing this).

> Refusing a rub-down search after already giving a strip-search. From the strip-search, I walked up a corridor with three staff and never spoke [to] or seen any other prisoners (Punishment – three days loss of wages, mattress and radio).

> These petty rules and the way they are enforced are surely going to cause a major incident (again!). As there has been a recent influx of new staff who are just finished training stints in borstals and YOI's their attitudes are all wrong.

[handwritten: exaggeration]

> Discipline is so bad in here you can only breathe when told to.

According to the report of the independent committee of inquiry:

[handwritten: is true?]

> certain of the offences as described in the Prison Rules are vaguely defined and some of the conduct described by some of the prisoners could easily be subsumed under almost any of them – disobeying orders, treating officers with disrespect, using insolent or abusive language, offending against good order and discipline. Many prisoners described behaviour which we can only assume was regarded by the prison officers and Governor as falling under one of these categories as the prisoners tell us they were awarded punishments – not getting out of bed to see the doctor, standing against a wall, not standing up for the Governor, trying to speak to the doctor, refusing to come off work and go to the cell while it was searched, hands in pockets (mentioned by several), possession of a prison rule book![11]

There were a series of formal sanctions invoked against those who broke the rules. They were placed 'on report' and appeared before the governor (or an authorized officer) the following morning (or on the Monday following a weekend incident). Prisoners on report were usually held in solitary confinement until the hearing:

> A prisoner is immediately taken to the separate cells on report. These cells are filthy and often cold. Discipline here in Peterhead is totally disorganised. Staff are unqualified to deal with troublesome prisoners and prisoners with problems. ← not true – cause staff qualified

It was at the hearing that the accused was faced with the full rigours of a system that denied him due process and legal representation. The officer making the complaint related the circumstances of the incident to the governor who, after hearing the prisoner's version of events, adjudicated on whether a breach of discipline had occurred. He could 'award' one of the following punishments if he decided that the prisoner was guilty:

1 Loss of remission (not over 14 days).
2 Loss of right to smoke or loss of earnings, in whole or in part (for not over 14 days). Once earning again, the prisoner may be required to pay for any damage or loss caused by him.
3 Loss of any other privilege (for not over 28 days).
4 Exclusion from working in association with other prisoners (not over 14 days).
5 Solitary confinement (for not over 3 days).
6 Restricted diet (not over 15 days).
7 Loss of mattress (not over 15 days).[12]

For more serious offences or 'repeated' offences, Prison Rules 43(2) allowed the governor, with the approval of the Secretary of State for Scotland, to report the offence to the prison Visiting Committee (VC) which could ' "enquire into the report . . . and may, if they find the prisoner guilty award . . . punishments" as laid down in [Rule 45(1)]'.[13] Members of the VC had a wider and more severe range of punishments available to them. These included:

1 Loss of remission (no limit).
2 Loss of right to smoke or loss of earnings, in whole or in part (for not over 28 days).
3 Loss of any other privileges (no limit).
4 Exclusion from working in association with other prisoners (for not over 28 days).
5 Solitary confinement (for not over 14 days or for mutiny 28 days).
6 Restricted diet (not over 15 days).
7 Loss of mattress (not over 15 days).[14]

In 1986, a total of 7663 punishments were 'awarded' in male prisons and 876 in female prisons. Table 5 provides a statistical breakdown of the particular punishments given. It is clear that in male prisons the most heavily 'awarded' punishment was loss of remission, which is a serious punishment. The next most frequent punishment was the loss of privileges, followed by 'other

Table 5   Punishments imposed in Scottish prisons, 1986[15]

	Male	(%)	Female	(%)
Forfeiture of remission	2024	26.4	142	16.2
Forfeiture of smoking	152	2.0	80	9.1
Forfeiture of payment for work	1285	16.8	278	31.7
Forfeiture of other privileges	1819	23.7	105	12.0
Payment for losses or damages	204	2.7	53	6.1
Exclusion from associated work	503	6.6	74	8.4
Cellular confinement	81	1.1	56	6.4
Deprivation of mattress	23	0.3	—	—
Other punishments	1572	20.5	88	10.0
Total	7663		876	

punishments' and loss of wages. The 1986 official figures did not provide the number of warnings given; these were subsumed under 'other punishments'. In 1985, however, official figures revealed that 1202 male prisoners were warned (16.4 per cent of the total).[16] Assuming a similar figure for 1986, it is clear that while offences in Scottish prisons were of a petty nature, as Table 4 noted, punishments were severe. There was, in other words, the 'minimal use of the least harmful forms of punishment'.[17]

Prisoners in Peterhead were highly critical of the punishment system, particularly the use of solitary confinement and segregation units:

I suggest ... [that] ... members of the Committee give long hard consideration to the present brain-child of penologists – isolation units, segregation units, punishment blocks, silent cells, as a sensible realistic answer to prison problems. Accepting that such odious units may serve in the short term to separate what the authorities term disruptive parties from main-stream population. Are they an unspoken admission of failure to re-educate and rehabilitate the disturbed occupants?

I stayed in the silent cell for twenty-seven days.

Kept in cell for three months with steel plates welded over window to exclude daylight – only allowed mattress and pot for seven weeks – had to wash with prison officers watching, holding riot-sticks.

Conditions in my cell here are really bad. Everything is damp. There is no ventilation. My clothes are damp and stay damp. The old ventilator has been filled with cement and even my bed is damp. I wonder why they filled the air vent with cement.

I've been locked up in this silent cell for eight days, which is unusual considering I've not caused any more damage. Anyway, this is not the average silent cell. This is a new addition. When you step into the cell, you see a box. That's the silent cell. Around this is all their strip-lights and big heaters. Also metal straps to keep the heat in. The inside is about three *square yards. There are two spy-holes and two small air vents. It's a human furnace. I've had headaches all week. Sitting here in this cell is like having a hand clasped around your throat. I find it very hard to breathe.*

There were a number of units in the prison used to isolate prisoners, including a ten-cell unit built in 1984, an annexe containing 21 prisoners with its own worksheed area and another 16-cell unit which had its own silent cell. This cell had no windows and was designed to hold prisoners regarded as seriously disruptive. Prisoners were segregated either after being formally charged or under Rule 36 which permitted the Visiting Committee or Secretary of State for Scotland to authorize the Governor to order a prisoner to work in his cell, and not in association, if it was 'desirable for the maintenance of good order or discipline or in the interests of the prisoner himself'.[18] This authorization lasted for one month and could be renewed indefinitely. In practice, the system was used against those regarded as 'subversive' or 'difficult'. The SCCL has noted that 'such cases have led to complaints of psychological disorientation and considerable distress'.[19] As one prisoner explained:

If a man smashes up his cell, there has to be a reason, a problem, personal or otherwise; so why not help him instead of making it worse by punishing him more. — Is there?

This treatment locked prisoners into a spiral of confrontation with the Peterhead authorities which, in turn, led to increasing punishment. Offences were often regarded as trivial, unjustified or fabricated. The Governor's hearing and the Visiting Committee's inquiry were equally despised as a 'kangaroo court' where proceedings were unjust, unfair and lacking any notion of due process: — ? going to say that.

It's one-sided. A prisoner can't put any defence. If an officer says coal's white, it's white.

The screw's word is always right . . . If you choose to speak against the charge . . . then the punishment is harsher. If you remain quiet, then you are still punished.

The powers that be would do well to introduce the right of independent [legal] representation where serious allegations of misconduct are made, with an accused permitted to call witnesses at an internal hearing. The present methods are unjust and, in most instances, unwarranted.

Prisoners, therefore, suffered punishments with an acute sense of grievance which

led to further 'offending' as a protest against the original 'unfair' treatment, often while the prisoner was still undergoing the original punishment (which suggests that the deterrent effect of the punishments was minimal). The cumulative effect of all of this often seemed to be that a significant number of prisoners spent months on end in solitary confinement and, having been identified as a security problem, several found themselves confined to cells under Rule 36.[20]

true. But what alternative? offered

The Scottish Council for Civil Liberties made a similar point when it noted that 'prisoners are subjected to a litany of petty and relatively trivial offences which may merit a varied list of punishments'.[21] The Council also indicated that the use of solitary confinement for extended periods, control units, punishment blocks and loss of remission were 'only open to token review, yet these punishments are more serious in kind than those meted out by the courts themselves, the most serious of which – loss of liberty – is subject to appeal'.[22] The prisoners' sense of isolation and grievance was compounded by what they saw as the lack of any coherent or even straightforward system for making complaints about their treatment. The frustration generated and neglect over complaints was another significant factor in the violent unrest in the prison.

MAKING A COMPLAINT

In theory, prisoners in Peterhead had a number of avenues open to them to complain about the prison's regime, including: requests to the Governor; seeing the Visiting Committee; petitioning the Secretary of State for Scotland; writing to MPs, solicitors, the Parliamentary Commissioner for Administration (Ombudsman), the Procurator Fiscal, local sheriffs and the European Court of Human Rights.[23] In practice, these avenues and access to them were strictly controlled and regulated. As the SCCL has pointed out, local sheriffs rarely exercise their right to investigate prisons, while 'the Ombudsman has had minimal contact with Scottish prisons'.[24] Furthermore: 'In the north of Scotland SCCL has encountered reluctance and even refusal to investigate serious complaints . . . On a number of occasions, the absence of criminal investigation has been inexplicable in terms of the criminal law.'[25]

Similar criticisms can be made about the role of the Inspector of Prisons in monitoring prisoners' complaints. The first report by the prison inspectorate on Peterhead was sent to the Secretary of State for Scotland in June 1982, nine months after the initial inspection was carried out.[26] The 27-page report contained no reference to prisoners' complaints or their lack of faith in the procedures, despite strong evidence coming from the prison at the time that the lack of action on complaints was a major factor in their alienation.[27] The Chief Inspector's second report on the prison, dated March 1987, did deal with the complaints system. He examined 38 petitions to the Secretary of State for Scotland and found that the average time taken to answer the complaint or request was five weeks. He concluded that some replies were 'lengthy' and 'explanatory' while others were 'inadequate in that they gave no reason for the decision reached'.[28] The Inspector also found that there was 'substance' to the complaints by prisoners concerning the Visiting Committee:

> Inmates interviewed displayed little faith in this system maintaining that the Visiting Committee were only another part of prison management. They also complained that too much time elapsed between making their complaint and receiving a reply. Invariably, too, they said, the reply was

given to them by a member of the Governor grade and not by the VC member.[29]

Like their counterparts in England and Wales (the Boards of Visitors), Visiting Committees in Scotland performed a dual function. Not only were they, in the words of the Chief Inspector, 'independent watchdogs'[30] who investigated complaints and inspected individual prisons but also, as noted above, they presided at serious disciplinary hearings. However, this dual role has been criticized by prisoners and academics as contradictory in theory and unworkable in practice.[31] Furthermore, in Scotland it has become clear that even on their own terms the Visiting Committees failed to fulfil their role as prison watchdogs. Both the 1987 report by the Chief Inspector of Prisons and the prison department report for the same year raised questions about poor attendance at routine meetings and the fact that members who were asked to make short visits to prisons did not 'feel well-equipped for the task, having had little or no training'.[32] The prison department report pointed out that in a 'few adult establishments' the VCs 'failed to carry out sufficiently regular or numerous rota visits during the year'.[33] More specifically, the Chief Inspector's report on the 1986 disturbance, while acknowledging that the nine members of the VC he met (out of 14) showed a 'general interest and concern for the whole prison', nevertheless noted that

> the Committee were not as familiar with the full extent of their statutory role as they might be, especially in the complaints procedure process. To some extent this had undoubtedly led to a loss of inmate confidence in the VC as a reliable impartial channel of complaint.[34]

It should also be noted that this critique and the issues raised by the Peterhead prisoners have been supported by research sponsored by the Home Office on Boards of Visitors in English prisons. This research concluded that the system was highly formalized; staff were usually present during the prisoners' applications to the Board; prisoners did not receive replies to applications; and that 'many prisoners were convinced that Board members did not investigate grievances at all, simply taking the governor's word that there was nothing amiss'.[35]

Prisoners at Peterhead expressed their grave disquiet about and distrust of the complaints system:

> *Another waste of time. Even when you are 100% right the prison is backed up to the hilt. The Governor backs his staff. The Department and Secretary of State back the Governor. I have been told the answer to my Petition, word perfect, prior to sending it.*

> *Do away with such phrases as 'At the Governor's discretion' 'Security reasons', (you can't even get a pen for security reasons), 'The Prisoner has no room for complaint', 'The Secretary of State does not wish to interfere' – all standard replies.*

The customary clap-trap by way of reply – 'No grounds for complaint' or a hollow admonition about using immoderate language. Fortunately for my sanity I am able to laugh at the inanity offered by the 'Sages at St. Andrews House'.

It must be remembered . . . that the whole purpose of the penal system is to curb a prisoner's right or desire to complain by 'subtle (and not so subtle) inferences,' that to do so will only prolong his stay in prison and that life will be made 'difficult' for him. These 'subtle inferences' (read threats) however, are becoming less valid nowadays as the totally ridiculous sentences and the certainty of no parole, much outweigh this 'pathetic carrot' and prisoners are beginning to realise just how much they have been conned over the years.

Prisoners were also sceptical about complaining to the police. There were a number of reasons for this. First, there was the bureaucracy involved:

In order to get an interview with the Police a prisoner has to use his weekly letter to contact them. Second Class Mail takes time.

Second, there was the view that the police would not be impartial in their investigations, a claim which has been made throughout the last decade about the police complaints procedure in general.[36] Third, police officers often investigated assault claims in the presence of prison officers. As one prisoner explained:

Two Aberdeen CID attended the prison and attempted to interview me in the presence of two warders – I refused to discuss the matter in the hearing of warders who, for all I knew, could have been involved in the alleged assault. The police left promising to discuss confidentiality with [the] fiscal and senior officer. They again returned when I sent a further letter to the Chief Constable; this time I was emphatically assured that the governor has the right to insist warders be present at the interview. I reminded them of the obvious prejudice in that any one of the warders present may have been involved or be prepared to relate my statement to others involved. I also informed the CID officers that I was fully entitled under minimum standards for treatment of prisoners (statute) [to] . . . a confidential interview with any police officer, court official, coroner's agent or any member of the authorities when I wished to complain of any matter concerning prison. The two CID ignored this point and insisted I give a statement in the presence of the warders; no statement was given. At a later stage the Chief Constable stated that I 'refused to give his officers a statement'. I complained to the Police Complaints Authority and received a reply 3 months later informing me that the PCA had no jurisdiction in Scotland.

In such cases:

> prisoners making allegations of assault against one or several prison officers face a legal barrier to proof in most cases. A critical imbalance in the power of prisoners to make charges against prison staff 'stick' has led to a disbelief in and distrust of the procedure.[37]

The system of punishment, lack of due process and the curtailment of complaints procedures all contributed to an atmosphere which alienated the population in Peterhead and made them more hostile to the prison authorities. As one prisoner pointed out:

> *I wrote petitions, I wrote to members of the Visiting Committee, I wrote to my MP, the Police, the PF [Procurator Fiscal], my lawyer, I had visits from the police and PF . . . and replies to my petitions and letters. At the end of the day it all turned out to be a complete waste of time . . . It seems there [are] two types of laws, one for prisoners and the other for staff, prisoners always get charged while the staff don't, plus it all takes months on our part but staff have things moving for them in a matter of days and on the prisoners' part there is always a lack of evidence against the staff. It's hardly surprising when you are dragged from your cell by a number of officers when the rest of the prison is locked up! No I've never felt happy with the outcome, if anything it's made me more bitter towards certain staff . . .*

The lack of confidentiality was compounded by the fact that prisoners could be charged under Prison Rule 42(16) for making 'repeated and groundless complaints' against prison staff. Finally, violent incidents between staff and prisoners usually took place with only one prisoner (the victim) present. As one prisoner explained:

> *The official channels of complaint are useless. Each time that I have been beaten it was done in private – no witnesses.*

Under Scottish law charges against prison staff concerning assault require corroboration. Prisoners in Peterhead were therefore confronted with one of the central contradictions of imprisonment. As lawbreakers they were confined in lawless institutions. As Graham Zellick has observed:

> Whatever attitudes one may have about crime and criminals it cannot be right that the law may be broken with impunity. That is why we sent people to prison in the first place. What kind of experience is imprisonment likely to be if those set in authority over prisoners express a contempt for the law and its processes different only in degree from the offences committed by those in their charge?[38]

Zellick's question was answered in November 1986 when the lack of legal rights within and accountability of the Peterhead regime provided further impetus to the prisoners' protest. The rule of law had failed to set the necessary parameters to protect those who, by its own liberal rhetoric, needed the fullest protection.

NOTES

1. Questionnaire response also cited in The Gateway Exchange, *The Roof Comes Off: The Report of the Independent Committee of Inquiry into the Protests at Peterhead Prison*, Edinburgh, Gateway Exchange, 1987, p. 82.
2. B. Sissons, *An Inside Job*, London, Freshfields, 1984, p. 88.
3. M. Fitzgerald and J. Sim, *British Prisons*, 2nd edn, Oxford, Blackwell, 1982, p. 75.
4. Scottish Council for Civil Liberties, *Facing Reality: The Scottish Prison Crisis in the 1980s*, Glasgow, SCCL, 1987, p. 27.
5. Ibid., p. 38.
6. Ibid., p. 39.
7. *Scottish Council for Civil Liberties Bulletin*, May 1987, p. 16.
8. Cited in Gateway Exchange, *The Roof Comes Off*, p. 78.
9. SCCL, *Facing Reality*, p. 29 (emphasis in original).
10. Scottish Home and Health Department, *Prisons in Scotland Report for 1986*, HMSO, 1987, p. 25.
11. Gateway Exchange, *The Roof Comes Off*, p. 80.
12. Ibid., p. 78.
13. Ibid., p. 77.
14. Ibid., pp. 78–9.
15. Scottish Home and Health Department, *Prisons in Scotland 1986*, p. 25.
16. Scottish Home and Health Department, *Prisons in Scotland Report for 1985*, HMSO, 1986, p. 25.
17. SCCL, *Facing Reality*, p. 32.
18. Gateway Exchange, *The Roof Comes Off*, p. 79.
19. SCCL, *Facing Reality*, p. 31.
20. Gateway Exchange, *The Roof Comes Off*, p. 81.
21. SCCL, *Facing Reality*, pp. 32–3.
22. Ibid., p. 33.
23. HM Chief Inspector of Prisons (Scotland), *Report of an Inquiry by HM Chief Inspector of Prisons (Scotland) into Prisoner Grievances at HM Prison Peterhead*, Scottish Home and Health Department, 1987, p. 41.
24. SCCL, *Facing Reality*, p. 24.
25. Ibid.
26. HM Inspectorate of Prisons for Scotland, *Report on HM Prison, Peterhead*, Scottish Home and Health Department, 1981.
27. See J. Boyle, *A Sense of Freedom*, Edinburgh, Canongate, 1977.
28. HM Chief Inspector of Prisons, *Grievances at Peterhead*, p. 46.
29. Ibid., p. 43.
30. Ibid., p. 42.
31. Fitzgerald and Sim, *British Prisons*.
32. Scottish Home and Health Department, *HM Chief Inspector of Prisons for Scotland: Report for 1987*, HMSO, 1988, p. 5.
33. Scottish Home and Health Department, *Prisons in Scotland Report for 1987*, HMSO, 1989, p. 20.

34. HM Chief Inspector of Prisons, *Grievances at Peterhead*, p. 43.
35. M. Maguire, 'Prisoners' Grievances: the Role of the Board of Visitors' in M. Maguire, J. Vagg and R. Morgan (eds), *Accountability and Prisons*, London, Tavistock, 1985, p. 154.
36. See Police Monitoring and Research Group, *Police Complaints Briefing Paper 4*, London Strategic Policy Unit, 1987.
37. SCCL, *Facing Reality*, p. 31.
38. Cited in Fitzgerald and Sim, *British Prisons*, p. 158.

CHAPTER 5

Discipline, freedom and outside contact

Any work connected with women is given low priority. Women connected with men in prison have even less . . . More than most of us they live in a world they didn't make.[1]

Prisoners no longer have faith in human nature. They cannot see a future without hope and being in prison with not an ounce of hope has resulted in terrible unrest and apathy.[2]

The glass screens that one Scottish prisoner remembered between prisoners and visitors in Barlinnie in 1983 seem exceptional even for Britain. But the relative infrequency and lack of privacy in visiting arrangements in British prisons combined with the much more restrictive rules governing letters and telephoning markedly diminish the prisoners' social bonds with the outside world and correspondingly deepen those within the world of the prison.[3]

Incarceration by its very nature separates the offender from the rest of the population, creating not only a physical but also a symbolic distance between the ascribed 'deviant' and those outside the walls. With the birth of the modern prison at the end of the eighteenth century this separation was justified by arguing the necessity of removing the criminal from the criminogenic influences of environment and peer group, thus allowing time for introspection, space for reflection and the possibility for change. As Michael Ignatieff has pointed out, only when temptation 'had been shut out by walls of stone and doors of iron could the inner voice of conscience begin to assume its sway'.[4] From the perspective of the confined this process, as Ignatieff recognizes, was psychologically painful. It was designed to be. For state servants and moral reformers separation was understood not simply in terms of benevolent reform but also in terms of discipline, and the infliction of psychological pain as punishment for transgressing the law. With the consolidation of the prison through the nineteenth and into the twentieth century the physical objects and human beings who brought familiarity, comfort and contentment to the offender's life outside the walls were replaced by a system that allowed access to them not as a *right* but as a *privilege* which could be removed at the discretion of prison managers. While letter writing and prison visiting in particular became the prisoners' main point of contact with the outside world they also became part of the state's armoury in the continuing struggle to maintain order and control. Allowing access to family and friends, therefore, was heavily circumscribed by the demands of discipline and regulation. Any breach of the many and all-embracing prison rules could be punished by the removal of outside contacts for a set period of time. By the late 1960s this contact was further compromised by the introduction of the parole system which, although providing the promise of early release, tied it to the good behaviour and conformity of the prisoners as defined and interpreted by a range of state servants.

What was central to prisoners' lives – personal relationships and their day of freedom – thus became governed and determined by a series of rules, regulations and standing orders whose interpretation was not only highly discretionary but also shrouded in secrecy.[5] This chapter explores the relationship between these procedures and the Peterhead prisoners at the time of the major disturbance in November 1986. The processes involved in visiting, letter writing and parole have been separated out for the sake of clarity. In practice, however, they are deeply intertwined, striking at the heart of prisoners' emotions in areas where they are at their most vulnerable.

PRISONERS' FAMILIES: VOICES FROM THE MARGINS

Male prisoners' families and those women with whom they have personal relationships are often forgotten in the debates around penal policy for long-term prisoners. The pressure group Families Outside has pointed out that those beyond the walls are not only invisible but also recieve little sympathy or support from neighbours, friends, other family members or the social services. Their suffering is both material and psychological. The children of the confined experience multiple disadvantages in relation to housing, schooling, heating and the provision of food. In addition, they suffer disproportionately from health disabilities including epilepsy, asthma, bronchitis, recurring chest infections, nocturnal enuresis, and physical and mental handicaps.[6] It has been estimated that in England and Wales over 500,000 children feel the impact of their father's incarceration sometime during childhood. No figures are available for Scotland but Families Outside maintains that 'there is every reason to believe that the picture is even bleaker in Scotland, where the incarceration rate per head of population is significantly greater'.[7]

For the partners of prisoners feelings of isolation, despair and guilt are common. This is compounded by harassment from neighbours, other members of the family and state agencies. This leads in turn to feelings of resentment towards their partner 'who as they see it, has "escaped into prison" while they are left with the responsibility of home, children and finance. They are in fact "serving a second sentence"'.[8] For prisoners, emotional links with the outside are complex and vary according to the family member or friend concerned. Ageing parents evoke a different psychological response compared to the feelings generated about children growing up with fading memories of their presence in the household. Similarly, marital or common-law relationships, their genesis and, more importantly, their future evoke unique, often very painful feelings and memories built on yearning and desire. For those in Peterhead these different psychological responses shared common emotional ground in that they were not residual feelings which were left behind at the point of incarceration. Rather they were deeply imprinted and branded on prisoners' consciousness and provided the propulsion for social action, particularly when they felt that relatives and friends were experiencing needless degradation and frustration because of the operation of the prison rules. This was a central element in the politics of protest in the winter of 1986.

VISITING THE CONFINED

Like every area of prison life, visits to Scottish prisoners are at the discretion of the prison authorities and are tightly controlled. The authorities have allowed no major concessions concerning the emotional needs and desires of the confined. This policy stands in marked contrast to the humanizing developments in visiting rights in a number of other countries. In some federal prisons in Canada, which contain prisoners serving two years or more, small houses or portakabins have been built within the grounds

> so that prisoners who are not allowed home can spend forty eight hours with their families once every three months. Those with no family are also allowed to use the facility for a weekend just to get a respite from prison life.[9]

In the maximum security prisons in Sweden visiting areas are provided which contain private rooms with a bed where visits of up to two hours a week 'take place in private'.[10] Finally, in the Netherlands, long-termers in closed prisons are allowed three visits of up to three hours a week. In addition they can have one 'private visit' each month 'with extra visits if the case can be made'.[11] The private visits enable them to have sexual contact and to be intimate and self-expressive with visitors. Accounts by Dutch prisoners have emphasized how family ties have been strengthened as a result of these visits. In the UK this development has been strongly opposed, particularly by the Prison Officers' Association whose members argue that it is open to abuse. However, as David Downes has pointed out:

> One reply to this criticism by a Dutch prison deputy director was that such abuses as, for example, drugs being brought into the prison, exist as a possibility with *any* visiting. In both systems, body searches can take place after visits as a check against illicit substances being brought in from the

outside. And the British prisoners were emphatic that both soft and hard drugs were as prevalent in the British as in Dutch jails. What *is* apparent is that the Dutch authorities regard the benefits of such visits as outweighing the costs.[12]

This latitude did not extend to those in Peterhead. Historically, the visiting facilities had always been a source of grievance for them. When Beverly Sissons taught in the prison between 1972 and 1977, there were no facilities for visitors 'except a small windowless waiting room and a lavatory in the gate house. The women with children found it difficult to travel as well as too expensive'.[13] Prisoners met their families for nine hours a year in these surroundings. As one prisoner pointed out:

Every two months they [the family] travel 120 to 180 miles to sit on one side of a 4 ft. broad table with a six inch board up the centre and officers around them as if they were criminals, watching their every move. I am serving a 14 year sentence, this means with good behaviour I serve 9 years 4 months, in this time I shall only see my loved ones 84 hours in almost a decade, this is ridiculous especially with the size of my family.[14]

The situation was equally bleak for those who accumulated their visits and travelled south to Barlinnie in Glasgow:

The cells kept for 'visiting prisoners' in Barlinnie were variously described to me as being 'flea-pits'; 'only fit for a polar bear' as they had no visible means of heat, and indeed no heat at all if I am not mistaken. They were also said to be 'dirty' and had 'lumpy mattresses'.[15]

Accumulated visits continued to be a source of controversy into the 1980s. In January 1986, one prisoner engaged in a hunger-strike to draw attention to the closed visiting conditions at Barlinnie:

Visitor and prisoner must bob their heads up and down . . . to communicate, the head going down to speak through the metal grille, then up to catch the other person's facial expression through the plate glass, and of course this prevents all physical contact.[16]

In 1986 the prisoners were allowed two visits each calendar month which lasted for one hour (except between 2 p.m. and 4 p.m. when they were allowed two hours). Visiting times varied between weekdays and weekends. During the week they could be visited at any time except between noon and 1 p.m. and between 5 p.m. and 6 p.m. All visits had to be finished by 8 p.m. At weekends visits were allowed on Saturday afternoon and Sunday morning or afternoon. As noted above, they could also accumulate visits and meet friends and relatives in a local prison nearer to home. This transfer could last for up to 28 days.[17]

The visiting arrangements were heavily circumscribed by the prison bureaucracy and the demands of security. Visitors required a Visiting Order, which they brought to the prison. The Governor could refuse visits from prisoners' friends, relatives who were not immediately family and 'anyone not known to the prisoner before custody'.[18] In addition, there was no provision made for access to meals, for families to take photographs or to exchange gifts at important times such as birthdays and Christmas. As the report of the independent committee of inquiry concluded: 'we appreciate that these views would result in anxieties over security, but believe that adequate search measures taken before and after visits would overcome such fears'.[19]

For prisoners and their families there were a number of problems associated with visiting which caused strain, depression and antagonism. The first problem for both groups related to the geographical location of the prison. As Chapter 1 noted, Peterhead is 34 miles north of Aberdeen. The majority of the prisoners, however, came from central Scotland, particularly the large conurbations of Glasgow and Edinburgh. Consequently, the journey to and from the prison could take between 12 and 16 hours:

My wife and daughter travel from Dunoon on a Saturday morning arriving at the Prison at approximately 2pm – fatigued. Our first visit on the Saturday is usually tense and to make matters worse we are separated by a four foot counter topped with eight inches of glass. These conditions are humiliating and only add to the tension . . .

There is never enough time but at Peterhead the consideration must be given to the visitors, often to catch a connection between trains, buses etc. The location itself is the obstruction and may act as a deterrent against close bonds between families. The visitors are always weary from travel, exhausted, the visit period is a respite from both sides of the barrier. It is a brief resting stop on the half-way mark for the visitors. I consider that they suffer from a form of exhaustion exposure. It takes time to unwind from the frustrations of long distance travel . . .

For those in solitary confinement visits could be particularly intense:

Considering the distance and inconvenience every two or three months I don't think the visits are long enough, although I'm aware the prison authorities permit extra times as is the norm in other prisons. But this only strikes some balance for the travelling time. Especially so, when in Solitary Confinement as you are disorientated at times, and feel alienated from everyone as you can't concentrate on conversations since you're not used to having conversations or contact with other people for months on end . . .

I don't get enough visiting contact with my wife and kids to keep a good relationship going; more so, when I'm in Solitary Confinement as my relationship has been terminated at present due to the distance and alienation at visits attributable to effects in part from Solitary Confinement; (Withdrawn after no contact with people)

The cost of the journey was an extra burden. According to a number of families the grants available from the Department of Health and Social Security were not only selective but also subjected them to a 'means test' to ascertain if they qualified for payment towards the cost of the journey:

> *By train takes so long. The train leaves Glasgow at 7.25am and they don't get home till 11pm. My sister has to pay for travelling but my mother gets help from the DHSS but this is very humiliating as it is Means Tested.*

> *I cannot criticise Peterhead Prison on the visiting hours as my family cannot afford the expense to come to Peterhead to visit me, as my Mother is an old age pensioner, and my Brother is unemployed, and I do not wish to cause my family any embarrassment by asking them to go to the Social Security for help in enabling them to visit me in Peterhead . . .*

> *I only get to see my Fiancée about twice a year because she lives in Edinburgh, is unemployed, is a single parent and has been refused DHSS Travel Warrants. She cannot afford to come and see me more than once or twice a year. That is not enough.*

The families were often kept waiting when they arrived at the prison as Visiting Orders were checked and visitors and prisoners were moved between the halls, waiting room and visiting area. This cut into the scheduled visiting time:

> *By the time they sort through the visit passes and work out who is going to what hall to collect people, then get them to the visit room, usually as much as half an hour has passed. Being in the (Punishment) Cells, I'm the last to be picked up for a visit and first to be returned. Once my wife waited forty-five minutes before I arrived.*

> *I have only had one visit since I came up here in October 1983, that was from my Daughter last June when she was only sixteen. She had just found out that I was her Father and wanted to see me. I had not seen her for thirteen years. She came up on a Saturday by train – missed the connecting bus and didn't arrive at the prison until 4.40 pm. They allowed me fifteen minutes with her . . .*

The physical structure of the visiting room reinforced the already strained relationship between visitors and prisoners. The visiting booth contained a fixed wooden base topped with glass. This prevented easy physical contact. The booths were separated by glass partitions. They could only hold two visitors which meant that friends and relatives rotated the seating arrangements in order to be close to the prisoner:

> *My Father died and my mother came to visit me to break the news, had to sit in tears while several members of staff looked on, also very frustrating as there was about two foot of wood and glass between us as I tried to console her . . .*

There was little privacy particularly in the booths closest to the supervisory staff. This resulted in pressing domestic and personal problems being internalized and remaining unspoken:

It takes 12 hours round trip by car to get there. Getting expenses (DHSS) is now easy but initially it was very difficult. The lack of privacy is not too bad if you can get in early – as far away from the Prison Officers as possible. It's humiliating because there are always Prison Officers watching. I have to get permission to give them a cup of tea or biscuit . . .

I'm taken from the hall 'The Search', 'Metal Dectector' 'Rub Down' – My visitors kept at the gate, then left in a room. Being in a prison such as Peterhead causes stress and despair that seems to boil at a visit. I personally try not to burden my family with worry . . .

One visit every four weeks with my wife and child is not enough to maintain effective contact with them. We are finding it increasingly difficult to relate to one another because of the four week gap between visits . . .

The discipline of the prison extended to the visitors:

Although the visits are long enough, my visitors do not relish being made to feel like criminals. They are stared at by screws constantly, are asked the make and number of their car, and on one occasion were stopped on the way out of the visits, and told to turn out their pockets and were searched by screws. I ended up getting three months for assaulting the screw for that particular incident . . .

Family members also complained about the inadequacy of the prison's communication system. Messages concerning the cancellation of visits were neither passed to them nor to the prisoners:

Recently there was a death in the family and I phoned up to say that I could not visit my son because of the funeral. I was refused another day to use my pass. I asked the prison officer to pass the message on to my son but this never happened. He had no idea why I missed the visit and was terribly worried because of my ill health. [20]

I had phoned the prison and asked if it was okay to visit my brother and the prison officers had said yes. His lawyer had to go up and see him on the Tuesday before. He got all the way up to Peterhead (from Glasgow) to be told by the officers that he had been moved the day before to Inverness. And yet they never phoned. My Mother had got everything ready for our visit and this is the way we heard of his transfer . . . [21]

The discipline and regimentation of Peterhead therefore extended beyond the walls and touched those acquainted with or related to its prisoners. The harrowing nature of the journey and the alienation engendered by the actual visit ensured that all visitors, from elderly parents to the youngest child, received the same symbolic message that not only were those inside beyond redemption but also they, too, had forfeited part of their dignity and humanity simply through being associated with them. This penal response, however, contained its own contradictions. For many of the prisoners, it was the final ignominy and ensured that any legitimacy the regime had was fractured by its drive to punish the innocent. Asserting this innocence and recapturing their visitors' dignity was as central to the 1986 demonstration as their own physical and mental treatment.

COMMUNICATING WITH THE CONFINED

Writing to and receiving letters from the Peterhead prisoners was also a complicated and often debilitating process. Writers were deeply enmeshed in a complex web of rules, regulations and standing orders which controlled the number, length and content of their letters. In addition, the Governor had discretionary powers to refuse prisoners permission to write to individuals or groups, particularly those not known to the prisoner before his confinement. Finally, all incoming and outgoing letters were censored.

The tone and content of the Prison Rules made clear to prisoners the extent and scope of the discretion allowed to prison managers in relation to letters. Rule 74 (1) of the Prison (Scotland) Rules indicated that all correspondence was subject to

> any such restrictions as may be laid down by the Secretary of State with a view to the maintenance of discipline and order, and the prevention of crime, and no other person (than friends and relatives) shall be allowed to communicate with a prisoner without the authority of the Secretary of State. [22]

In the Abstract of the Rules, published in 1976, the prison department informed prisoners that 'every letter to or from a prisoner except certain categories of prisoners shall be read by the governor, or by an officer deputed by him for the purpose'. [23] This allowed the governor to stop 'any letter on the grounds that the contents are objectionable'. [24] What was objectionable was never defined. Prisoners were also told that letters and visits were 'privileges which may be forfeited as a punishment'. [25] As with prison visits, other countries have pursued more liberal and ultimately less alienating policies with regard to letter writing. In the Netherlands:

> there is no limit to the number of letters prisoners can write or receive. There is random censorship, but it is not a pretext for limiting correspondence. Postage has to be paid for, but the more generous wages mean this is no problem. [26]

In Peterhead there was little scope for developments of this kind. In 1986, prisoners were allowed one free letter a week. Additional letters had to be paid for from their wages. As Chapter 2 noted, wages in the prison were very poor. Prisoners could not afford to buy extra letters. Alternatively, they had to make difficult and psychologically burdensome choices between buying letters and everyday items for their personal use. The prison authorities offered little financial support in this area. State expenditure on postage was minimal. In the financial year ending in March 1987, the prison department spent £71,000 on postage in Scottish prisons. This was 1.4 per cent of the budget for 'administration'. It compared with £3,161,000 (61 per cent) spent on administrative pay and allowances; £150,000 (3 per cent) on travelling and subsistence; £824,000 (16 per cent) on transfer and detached duty expenses; £132,000 (2.5 per cent) on stationery and printing; and £94,000 (1.8 per cent) on what was termed 'miscellaneous'. Overall, postage constituted 0.13 per cent of net expenditure for the year which was £55,498,000.[27]

Prisoners were concerned about the censorship of mail and the use to which private information was put in order to disempower them:

> *Apart from accumulated visits that is, I depend mostly on letters to keep me in contact with my family but how can you write your personal feelings when you know that the letters are being scrutinised by an ordinary prison officer who has been given the job of mail censor?*

> *Gossiping staff, contents of domestic mail and interference with legal matters etc. etc. . . .*

> *For some absurd reason the envelopes in which our letters come are withheld from us and once one of these private items (my envelope) which had my Sister's name and address on the back was found by another prisoner and handed to me after he had found a number of them lying about the hall . . .*

They also maintained that mail was withheld, delayed, or in some cases simply disappeared from their property. Outside agencies such as the Scottish Association for the Care and Resettlement of Offenders, the Scottish Council for Civil Liberties, Families Outside and the Gateway Exchange supported the prisoners' allegations. These agencies utilized recorded delivery to ensure that the mail reached the prison. Prisoners pursued a similar strategy. They requested certificates of posting for outgoing mail. In 1986 they obtained 2900 certificates of posting, or around eight every day. As one family member explained:

> William has to get proof of postage because several of his letters didn't get out. The reasons given for this was that the letters had been full of lies. At times I knew for a fact that his letters had just vanished and he has not been informed why . . .[28]

The controls around visiting and letter writing made a direct contribution to the individual atomization and the collective alienation felt by the prisoners in Peterhead. Official claims that the regime was based on sensitivity and care were belied by the treatment of prisoners, their families and their friends. For prisoners, it was the latter's treatment which turned the screw of Peterhead still further. However, as this book has made clear, it was an issue on which they refused to be broken.

DISCIPLINE, EARLY RELEASE AND PAROLE

The parole system in Scotland is a complex and contentious process. The system was originated in the White Paper, *The Adult Offender*, published in 1965.[29] The paper's proposal became law under the Criminal Justice Act 1967 and the parole system came into operation on 1 April 1968. The Act established a separate Parole Board for Scotland. It has 14 members who sit at the apex of a convoluted process which begins five months before the date of possible parole when the prisoner is allowed the opportunity to identify why s/he should be released. If willing, the prisoner is also allowed an interview with a member of the Local Review Committee (LRC) of the prison in which s/he is confined. The LRC consists of the governor (or deputy governor) of the prison concerned, a social worker and at least two others who are deemed to be independent members. The LRC makes a recommendation for or against parole on the basis of the information before it. The Committee's recommendations and the papers are passed to the Scottish Home and Health Department where the cases are again considered by officials acting on behalf of the Secretary of State for Scotland. At this stage some cases recommended for early release by the LRC may be refused, and others which were initially refused may be supported. Finally, the full Parole Board considers all cases formally submitted to it by the Secretary of State and makes a recommendation about the suitability of a prisoner for parole and the date on which it should be granted. Unlike the system in England and Wales, no prisoner can be released by the Secretary of State on the sole recommendation of an LRC – 'the case of everyone who is released must first be reviewed by the Scottish Parole Board'.[30] The government-appointed Carlisle Committee, which reported in November 1988, noted a number of other differences between the two systems including the fact that 'the paroling rate in Scotland has consistently been lower than in England and Wales'.[31] In 1969 the rate was 16 per cent in Scotland, compared with 25 per cent in England and Wales. In 1983 it was 39 per cent in Scotland but 53 per cent in the South. By 1987 the gap had become wider when the figure in Scotland was reduced to 28 per cent, while in England and Wales it rose to 59 per cent. In addition, more prisoners opt out of consideration in Scotland, 'about 12% as against 4% for the 2 year plus group in England and Wales'.[32]

If granted parole the prisoner is released on the qualifying date or as soon as possible thereafter. If the prisoner misbehaves between receiving parole and the release date the release may be postponed or cancelled. Once released, the prisoner has to observe a number of conditions in the parole licence which, if broken, can mean that the licence is revoked. These conditions include: being placed under the supervision of a social worker; keeping in touch with the social worker; informing the social worker about a change of address or loss of job. The Parole Board also maintains that a licensee 'shall be of good behaviour and shall keep the peace [and] he shall not travel outside Great Britain without the prior permission of his supervising officer'.[33]

Finally, life sentence prisoners remain on licence for the rest of their lives. The Secretary of State cannot order release without the Parole Board's recommendation. Additionally the Lord Justice General and, where possible, the trial judge must be consulted about the release of prisoners who fall into this category. In 1986 there were 332 life sentence prisoners in Scottish prisons, which was 9.6 per cent of the average daily population of adult prisoners.[34]

THE SYSTEM IN PRACTICE

Since its inception the parole system has been subjected to a range of criticisms, including: its arbitrary nature; the bureaucracy involved; the lack of prisoners' rights both during the process and after release; the denial of appeal procedures; the tension involved for prisoners and their families; and the lack of information and secrecy which allows the authorities to withhold the reasons why prisoners have been refused early release. Critics have also argued that the system quickly became a mechanism for managing and controlling individual prisoners. The power invested in individual members of staff who could make representation to the Board meant in practice that only those prisoners who conformed to official and managerial desires stood any chance of early release. As one early critic of the system noted:

> The parole scheme . . . despite the liberal rhetoric, has been and continues to be used primarily as a management tool to further control over the incarcerated. It is designed to control people's behaviour; prisoners are explicitly worried that people who cause 'trouble' will not qualify for parole.[35]

From its introduction in Scotland in the late 1960s the system has been highly contentious. Initially prisoners refused to cooperate by declaring themselves to be ineligible. In 1969 the Parole Board pointed out that of the 702 prisoners who were eligible for parole during the year, 152 (21.7 per cent) made no application for early release. The Board was 'seriously concerned' about the situation, particularly as a 'high proportion came from Peterhead and Aberdeen'. The independent inquiry outlined the reason for the lack of cooperation, citing research, conducted at Edinburgh University which found that

> the realisation among the prisoners concerned that their chances of selection for parole, based on life-style, record and response to training in prison are slight indeed. Their assessment is not unrealistic, it is not infrequently supported, albeit tacitly, by the staff of the prisons, who when asked by a prisoner 'what are my chances of parole' will reply 'well what do you think?'[36]

This continued into the early 1970s when 'opting out' reached its peak. Between 1970 and 1973, 28 per cent of those eligible opted out of consideration. Since then, the number opting out has declined as more prisoners allowed their cases to be put forward for review. It still remained higher than the rest of the country, however, averaging 12 per cent between 1976 and 1985.[37]

The prisoners' reluctance to be considered for parole was compounded by the conservatism of the new Board in Scotland. As noted above, the Carlisle Committee recognized that the paroling rate in Scotland has been consistently lower than in England and Wales. This conservatism was established early in the Board's life. In 1972, 139 prisoners were released on licence, prompting the Board to comment that this was 'only a very small part of the total number released from Scottish Penal Establishments . . . it is evident that some men may be spending longer in prison than is necessary in terms of rehabilitation'. [38] This conservatism continued into the 1980s. At the same time, the long-term prison population also continued to climb. In 1971 there were 641 very-long-termers in Scottish prisons; by 1986 there were 1496. In 1971 there were 100 lifers; by 1986 there were 400. Between 1985 and 1987 there was a 40 per cent rise in the number of long-term prisoners. [39] Finally, the prison department made it clear to prisoners in the bluntest terms how it saw the operation of the system. In the *Abstract of the Rules and Regulations for Convicted Prisoners* issued in January 1976 the department pointed out that:

> No prisoner is entitled to parole nor will he be automatically released on parole. Parole cannot be earned simply by keeping out of serious trouble in prison, although prisoners guilty of serious misconduct are unlikely to be paroled. There is no need to apply for parole; every case will be considered and parole granted to those selected after very careful consideration. Parole means release on licence and any person breaking any condition of the licence may be recalled to prison. [40]

For those in Peterhead, such sentiments only reinforced the view that the prison was a place of no hope from which it was very difficult, if not impossible, to obtain early release. From October 1983 these difficulties were intensified by the changes in the parole system announced by Leon Brittan. As Chapter 7 notes, these changes not only increased the number of long-term prisoners but also exacerbated the already tense situation in the long-term prisons. As the National Association for the Care and Resettlement of Offenders pointed out, Brittan's proposals created two parole systems:

> one in which cases are examined on their merits and another in which parole is refused other than in exceptional circumstances. The result is a serious and arbitrary distortion of judicial intentions . . . We consider that these changes are intrinsically unjust and counter-productive in their stated aim of combating violent crime. [41]

In May 1984 the Secretary of State for Scotland indicated to the Parole Board that he would not release prisoners serving five years or more for crimes of violence or drug trafficking 'except in cases where the circumstances were exceptional'. [42] In practice this meant that while the Board continued to see cases, it had to now 'identify exceptional circumstances, to the satisfaction of the Secretary of State, before it is invited to consider making a recommendation for parole'. [43] Similar rules were made for those who murdered police and prison officers, children and those who killed by using a firearm. For all of these categories the first function of the Parole Board 'was to identify exceptional circumstances before it would be invited to consider advising release on parole where under 20 years would be served'.[44] The Chief Inspector of Scottish Prisons pointed out that 'very many Governors, staff and inmates had been shocked by and dismayed with'[45] the changes:

> The prisoners felt unjustly treated in that the effect of the announcement was retrospective, that what they believed were realistic expectations had been thwarted and what light there had been at the end of the tunnel had been extinguished.[46]

The Chief Inspector concluded that prisoners and staff perceived the new policy as 'repressive and iniquitous'. He was equally forthright in his general review of Scottish prisons for 1986 when he pointed out that the objective for the changes in the parole procedures was 'to deter serious crime but within the prisons the man of violence who becomes a "no-hoper" may also become a serious danger to prison officers and other prisoners'.[47]

For those in Peterhead the changes simply underlined the collective view that not only was Peterhead a prison of no hope but also any incentive towards positive behaviour had been taken away:

> *The incentive, bogus as it was, has been taken away from all and sundry, or nearly, hence, the lack of reaction by way of behaviour seemed to be, in the past, reformative. Nobody seems to give a shit anymore; and it's going to get a helluva lot worse before it gets better. The sentences are longer now than ever.*

> *Prisoners convicted of crimes of violence and those involving firearms and drugs are beginning to realise that they will not be afforded an opportunity for early release, unlike other prisoners. Prison apartheid is how I would describe it.*

> *Prisoners morale is low because of this. There is no hope as it is anyway and most prisoners cannot see the light at the end of the tunnel.*

They were also clear about the link between the changes and the demonstrations:

> *Each year, for quite a few years, I have lived in a state of nervous tension for between four to six months of each year, waiting for a reply to my application for parole. The stricter interpretation of the criteria governing release on parole [has] led to a feeling of hopelessness in many categories of prisoners which, in turn, has contributed to the general unrest in prisons.*

> *Unquestionably, the recently stated policy to curtail parole for the general prison population and to deny same to certain categories has been a contributory factor in the recent series of disturbances.*

> *Now that some prisoners know that they have no chance of parole, violence has increased and the whole atmosphere has become markedly hostile.*

The increase in the level of hostility was underpinned by a feeling of hopelessness which was likely to be turned against prison staff and property:

> *No-one who has violence attached to their crimes stands a chance, so have nothing but many years in prison to look forward to, so, in most cases, or some cases, they don't care what happens or what they do.*

> *Most guys that I know personally say that if there isn't any parole for certain people, then they don't have anything to lose.*

> *Most people I have spoken to feel bitter. Every day in prison is more punishment, but there was always the parole system, no matter how unfair it was . . . everyone knows that a Judge takes parole into consideration when passing sentence, but now it's all time.*

> *The changes have left a lot of prisoners serving long terms feeling bitter and without hope.*

For many, the changes in parole signified the end of the road.

This chapter has pointed to highly sensitive areas of prison life which had a significant impact on Peterhead prisoners in 1986. Freedom, emotional ties and contact with the outside for the confined were more than abstract concepts. They were deeply held and vibrant, but often debilitating, feelings which cut into their consciousness and informed their attitudes towards the prison regime. To see the discipline of the regime reach beyond the walls and into the lives of family and friends caused many of them searing emotional pain. It was the final impetus towards confrontation with the system which, from their perspective, directly contributed to the irretrievable disintegration of relationships that were already brittle or fractured.

The emotional needs of long-term prisoners and their families have never been deeply researched by academics, state bureaucracies or the media. In the latter's case these needs and their place in the events leading up to the 1986 demonstration were either ignored or under-reported. The next chapter analyses the nature of the media's coverage of the demonstration and the pathological discourses which underpinned this coverage. If 1986 was the end of the road for prisoners, then the majority of media commentators ensured that those outside understood that the road was of the prisoners' own making, hewn from their unreasonable demands on the system.

NOTES

1. Kay Carmichael, cited in Families Outside, *Annual Report 1986*, The Families Outside Project, 1986, p. 4.
2. Questionnaire response cited in Gateway Exchange, *The Roof Comes Off: The Report of the Independent Committee of Inquiry into the Protests at Peterhead Prison*, Edinburgh, Gateway Exchange, 1987, p. 59. All other prisoners' responses in this chapter are in italics.
3. D. Downes, *Contrasts in Tolerance: Post-war Penal Policy in the Netherlands and England and Wales*, London, Clarendon Press, 1988.

4. M. Ignatieff, *A Just Measure of Pain*, London, Macmillan, 1978, p. 177.
5. S. Cohen and L. Taylor, *Prison Secrets*, London, Radical Alternatives to Prison/National Council for Civil Liberties, 1978.
6. Families Outside, *Annual Report 1987*, The Families Outside Project, 1987, p. 15.
7. Ibid., p. 6.
8. Ibid., p. 8.
9. V. Stern, *Bricks of Shame*, Harmondsworth, Penguin, 1987, p. 107.
10. Ibid.
11. Downes, *Contrasts*, p. 175.
12. Ibid., p. 176.
13. B. Sissons, *An Inside Job*, London, Freshfields, 1984, pp. 34–5.
14. Personal communication to the Scottish Council for Civil Liberties.
15. Sissons, *Inside Job*, p. 85.
16. P. McKinlay, *Scottish Prisons: Lift the Lid*, Edinburgh, Fight Racism/Fight Imperialism, 1986, p. 10.
17. Families Outside, *Annual Report 1986*, p. 27.
18. Stern, *Bricks*, p. 107.
19. Questionnaire response cited in Gateway Exchange, *The Roof Comes Off*, p. 66.
20. Ibid. p. 66.
21. Ibid.
22. I. McDonough, *Prison Regimes in Scotland – A Preliminary Report*, Glasgow, Scottish Council for Civil Liberties, 1982, p. 2.
23. *Abstract of the Rules and Regulations for Convicted Prisoners*, January 1976, p. 6.
24. Ibid., p. 6.
25. Ibid., p. 5.
26. Downes, *Contrasts*, p. 174.
27. Scottish Home and Health Department, *Prisons in Scotland: Report for 1987*, Cm 551, HMSO, 1989, p. 27.
28. Gateway Exchange, *The Roof Comes Off*, pp. 65–6.
29. Scottish Office, *The Adult Offender*, White Paper, Cmnd 2582, HMSO, 1965.
30. Home Office, *The Parole System in England and Wales: Report of the Review Committee* (Carlisle Report), Cm 532, HMSO, 1988, p. 18.
31. Ibid., p. 18.
32. Ibid.
33. Scottish Office, *Report for 1984 – Parole Board for Scotland*, HC 494, Session 1984–85, HMSO, 1985, p. 14.
34. Scottish Home and Health Department, *Statistical Bulletin No. 7*, Government Statistical Service, 1988, p. 4.
35. M. Fitzgerald, *Prisoners in Revolt*, Harmondsworth, Penguin, 1977, p. 59.
36. Cited in Gateway Exchange, *The Roof Comes Off*, p. 28.
37. Scottish Office, *Report for 1985 – Parole Board for Scotland*, HMSO, 1986, p. 10.
38. Cited in D. MacDonald and J. Sim, *Scottish Prisons and the Special Unit*, Glasgow, Scottish Council for Civil Liberties, 1978, p. 20.
39. C. Jones, 'The Crisis in Scottish Prisons,' *Scottish Council for Civil Liberties Bulletin*, October 1987, p. 13.
40. *Abstract of the Rules and Regulations*, p. 11.
41. National Association for the Care and Resettlement of Offenders, *Parole: The Case for Change*, submission to the Parole System Review, December 1987, p. 11.
42. HM Chief Inspector of Prisons (Scotland), *Report of an Inquiry by HM Chief*

Inspector of Prisons (Scotland) into Prisoner Grievances at HM Prison, Peterhead,
Scottish Home and Health Department, 1987, p. 63.
43. Ibid., p. 63.
44. Ibid.
45. Ibid., p. 64.
46. Ibid.
47. Scottish Home and Health Department, *HM Chief Inspector of Prisons for Scotland: Report for 1986,* Cm 260, HMSO, 1987, p. 15.

CHAPTER 6

Media construction of prison protest

The preceding chapters provide a detailed historical and contemporary overview of long-term imprisonment in Scotland, specifically at Peterhead. Gaining access to prisoners' accounts of life inside Peterhead prison presented a unique and revealing opportunity to consider the 'view from below' against official discourses and explanations, and against common-sense assumptions and prejudice. Most people's understanding of what actually happens in a remote, long-term prison such as Peterhead is informed by this 'mix' of official commentary and common-sense assumption. Unless people are involved directly with imprisonment the issues are as distant and hidden as the regimes themselves. When disturbances or protests occur at prisons, however, the issues become more public, more dramatic and more engaging. In short, they become news. Rooftop protests, fires in the halls and hostage-taking can be seen as the desperate actions of frustrated, brutalized prisoners to whom all other forms of negotiation and protest have been denied. They can be interpreted as being clear evidence that something is profoundly amiss in the prison system. Alternatively, they can be presented as the 'real', 'live' versions of endless film and television movies obsessed with the 'pathologically violent', the 'criminally insane' and the triumph of 'good' over 'evil'.

In gaining access to information on the disturbances and protests which regularly occur in prisons public opinion relies heavily on media coverage. The relationship between the media and the Prison Service is already in place. For news coverage is the sole source of access to the prison system and, given the obsessive official secrecy concerning closed institutions, the media has the potential to play a significant, possibly definitive, role in making the prison system accountable to the public. Given the seriousness of the 1986 and 1987 protests and the sheer weight of press coverage devoted to the events it is important to consider the questions of accuracy and balance in the making of 'prison news'. Not only does the media have a role to play in providing information, in situations such as Peterhead they are directly interventionist.

The coverage sets agendas, it prioritizes contrasting accounts, it legitimizes informants, it selects material and defines relevance, but most of all it reconstructs events. The media, quite literally, becomes the lens through which issues are brought into sharp focus.

This chapter considers critically the role of the media during and after the 1986 and 1987 protests, examining particularly the process by which serious protests involving hostage-taking and arson became reconstructed as 'prison riots' by a violent minority. It is also concerned to demonstrate the close liaison between the prison authorities and other 'official' bodies and the media, especially in terms of the weighting this provides to the 'view from above' (official sources) compared to the 'view from below' (prisoners' accounts). First, however, it is important to discuss recent critical research into the ideological role of the media and its significance in the making of crime news.

CRITICAL RESEARCH ON THE IDEOLOGICAL ROLE OF THE MEDIA

While there is considerable research on how people 'feel' about crime, few researchers have 'empirically examined the sources of information from which people gain their ideas about crime or the nature of the impressions presented in them from which they select their opinions'.[1] Within existing research on the relationship between crime and the media, there has been no specific coverage of prisons, imprisonment and prison demonstrations.[2] Previous critical media research, however, has identified central themes relevant to such an analysis. The importance of the media is well established in sociological inquiry, particularly in terms of its ideological function, institutionally related to the definition, maintenance and reproduction of dominant social relations and power centres within society. Critical media research recognizes the significance of the media as a supplier of *information* within already established political contexts. Analyses of the content of media output, combined with the processes of production within the constraints of ownership and control, have identified the role of the media in developing and reproducing ideological construction across a whole range of issues.[3] Such work has recognized the significance of how 'The media do not merely "reflect" social reality, they increasingly help to make it'.[4]

Central to critical media research has been recognition of the 'agenda-setting' role of the media, of how they are part of a framework within which events, issues and problems are debated and analysed.[5] For the media regularly set the agenda and lay the emphases for the 'latest' public debate and subsequently provide an arena in which it takes place. It is the prescription of an agenda which establishes boundaries and limitations concerning what is to be included and develops a conceptual framework which determines what is 'legitimate' and non-legitimate information within media production: 'The media do not just transmit neutral information; they present a particular set of images about what the social world *should* be like.'[6] The media interpret and reconstruct 'real reality' to create what is in fact 'media reality', a process which in turn frames and contextualizes the future responses of the media, thus perpetuating the legitimacy of 'media reality'.[7]

Focusing, for example on industrial disputes and political issues, critical research has examined the process of agenda-setting using content analysis.[8] A substantial body of work has examined the media presentation of class, race and gender, and the reinforcement of wider power relations and oppressive structural forces through stereotyping.[9] There has been considerable analysis of news coverage, examining the processes of selection and presentation. How this process affects the end product, the news bulletin or newspaper raises the crucial issue of accuracy and balance in the production of news. The emphasis on news coverage is derived in the relative power news media hold due to their 'privileged status as reality and truth' in society.[10]

It is generally accepted that the public has a 'right to know' about crime, yet 'the responsibility for informing them rests almost exclusively with a competitive and commercial press'.[11] As has been established, it is in this context that news is 'manufactured' or created by journalists through their interpretation and selection of world events, and not simply 'discovered' and 'recorded'.[12] Empirical work has concentrated on the organization of news production and analysed the models of society used as categories for selection procedures. This work has examined critically the relationship between state institutions and the media[13] and the flow of information – and disinformation – from the police, the army, the civil service, political organizations and other 'authoritative' sources to the media and its subsequent use as 'independent' news. Such individuals and organizations are reported faithfully and consequently become the 'primary definers' of social and political events, issues and problems. The media assume the role of 'secondary definers' through selection and presentation of information, with the possible exception of serious investigative journalism.

Clearly what constitutes 'the media' is not homogeneous. Apart from the distinctive qualities of the press, radio and television the relative status of each newspaper, radio station or television company differs within each medium. 'News' is selected and presented differently in the 'tabloids' than it is in the 'qualities', on local radio than on national radio, and so on. Priorities are determined by perceived audiences at different times and by restrictions on time and space. Yet what remains consistent, whatever the medium, is the significance of *sources of information*. The legitimation and use of acceptable sources within news production are processes central to the construction and presentation of issues to the public.

THE PRODUCTION AND CONSTRUCTION OF 'CRIME NEWS'

There is no limit to what might be reported, the number of observable describable events is infinite . . . We often fail to realise what a very, very limited selection of events it is that appears on our tables at breakfast time. On some days, whole continents do not rate a mention.[14]

This ex-journalist's comment illustrates that central to news production is the process of selection. Journalists and editors hold discretionary power in making selections for daily newspapers or television bulletins. A range of studies has examined this process, focusing on the bureaucratic and organizational constraints which surround the production of the news, and on the work practices of journalists which influence the selection and presentation of events.[15] The organizational routines of news production impose emphases on certain types of event. The 'round-the-clock' production of news, 24 hours a day, for instance, favours covering what is 'immediate' or 'new', or alternatively an event over a period of time which suddenly reaches a climax. A routine method evolves, within the different broadcasting and press media, organized around production, at regular intervals, of either the news bulletin (television and radio) or the newspaper. This ensures two things: that events become 'routinized' and no longer appear as haphazard as they are in reality; and that there develops a continuity in news production to cover changes in personnel.[16] Within this overall structure of news organization individual journalists work as general reporters, covering a range of 'routine' stories whenever they are on shift, or as specialist correspondents. Those who cover 'crime issues' usually are 'crime' or 'home affairs' correspondents or, occasionally, 'legal affairs' or 'court' correspondents.

The 'newsworthiness' of any event is based on the 'news values' held by journalists.[17] It is difficult to define what is 'newsworthy'. It has been a traditional claim by journalists that they have a 'professional sixth sense' or a 'nose for a story'.[18] Several studies have shown, however, that news values are, in part, a product of 'newsroom culture'; journalists learn the tricks of the trade literally 'on the job'.[19] Ex-journalists have indicated that their basic training guides them towards common 'basic ingredients' of a news story – conflict, hardship, danger to a community, novelty, scandal and individualism.[20] Steve Chibnall has identified eight imperatives which are not strictly laid down 'rules', but indicators of the elusive 'newsworthy' criteria.[21] *Immediacy* is perhaps the most obvious – an event has to be 'new' to become news. A second is *dramatization* – where an event is visible and spectacular it will be emphasized and often given more space as a consequence. A third is the *personalization* of a story, whereby leading individuals are emphasized at the expense of the context of the events. Fourth, *simplification* of events around 'common-sense' assumptions is an ongoing process and often a consequence of dramatization and personalization. Fifth, incidents will often be reported at the level of *titillation*, emphasizing sexually related stories, or 'sexualizing' the ordinary and the mundane. An element of this is the converse narration, which expresses hypocritical indignation at the activities or lifestyles of celebrities or personalities, while often describing details in a titillating way. Sixth, there is an underlying *conventionalism* in news reporting, where new events are assessed in relation to previously established frameworks of meaning or an overall 'world view'. Seventh, the search for *novelty* is an aspect of this, looking for a 'new angle' on what is really 'the same old story'. Finally, the construction of news is strongly informed by the *structured access* of journalists to 'institutional experts'.

111

The effects of professional news imperatives can be adverse. Their continual emphasis is often adopted at the expense of broader, structural analyses of events, thus diverting attention away from the 'serious' to the 'superficial' elements of news. This has led to an unhealthy competitiveness which has become reliant on speculation.[22] A further related concern is the persistent emphasis on the statements of those in authority or power positions which are viewed as more credible, convenient and therefore afforded more space than alternative accounts. To some extent the 'balance' of these criteria reflects the status and style of the newspaper (i.e. 'tabloid' or 'quality' press).[23] A study of Canadian newsrooms describes how journalists use a 'vocabulary of precedents' to guide their work.[24] By this is meant 'what previous exemplars tell them should be done in the present instance', which mirrors Chibnall's description of 'conventionalism' as 'coming to terms with new realities in old ways'.[25] These precedents revolve around three areas which inform the working culture of journalists: 'recognition knowledge' of what is a story (newsworthiness, good visuals, and so on); 'procedural knowledge' or how to handle a story; and 'accounting knowledge' or how to put the story together. Within the construct of 'precedence', however, there is negotiation and conflict over values and practices.[26] Organizational practices remain dominant, and Whitaker argues that journalists fit into well-established and closely regulated working practices which come to dominate their news-gathering potential.[27]

In relation to crime reporting and the construction of crime news, most journalists have no direct access to cases and in terms of the 'vocabulary of precedents' they learn to rely almost exclusively on information divulged to them by those at an official level.[28] The police are the 'primary definers' of the 'significance' of any particular crime and its 'newsworthiness'. In that sense the role of the police is that of a 'control agency' which adopts three news management goals: to facilitate their work; to protect their public image; to promote their aims and ideologies. The combined effect of pressures of time and demands of impartiality on news production processes has given 'a systematically structured *over-accessing* to the media of those in powerful and privileged institutional positions'.[29] Primary sources of information on 'crime' for journalists come from the police, court reports and the Home Office or Scottish Office. Government officials, civil servants, opposition spokespersons, and independent commentators (from community or pressure groups) are used as 'secondary' sources.

Research on police sources has illustrated how access to information is severely restricted.[30] Journalists who consistently doubt police information are likely to find future access restricted and could face prosecution.[31] This process virtually guarantees the adoption of an uncritical attitude towards such information, and limits accounts from other sources.[32] The information presented to journalists is preselected and ranked by the police from a range of potential 'crime news'. This selection is based to some extent on what the police consider journalists will *want* to cover as news, and this informs the day-to-day practices of police press officers. An examination of police press releases reveals similarity in tone and style to press reports. The impact of such news processes can be that 'crime news is really police news'.[33]

The problem of 'primary definers' and the dominance of official sources in the making of crime news extends to the relationship between journalists, the police and the courts, and its effect on definitions of and responses to 'serious' crime. Put another way: 'through their interactions and reliance on official sources, news organisations both invoke and reproduce prevailing concepts of 'serious crime.'[34] Research has suggested that individual crimes become 'crime waves' due to the methods by which news is organized around news *themes*.[35] 'News themes' are the combined and heavy coverage of a number of incidents which journalists report as a 'single topic'. This imposes an organizational, presentational order on quite disparate incidents and events. Crime is rarely reported unless it fits within an established theme, where it can relate to an emerging trend in criminality or law enforcement.[36] Further studies confirm that 'crime news' is restricted to a *selection* of potential events that could be reported.[37] They demonstrate that crime news which is organized around 'themes', and sometimes a 'crime wave', overemphasizes certain types of crime and heightens the public's fear and anxiety. This is particularly the case with crimes involving violence and sexual assault. 'Crimes of the powerful', such as corporate crime, police corruption or abuse of power are underemphasized.[38] Certainly the influence of the news production process, encompassing the news management and social control potential of state agencies, is considerable in establishing what constitutes 'serious crime'. This in turn sets the priorities, if not the agenda, for policy within the criminal justice process.

Thus bureaucratic and organizational procedures have a significant effect on the production of news. The news coverage of issues relating to imprisonment can be analysed in the same way. Of particular importance are the news management capabilities of official personnel within the Prison Service, Home Office and Scottish Office, which have close parallels to those of the police outlined previously. There are two main areas of work for a journalist covering prisons: either straight news reporting of specific events, or in-depth work as a features writer, home affairs correspondent or documentary researcher. These are complementary roles but are distinct at an operational level. The former is perhaps the more familiar as it informs the public in a routine way about the prison system. The latter, however, is equally significant, given that specialist journalists work regularly and intensively within official channels. Possibly more than with other social issues, the public is totally dependent on the media to provide information on what is happening in prisons and what is being planned or developed in penal policy.[39] This is given further emphasis because of the lack of information available from other sources, particularly the state agencies concerned, on any closed institutions including prisons.[40]

This analysis will concentrate on *press* coverage of prison protest due to the difficulty of embarking upon a detailed assessment of broadcast bulletins transmitted several years ago. Although research has stressed the primary source of television news for public information on issues and events,[41] significantly other empirical work on crime news has found that regional newspapers are the main source of information about *local* affairs.[42] It is legitimate, therefore, to concentrate analysis on the practices of press journalists, particularly those working on the national Scottish newspapers.

In reporting major prison incidents, an assignment may fall to a shift reporter, or a regular home affairs writer. When a rooftop incident suddenly occurs, whoever is available is sent to cover the story and if the situation is prolonged several individuals work on a rota basis. 'Covering the story' in such cases means spending the majority of the time based at the prison where the incident is taking place. Journalists follow visually what is happening 'on the roof' and receive official statements at regular intervals, usually from a Scottish Information Office (SIO) press officer. This information is then sent back to the newspaper and compiled into a report about the 'latest developments'. Statements from interviews with officials from other notable organizations such as the Scottish Prison Officers' Association, the government and the Scottish Office often will be added to these 'on-the-spot' reports, providing background information. Journalists, then, are compelled to rely heavily on official statements both at the prison and from elsewhere, to compile substantial news stories. Such statements, however, reflect the vested interests and the blanket control of information which officials therefore enjoy, and ensure the limited nature of routine news coverage. The restrictions placed on producing prison news cause concern among some journalists. As one has commented:

> Where the problem arises is that you cannot tell from standing a quarter of a mile away looking at what's happening on the roof what led up to that incident and how it was resolved, the aftermath – anything from *inside*.[43]

Consequently, routine news coverage is restricted in its ability to present more than a point-by-point account of a prison incident. As the same journalist said:

> It is sad but true that in most cases in terms of the general news coverage there is not a lot of place for analysis anyway . . . It is a markedly different job from someone who will try to put the events in context.[44]

There are additional problems in the process of routine news reporting. It can lead to an over-reliance between journalists, who develop a clique, despite the competition between papers. The pooling of information and comparing of 'angles' is not unique to the news coverage of prisons but it has specific problems. In an environment where such a tight control prevails on the management of information, such over-reliance can promote an artificial homogeneity in the reporting of prison incidents, prisoner motivation and institutional responses. How much of a problem this becomes depends on the responsibility of individual journalists to 'produce your own analysis of what it all means'.[45]

PETERHEAD: CONSTRUCTING THE 'POWDERKEG'

The context within which the 1986 protest at Peterhead was reported was well established prior to the event. In 1984 the rooftop demonstrations produced news coverage which was clear in its assumptions: 'RIOT PRISON',[46] 'THE PETERHEAD POWDERKEG',[47] and 'TIME-BOMB PRISON'[48] are three typical headlines. They represent unambiguous examples of the tone which came to dominate much of the coverage. Peterhead was described as 'Scotland's toughest jail' and as a '"hard men" jail'[49] which 'houses Scotland's most violent prisoners'.[50] The inference was clear: 'Behind its walls the violence simmers among its hard men'.[51] Prisoners at the jail consistently were portrayed as 'hard men', 'violent inmates' and even 'the toughest, most brutalised dregs of Scotland's criminal strata'.[52] This overwhelming generalization was then placed alongside their actions – that is, prisoner protest or political protest was redefined as 'riot'. For within the context of pathological criminality and violence *rational* protest was inconceivable. The media were locked into a construction of events which explained and reported prison protest as a direct manifestation of prisoners' violent tendencies. Certainly it prepared the ground for the coverage of the 1986 demonstration.

Examination of the press coverage of the 1986 demonstration at Peterhead provides immediate illustrations of the general problems in the media constructions of prisoner protest. The choice of language, such as 'riots' and not 'demonstrations', immediately positions the reader in relation to how s/he will perceive and understand events. Other problems with language stem from its sensationalist and dramatic use which overemphasizes any violence or aggression while underemphasizing or ignoring grievances voiced by the protesters. Combined with this is a concentration on any hostages taken which individualizes the protest and polarizes events into the 'good' of prison officers against the 'evil' of the prisoners. Finally, explanations given for demonstrations rely heavily on well-established official statements which blame a small minority of pathologically violent men. This stands in stark contrast to the space afforded to alternative accounts from prisoners themselves, their families, campaign groups and critical individuals outside the prison system.

The 1986 Peterhead prison siege was, at the time, the most serious of its kind, lasting a record 93 hours. It marked a general shift by prisoners to public displays of protest, going 'on the roof' and taking hostages. Nine days before the Peterhead siege started there was a hostage-taking at Saughton prison, Edinburgh, which the *Evening Times* related to Peterhead. The piece, headlined 'POWDERKEG PRISON' was subtitled 'Peterhead time bomb on a short fuse'. It described the prison as 'Scotland's toughest jail. It is where the thin blue line of the prison system takes on the "hard men" of society, sometimes head on.'[53] The report gave examples of previous incidents at Peterhead and showed three photographs of the aftermath of events at the jail, captioned 'DESTRUCTION'. Other captions, such as 'BATTLES', 'TENSION', 'STABBED', made the parallel with war. The justification for this full page spread on Peterhead was that the Saughton protesters had complained specifically of violence there and in particular the use of excessive punishments in B Block. Instead of highlighting these complaints, however, the report represented Peterhead as a prison full of violent, unstable, irrational men who embarked on physical destruction instinctively and without provocation. In the report on Saughton, only one protester was quoted, saying 'what we have set out to do is bring forward the corruption and brutality of the prisons'. There was no comment made on this statement, nor was it related to the accompanying piece on 'powderkeg' Peterhead. While the report on Saughton included a suggestion from prisoners of genuine grievances against the Scottish prison system, the feature on Peterhead ignored such motivations, preferring to seek explanations in established notions of mindless violence by a pathologically criminal element among Peterhead's prisoners.

In its coverage the *Evening Times* simply reproduced a previously established code of practice in the representation of Peterhead. A full two years earlier the newspaper had used exactly the same headline 'PRISON POWDERKEG'.[54] The first paragraph, known as a 'slant-first', was almost identical: 'Peterhead is the time-bomb of the Scottish prison system, where the country's toughest criminals live on a very short fuse.'[55]

This paper was by no means alone in its repeated use of such jargon. From the same incident in 1984 the *Daily Record* headlined its coverage as 'TIME BOMB PRISON',[56] the *Glasgow Herald* used 'The Peterhead Powderkeg'[57] and both used the description 'Hard Man Jail'.

These examples set the tone for the coverage of the November 1986 hostage-taking at Peterhead. They provided a powerful illustration of how Peterhead's reputation was constructed, maintained and reproduced. Because the siege began on a Sunday afternoon, on 9 November 1986, newspaper coverage only began in earnest the following day. The *Evening Times* used the front page headline 'MASK OF DEFIANCE' alongside a large photograph of a hooded figure. The slant-first ran: 'The dark hooded figure squatting on a prison roof is a symbol of defiance . . . And his baton carries the message: "Don't come close".'[58] The report described how the siege had started and the 'orgy of destruction' that had followed at the jail. Similarly, the *Daily Record* had used the headlines, 'TERROR ON THE TILES' and 'Masked Men in Orgy of Destruction'.[59] The dramatic use of pictures and language emphasized a climate of violence and fear for the hostage. It portrayed the prisoners involved as 'other' – irrational, 'hard men' – summed up by the headline 'These Men Have Nothing To Lose'.[60] The *Daily Record* exemplified this in a piece entitled 'The Deadly Past of Leaders' which gave substantial details of the offences for which the men involved were convicted.[61] Even comments made in court by judges when passing sentence on the men were included. This added further, seemingly authoritative, evidence to the general portrayal of the prisoners as abnormal, irrational, dangerous and pathologically violent. Both papers focused on the plight of the prison officer taken hostage, John Crossan. Large front page headlines proclaimed 'THE HOSTAGE', 'Held by knife man on the wrecked roof of riot prison';[62] and 'FEAR OF THE HOSTAGE', 'Warder's Family Tell of Prison Anguish'.[63] Each report gave substantial coverage to personal details of the officer and his family. This theme intensified as the siege continued. By the Wednesday the *Evening Times* front page headline was 'TEARS AND FEARS', 'Police warn of threat to life of prison hostage'.[64] The first paragraph read: 'Fears increased dramatically today for the life of the young prison officer . . .

116

Tension rose sharply after more than thirty inmates clambered on the wrecked roof of the prison'.[65] The caption accompanying the photograph added: 'HIGH TENSION . . . Tearful hostage John Crossan is put on parade on the wrecked roof of Peterhead. He is a man alone with his fears'.[66]

The headline in the *Glasgow Herald* took the same theme – 'Peterhead siege on knife-edge' – reporting that the prisoners 'appeared angrier'.[67] There was considerable contrast, however, in the report in *The Guardian*.[68] The headline 'Prisoners at siege gaol show warder on roof' was followed by a report which stated that the hostage 'looked solemn' and that 'the prisoners seemed on reasonable terms with Mr. Crossan who did not show any signs of fear'. This comparatively different style and content demonstrates clearly how newspapers make conscious choices to overemphasize certain aspects of events turning the story into a drama, appealing to the human interest element and, in the process, swaying readers towards a particular focus of concern while denying the potential of a quite different reality. This is not to deny the seriousness of hostage-taking, the threat to the individual or the deep hurt caused to his family but the contrast between *The Guardian* coverage and that of other papers is instructive.

The personalization of the protest in terms of the hostage reached its height in the report by the *Daily Record* on 13 November 1986. In a centre-page spread the headline read 'A MAN ALONE' alongside a full colour photo of the officer and protesters on the roof at Peterhead. It was sub-titled 'Face to face with hatred John can only wait and hope'. The report was a clear example of establishing newsworthiness through high drama:

> High on a dawn-cold prison roof yesterday a young man was taken over the edge of despair. Around him a crowd of angry men, their faces ugly with menace, paraded him for all to see . . . a helpless victim, their contempt for his life was total. And the young man's anguish was extreme . . . He was in obvious distress. His body shook and his shouted plea was filled with emotion.[69]

This flamboyant report can be contrasted to another of the same day. The *Glasgow Herald* described Crossan as 'clearly under strain' and quoted him as shouting through a makeshift megaphone. The report stated:

> 'We are up here to negotiate for the release of me and the other guys but they are not even listening' he shouted to the journalists on the roadway, about 100 yards away. Then Mr. Crossan appeared to break down and cover his face with his hands, wiping his eyes.[70]

This description, as well as using more temperate language, framed the officer's despair quite differently. Far from being associated solely with his captors' aggression it suggested that his desperation was related directly to an inability on the part of the prison authorities to negotiate adequately with the protesters. It is significant that immediately after Crossan had shouted, attempts were made by prison officials to drown out further communication by turning on a prison generator. Ultimately a news clampdown was imposed by the prison authorities and journalists were removed from within sight of the jail. Some were threatened with arrest if they did not leave. Rather than relating this to the nature of the statement made by Crossan, various reports uncritically reported the Scottish Office justification for the removal of journalists because they were 'hampering negotiations' and putting the hostage's 'life in danger'.[71]

Sympathy for the prison officer's situation was further generated in news reports' favourable representation of prison officers' work. While the 1986 siege was in process, the *Evening Times* carried a special two-page feature headline 'TRAINED FOR A LIFE BEHIND BARS'. The first paragraph emphasized the demanding nature of the work: 'There is no mistaking the sense of pride that goes with the uniform. A swelling pride that comes from training for one of the toughest jobs around.'[72] The report constructed a favourable image of prison officers and their work. It made no comment on any of the critical issues raised about standards of recruitment, inadequate training, allegations of harassment or brutality. This was in sharp contrast to the portrayal of individual prisoners involved in the protest. As previously mentioned, many reports concentrated on details of prisoners' convictions and the constant use of violent imagery. While prison officers were caring, committed and dedicated, the prisoners were 'desperate men', 'masked men', 'hard men', who instinctively turned to 'threats', a 'menacing show of defiance', and were forever 'sneering', 'jeering' and 'cursing'.

The generalization of negative, indeed violent, imagery of those involved in prisoner protest enhances and underwrites the drama and tension necessary to command the contrived attention of the newspaper's readership. Further, it is an essential mechanism in legitimating the official response that behind all prison protest lies a minority hard core of violent men whose objectives are to disrupt the regime, intimidate other prisoners and injure prison officers. A clear example of this was the report on the ending of the siege which was facilitated by the involvement of a journalist from the *Daily Record*, Ian Cameron. The protesters requested to speak directly to a newspaper reporter and agreed they would release the hostage and end the siege if this request was met. The reporting of this meeting was used to its full dramatic potential by the newspaper. It was, of course, a massive and impressive scoop, an exclusive without parallel. The front page headline boomed: 'FACE TO FACE WITH A KILLER', 'Ordeal of *Record* man who helped end the siege', and it continued with suitable dramatization: 'For forty frightening minutes, *Record* reporter Ian Cameron sat face to face with triple killer Andy Walker . . . alone.'[73] Inside there was a two-page account from Cameron of his interview with the protester, whom he described as the 'pint-sized bearded murderer' and a 'triple killer'. His 'exclusive' started:

> I have never been so scared in all my life. For forty minutes I was alone with one of Scotland's most callous mass murderers . . . It was his huge green eyes that almost hypnotised me – eyes which flashed with anger one moment and with despair the next . . . He had almost violent changes of mood.[74]

When quoted by the *Glasgow Herald*, however, Cameron's words were considerably tempered. He described the incident as 'very unnerving' and Walker as 'quite a small man. I was expecting a giant – an ex-Army corporal who killed three people'.[75] It is clear that the general coverage of the 1986 siege was sensationalized throughout and that the media played a significant part in generating massive hostility against those confined in Scottish prisons. The specific grievances publicized by the prisoners and the broader issues concerning the endemic problems of Peterhead's regime were lost in a coverage which almost universally concurred with official explanations of persistent unrest. This portrayal of prison protest was no more than a 'good versus evil' drama, played out in the daily tabloids. It was a distinction compounded in the coverage of the end of the 1986 siege. Prior to the surrender of the protesters, the roof of the prison was set ablaze by the prisoners. This happened because the interview with Cameron ran over time and the men feared that they had been betrayed when Walker did not return. Much of the coverage failed to report this significant turn of events, preferring evocative imagery: 'Blazing but bloodless end to jail siege' and 'Rebels set fire to prison as hostage is released'.[76] The *Daily Record* had its own misleading explanation: 'FLAMES OF REVENGE', 'Ordeal ends in one last act of hate'.[77] The first paragraph again resorted to poetic metaphor: 'The grey fortress that is Peterhead jail returned to an unnatural calm last night', thus suggesting that the jail was not 'naturally' without unrest. The picture caption consolidated the now established violence of the prisoners: 'THE FINAL DEFIANCE . . . the siege is over but the flames of hate roar through A Hall'.

In the days following the ending of the siege the hostage's ordeal became the primary focus of media attention. The *Daily Record* reported 'MY DAYS OF HELL: by the Peterhead Prison Hostage' and claimed 'Another Record Colour Exclusive'. The first paragraph opened: 'Prison officer John Crossan spoke yesterday of his four nightmare days as the hostage of Peterhead'.[78] The subsequent report contained several statements from Crossan which undermined the dramatic coverage of his confinement. The report quoted him as saying:

> There were times during the siege when I was terrified . . . Yet there was no aggro directed at me, though there are a lot of grudges against some staff. The men imprisoned in Peterhead are human beings with family and other problems like everyone else, including myself. They also have grievances which at least should be aired in public.[79]

Therefore, the prison officer who was taken hostage, the only non-prisoner close to the siege, provided a quite different account of the events, the prisoners' attitudes and the context of the protest than those accounts which had dominated the media throughout. Fundamentally this raises serious questions about how prisoner protest was interpreted and how accounts focusing on 'violence', 'hatred', 'evil' and 'nightmares' came to be written. John Crossan was the individual most directly threatened by the prisoners' actions yet his emphasis bore no resemblance to those accounts which had apparently so authoritatively and dramatically recorded his ordeal from a distance.

As discussed in an earlier section, how news reports weight their explanations of prison protests concerns the individuals they turn to for comment. Of the newspaper coverage researched, the overwhelming majority took for granted, and printed verbatim, statements from Scottish Office and Scottish Prison Officers' Association (SPOA) spokespersons. The degree to which this is done depends on the particular paper or, in the case of broadcasting, which particular news bulletin the report appears on. In the 1986 press coverage, as already mentioned, Peterhead's 'reputation' preceded it. Stock phrases were churned out and explanations for the protests were recycled. The *Daily Record* report warrants quoting in full, by way of illustration:

POWDERKEG OF VIOLENCE
Peterhead Prison is home to the country's most dangerous and desperate criminals . . . thugs, killers and terrorists. Given the nature of the inmates the regime has to be tough.

HAVOC
It has been branded Scotland's powderkeg prison and, at best it exists under an uneasy calm. A recent report said: 'The staff perform a duty demanding a high degree of skill in difficult and often dangerous circumstances.'

Prison department chiefs believe much of the trouble which plagues the jail is instigated by a small number of inmates who are prepared to create havoc.

Relatively minor grievances, real or imagined, are considered sufficient by some for disturbing the routine. The authorities have tried to combat the problem by spending £500,000 on a special 10-cell unit to segregate the troublemakers.

But that doesn't appear to have solved the problem. The worst violence has been in the last decade and this is the 12th major incident since 1975.[80]

This entire account took for granted, and reported as fact, a series of assertions originating from the prison authorities. A Scottish Office annual report which praised prison officers was emphasized. The suggestion that violence was due to a hardened minority who were 'by nature' disruptive, was asserted six times in five short paragraphs. Legitimacy was given to the idea that the authorities were doing all they could to 'combat the problem', with the stress placed on the amount of money spent on a segregation unit at Peterhead. The contradiction in this effective piece of public relations comes in the last sentence – despite all positive efforts, the protests continued.

Even after the 1986 siege ended, favourable reports on the way the prison authorities handle such events continued to be published. The *Evening Times*, for example, headlined a report 'Prison Riots Probe to Start on Monday'.[81] This and the article which followed suggested that the prison authorities would deal adequately and thoroughly with grievances raised by prisoners in the protest. The *Glasgow Herald*'s coverage[82] focused on the issue of conditions at Peterhead and allegations of brutality. However, the reporter, Graeme Smith, emphasized official statements which undermined the prisoners' grievances.

Over half the report quoted Ian Lang (Scottish Home Affairs Minister), and John Renton (SPOA). The remainder of the piece was divided between a description of the end of the protest and an account by Ian Cameron of his involvement. Ian Lang was quoted as saying that because so few prisoners were involved in the protest it could not have been about conditions at the prison. Rather it was 'the actions of a small minority'.[83] Renton was quoted at length, countering accusations of brutality by prison officers:

> The suggestion that Peterhead creates violent people is a false one and the fact is that those prisoners who are violent at Peterhead were violent before they entered prison. The problem they have is that they are unable to cope with the heavy sentences that have been imposed upon them and must look for scapegoats for their own deficiencies of character.[84]

Renton also commented on criticisms of the regime as being made by people 'outside the prison system . . . who pretend to have the interests of the prison service at heart'.[85] This was the only reference to alternative accounts or informed opinion concerning the protest and it was dismissed simply by quoting John Renton. Similarly, *The Scotsman* quoted Ian Lang and John Renton substantially.[86] Its report did cover an all-party call for an independent inquiry or Royal Commission into the Scottish prison system. Renton's scathing response to this proposal, however, and his criticisms of others were also well documented as 'the whimperings of know-all do-gooders who have little to offer society other than their pessimism'.[87] Renton continued, commenting that prison officers were being 'pilloried for no other reason than the fact that they do a magnificent job on behalf of society'.[88]

Such reporting contrasts vividly with the space and legitimacy afforded to prisoners' grievances. Throughout the siege much of the coverage included photographs of the prisoners' banners proclaiming specific messages such as 'Brutality: We Need Help'; 'Living Death Must End'; 'Long Term Mental Torture'; 'Saughton History; Peterhead Now'; 'We Are All Hostages'; and 'They Treat Us All Like Animals'. Yet none of the reports attempted to examine the meanings and motivation behind these displays. The obsessive questioning, particularly in the tabloid newspapers, as to why the men behaved as they did, at no time considered the messages which were waved before their eyes. Some news coverage gave space to the grievances expressed by men at the jail, but only after the siege had ended. The *Sunday Mail* carried a piece headlined: 'Banged Up and Ready To Explode; Prisoner's-eye View of Peterhead'.[89] The article related the experiences of one man at the prison but it was judged that to justify such a statement some assessment of his credibility had to be provided. The first paragraph stated:

> Steve is no angel. He's a not-so-old lag with a violent record. His last sentence was 6 years for robbery . . . He makes allegations that would be denied by prison authorities. But it shows the state of mind that led to the violence.[90]

The reader was left in no doubt that Steve was not necessarily to be believed but he provided a good example of the 'state of mind' of Peterhead prisoners and the pathologically violent disposition that put them inside in the first place. *The Observer* provided the only news reporting which emphasized the conditions at the prison in a piece titled: 'Riot jail inmates plead for end to brutality'.[91] The report described how prisoners 'have been pleading for two years for reforms to a regime that they claim is increasingly brutal and repressive' and it included critical comments from prisoners, academics and others on conditions at Peterhead. The same day the paper ran a strong editorial entitled 'Jails: a failure of will' which made connections between the immediate protests and the overall crisis in penal policy.

Within a year the drama of the 1986 hostage-taking and the coverage were repeated as prisoners returned to the roof in September 1987. Immediately the focus was on the prison officer, Jackie Stuart, his age and his family. The *Daily Record*'s headline read 'GRANDPA COURAGE'.[92] The first paragraph continued: 'Stripped to the waist, surrounded by violent men, hero grandfather Jackie Stuart is paraded as a human trophy.'[93] The themes, now pre-eminent in the reporting of prison protest, were already in place as 'good' was set against 'evil': 'As Scotland's powderkeg prison erupts again . . . one man is left to bear the brunt of the prisoners' frenzy.'[94] Clearly it has been established that the 'human tragedy' angle was one which could be exploited and developed more fully.

The *Evening Times* coverage moved from the specific plight of Jackie Stuart to focus on prison officers' families under the headline: 'Women Who Live With The Dangers'.[95] The article focused on the job of prison officers as being dangerous, unpleasant and a constant strain on their families who 'know only too well the agony that the hostage's wife is going through'.[96] The wife of a prison officer described her husband's job in the following terms:

> 'Prison warders are subjected to daily insults from inmates and they know they could be taken hostage at any time. When they open the cell doors in the morning they get the contents of chamber pots thrown in their faces and I've heard of many prison warders getting a kicking from prisoners,' she said.[97]

This personal account emphasized exclusively the issue of the hostage-taking and generalized this incident to focus on the 'plight' of prison officers and routine suffering of the job. The broader issues concerning the motivation of the prisoners and their grievances were virtually ignored.

By the second day the 'drama' surrounding the hostage was the sole issue. The *Daily Record*'s full front page proclaimed: 'HAMMER OF HATE: "HE'LL GET IT" THREAT TO BRAVE HOSTAGE'.[98] It went on to describe how:

> The life of hero prison officer Jackie Stuart last night hung in the balance. The three remaining hardline prisoners holding him hostage at Peterhead prison yesterday treated him like an animal. And for a few harrowing seconds it looked as if his captors were going to kill him.[99]

The *Evening Times* chose the same emphasis: 'TEARS ON THE ROOFTOP . . . Prison hostage Jackie Stuart appeared sobbing on the roof at Peterhead today. And there are now fears for the officer's life.'[100] The focus on the hostage was also developed in *The Independent*, which carried the headline: 'ROOF-TOP ORDEAL OF PRISON SIEGE HOSTAGE'.[101] What followed was very much in line with the style of the tabloids, describing the prison officer as

> slumped across a cellblock roof yesterday, his forehead resting on an arm. He seemed an old, exhausted man. For a few seconds he raised his head and moved his hands in the air, as if waving helplessly to colleagues in the prison yard. Then he pulled up the collar of his blue jacket against the cold easterly breeze and bowed his head on to his arm. His shoulders heaved as if he were crying.[102]

The report failed to question why prisoners, in full knowledge of the heavy sentences handed down to those in the previous siege, had staged a repeat protest. There was minimal coverage of the grievances, of the nature of the protest or of the broader context of possible negotiations. Yet, on the same day, *The Scotsman* carried an article headed 'Hopes rise for jail siege breakthrough'[103] which attempted to make sense of the issues.

The themes of the 1986 coverage, even the words used, were reiterated throughout the protest but the papers were provided with a new angle when it ended with the SAS allegedly storming the prison. The use of the SAS provided a victorious, celebratory and military conclusion representing a full expression of 'good' over 'evil'. The *Sunday Post* headline boomed: 'SAVED BY THE SAS', 'Rioters are Routed in Eight Minutes'.[104] Other reports followed this line with these headlines: 'SAS Rescue Hero Jack';[105] 'Delight as freed jail hostage is reunited with grandchildren';[106] 'Sprung by the A-Team: Siege is over as SAS go in with grenades';[107] 'Maggie Sends in the SAS'.[108] The *Scotsman* led the way in demanding an inquiry into Scottish prisons in an editorial headlined 'Prisons inquiry is unavoidable'.[109] *The Independent* also ran a piece, 'Prison at "the end of the line"'.[110] The *Glasgow Herald, Scotsman, Guardian* and *Independent* on the same day[111] highlighted the prisoners' demands for a public inquiry to bring about the end of the protests, but the prisoners were not afforded rational motivations for their behaviour by other press coverage. The *Sunday Mail* recognized that the prisoners had grievances in an editorial titled 'Siege of Shame',[112] but its description of events detracted from this issue:

> the whole of Scotland has been shocked by the disgraceful scenes this past week . . . [the hostage was] paraded like a dog and his life threatened by a bunch of convicted criminals. All the while they revelled in the publicity their reign of terror received . . . And there is no public sympathy for a bunch of nutters grabbing and terrorising a prison officer – no matter how genuine their grievance.[113]

Only *The Observer* gave any emphasis to or expressed *real* concern about prisoners' allegations of mistreatment and general conditions at the prison in its piece headlined 'Grim dossier of brutality at Peterhead'.[114]

The lack of attention paid to prisoners and other outside commentators on the prison protests in press reports is underlined by coverage given to the independent committee of inquiry into the protests at Peterhead prison, which produced its report, *The Roof Comes Off*, in November 1987. The limited coverage given to the report reflects the legitimacy afforded to alternative accounts. Several news reports sought to undermine the credibility of the inquiry by quoting extensive criticisms from the Scottish Office and by questioning its authority to pass criticism.[115]

Finally, the coverage of the trials of the prisoners involved in the 1986 and 1987 protests demonstrate the well-worn thesis of criminal violence. The headlines were unequivocal and reflected solely descriptions preferred by prison officers at the trials: 'Gaol rioters "threatened to mutilate hostage"';[116] Hot fat was thrown at officer in jail riot';[117] 'Stabbed officer feared he would die';[118] 'Prison officer tells of threat to set him on fire';[119] 'Prison riot jury hears of inmate's bloodbath threat'.[120] The greater percentage of column inches was devoted to prison officers' statements about events and about prisoners' motivations. One officer was quoted as saying: 'you could put them in a 4-star hotel and they would be up on the roof'.[121] From such specific examples the problematic nature of routine news coverage is clearly illustrated. In the case of reporting Peterhead the search for the dramatic headline or photograph, the 'new angle', or the emotive description led to an over-simplification of complex events.

Throughout the news coverage of the 1986 and 1987 Peterhead protests and the subsequent trials little mention was made of the debates around penal policy, leaving 'explanations' for the protests within the preconstructed context well rehearsed within official circles. In this scenario the demonstrations were 'riots' incited and carried out by a 'handful of pathologically violent men' who were 'out of control' and 'hell-bent on chaos'. They intimidated others into an 'orgy of destruction' and their actions were motivated by 'violence' and 'hate'. Their depraved lack of humanity was self-evident in the taking of hostages and the 'threat to life' and 'terrorism' of these actions. Finally, when all else failed, they underlined their 'meaningless destruction' by setting fire to the prison. This, in 1986, had been the final act of 'evil', a prophecy self-fulfilled. These dramatic, impressionistic, sensationalized and certainly newsworthy statements dominated the coverage and concurred exactly with the prison authorities' position on long-termers at Peterhead: hard, violent men who need a tough, uncompromising regime. Against these powerful messages, spanning official sources and media coverage, any critical, informed and penetrative analysis becomes difficult, if not impossible. Certainly the 'view from below' remained trapped within the walls of the punishment block.

PUBLISH . . . AND BE DAMNED

In the earlier discussion of the production and construction of crime news a set of criteria was outlined against which the newsworthiness of stories is established. These were: immediacy; dramatization; personalization; simplification; titillation; conventionalism; novelty; and access to 'experts'. With the exception of titillation – although there is evidence to suggest that people are titillated by the threat of violence and the 'excitement' of public tragedy – the Peterhead protests met the criteria perfectly. They were 'immediate' and visible, a drama unfolding before a mass audience. The imagery of 'riot', the reported violence of the men, provided a dramatic backcloth culminating with the 'storming' of the prison by the SAS. In terms of simplification, the coverage appealed to the common-sense assumptions and prejudices of its mass audience, using the 'novelty' of the hostages to develop highly personalized coverage in terms of the prison officers and their families. Certainly such personalization occurred at the expense of reporting the wider context of the events. The news coverage also established its own 'conventionalism' even in terms of the repeated use of metaphor and rhetoric. In that sense a 'vocabulary of precedents', in handling the stories and putting them together, and a framework of organizational practices were established.

How these organizational practices, particularly the relationship between media and the authorities, came to be institutionalized and how access to official sources ('experts') came to be structured is central to a critical analysis of the media role in reporting prison protest at Peterhead. In Scotland journalists have to rely on the Scottish Information Office (SIO) to provide press releases and organize press conferences on all aspects of Scottish home affairs including the operation of the Prison Service. This provides the SIO with considerable discretion in the management of news and has led journalists to refer to the SIO as the 'Scottish Mis-Information Office'. Interviews with journalists indicate that there had been some naive trust in the information provided by the SIO, but recently there has been a more general awareness that information is regularly 'stage-managed'.[122] Allegations include: late notification, especially on Fridays, thus preventing full coverage or a counter-view; and provision of 'summarized' reports with subtle manipulation of overall context. One journalist said: 'they will mislead by omission whereas they used to, for a while, by commission'.[123]

Historically, the management of news by state institutions is well documented.[124] Law enforcement agencies, as discussed earlier, enjoy extensive discretion in news management because of their near monopoly of information and protection under secrecy legislation. Successive Thatcher administrations have strengthened still further state powers to withhold, or selectively to release, information.[125] While some journalists have become more aware of news management, state agencies have become increasingly wary of investigative journalists. As one journalist stated, 'the rules of the game have changed' and a 'mutual watch' is kept between the two parties.[126] Individual journalists can find themselves monitored by the departments with which they have to work[127] and 'critical copy' can lead to real problems of access: 'in recent years they have been keeping a kind of hostility rating for named journalists. Depending what your track record is with them you are deemed either hostile or friendly.'[128]

An adverse track record can result simply from asking 'too many questions', not taking official statements at face value, and cross-checking answers with other services. 'Unfriendly' journalists can find their jobs made more difficult in several ways. These include: submission of 'written questions' prior to interview or press conference; delaying interviews in order to provide a block statement; denial of stories and naming of the journalists to discredit their work; selective invitations to 'off-the-record' briefings, creating media 'insiders' and media 'outsiders'. Off-the-record briefings were used throughout the prison protests, allowing the prison authorities to give background information on specific issues to selected journalists. It enabled a point of view to be fed to the media without any source being named and without accountability. As Robbie Dinwoodie, at the time home affairs correspondent for *The Scotsman*, stated:

> What I don't think you can do is accept anything they give you without making clear that this comes from the department. What 'off-the-record' in its most highly developed form means is that you accept assertions and opinions, things that you can't substantiate, as independent free-standing 'facts' and that's supremely dangerous. [129]

It was his judgement that concerns over the use of 'off-the-record' briefings were a reflection of general developments in news management in the 1980s: 'News management has become more overt – government spokespeople in all departments have had their job more heavily politicised – both sides know what's going on and it has become a tactical battle.' [130] For a journalist identified as 'unfriendly' by the SIO, using briefings which could not be attributed was a 'famous way of gagging you'. Robbie Dinwoodie saw this as part of a broader problem within state departments where there was 'a refusal to accept that criticism can be intended as constructive' and a 'tendency to view anyone who is perceived as critical to be automatically hostile'. [131]

This can also lead to repercussions in the relationship between journalists and their newspapers. The pressure that owners and directors place on editors occasionally brings criticism that individual journalists are too partisan. This is compounded by the tendency for quality newspapers to maintain a strict division between news reporting and in-depth features. There is considerable editorial pressure to omit what is seen as 'subjective comment', an issue difficult to resolve as Dinwoodie pointed out:

> comment and analysis are so close that it can be very hard to tell the difference. What I would have regarded as a piece of necessary analysis and context someone above me at the paper could regard as a personal comment. [132]

The frustration of having to accept editorial censorship of controversial or 'counter-view' analysis is clear in considering the reporting of the protests. Alternative accounts rely on letters from prisoners, often smuggled out, and the use of such information depends on the editor's position. Journalists commented that there was a clear reluctance among editors to incorporate such information into their reports on the assumption that prisoners' accounts 'lack credibility'. Clearly it was considered that to attach credibility to prisoners' accounts not only might bring criticism of the editorial policy but also could disrupt relationships with the SIO. These are powerful constraints on a balanced production of news with 'exclusion' from the coterie of media insiders a high price to pay for publishing accounts which might show state departments, their policies and their officials in a poor light. With high competition, financial stringency, staff cuts and increased workloads forming the 'rationalized climate' of news production, the 'disruptive' journalist can easily be dispensed with. This is a point not lost on the SIO.

Given the constraints of news production, the stage management of events by state departments staffed by press, information and public relations officers, the creation of 'insiders' and 'outsiders' and the agenda-setting devices so deeply entrenched, it comes as little surprise that prison news, particularly related to mass protest, is limited. During the 1980s a few journalists made serious attempts to break the boundaries and put prison protest within a more informed and considered context about penal policy in Scotland. At *The Scotsman* Robbie Dinwoodie mobilized what he considered to be that newspaper's 'long history of a hostile stance to any authoritarian streak'.[133] More than any other journalist he took the issues beyond the superficial criteria which have come to dominate the selling of news, and his feelings about the journalist's role in the prison debate are clear:

> If the press and broadcasters can do more to keep these grievances [of the men], and the whole debate as to what kind of prisons society wants, going then there is less likelihood of there having to be riots and roof-top protests.[134]

What is evident is that the struggle to increase accountability within the prison system is matched by a struggle to increase access to information outside. Access to what is happening within prisons should be a democratic right, and Dinwoodie was sceptical of the 'new-image' Scottish prison department and its potential for change in terms of news management: 'The trouble is, that without a lot of correctives, like a better system of internal justice and much greater accountability and scrutiny, you can't trust a closed system.'[135]

NOTES

1. S. Sherizen, 'Social Creation of Crime News: All the News Fitted to Print' in C. Winick, *Deviance and Mass Media*, London, Sage, 1978, p. 203.
2. A paper from Australia indicates the problems of media coverage of deaths in police and prison custody: R. Hogg, 'The Media and State Deaths' in M. Hogan, D. Brown and R. Hogg (eds), *Death in the Hands of The State*, Redfern, New South Wales, Redfern Legal Centre Publishing, 1988.
3. S. Cohen and J. Young (eds), *The Manufacture of News; Deviance, Social Problems and the Mass Media*, London, Constable, 1981; S. Hall, C. Critcher, T. Jefferson, J. Clark and B. Roberts, *Policing the Crisis: Mugging, the State and Law and Order*, London, Macmillan, 1978; J. Curran and J. Seaton, *Power without Responsibility*, London, Methuen, 1981.

4. Curran and Seaton, 1981, *Power*, p. 228.
5. Cohen and Young, *Manufacture of News*.
6. Ibid., p. 430, (emphasis in original).
7. T. Bennett, 'Media, "reality", signification' in M. Gurevitch, T. Bennett, J. Curran and J. Woollacott, *Culture, Society and the Media*, London, Methuen, 1982.
8. Glasgow University Media Group, *Bad News*, London, Routledge and Kegan Paul, 1976; GUMG, *More Bad News*, London, Routledge and Kegan Paul, 1980; *Really Bad News*, London, Writers and Readers, 1982; M. Hollingsworth, *The Press and Political Dissent*, London, Pluto, 1986.
9. See in particular, K. Davies, J. Dickey and C. T. Stratford (eds), *Out of Focus; Writings on Women and the Media*, London, Women's Press, 1987; P. Cohen and C. Gardner (eds), *It Ain't Half Racist Mum: Fighting Racism in the Media*, London, Comedia, 1982; P. Golding and S. Middleton, *Images of Welfare*, London, Macmillan, 1982.
10. S. E. Bird and R. W. Dardenne, 'Myth, Chronicle and Story: Exploring the Narrative Quality of News' in J. W. Carey (ed.) *Media, Myths and Narratives*, London, Sage, 1988, p. 82.
11. J. Ditton and J. Duffy, 'Bias in the Newspaper Reporting of Crime News', *British Journal of Criminology*, vol. 23, no. 2, April, 1983, p. 159.
12. Cohen and Young, *Manufacture of News*.
13. Hall *et al.*, *Policing the Crisis*.
14. B. Whitaker, *News Ltd.: Why You Can't Read All About It*, London, Comedia, 1981, p. 23.
15. See most notably S. Chibnall, *Law and Order News*, London, Tavistock, 1977; R. Erikson, P. M. Baranek, and J. B. L. Chan, *Visualising Deviance*, Milton Keynes, Open University Press, 1987. For an overview of this literature, see L. Masterman, *Teaching the Media*, London, Comedia, 1985; R. Negrine, *Politics and the Mass Media in Britain*, London, Routledge, 1989.
16. J. Burgess, 'News from Nowhere' in J. Burgess and J. R. Gold (eds), *Geography, The Media and Popular Culture*, Beckenham, Croom Helm, 1985, p. 195; Negrine, *Politics and the Mass Media*.
17. See Chibnall, *Law and Order News*; Erikson *et al.*, *Visualising Deviance*; Masterman, *Teaching the Media*; Negrine, *Politics and the Mass Media*.
18. Erikson *et al.*, *Visualising Deviance*.
19. Chibnall, *Law and Order News*.
20. D. McShane, cited in Hollingsworth, *The Press*.
21. Chibnall, *Law and Order News*, pp. 30–5.
22. For an analysis of this increasing trend in tabloid journalism, see J. Jenkins, 'Sex and Vice Exposé: "Make It Up"', *New Statesman*, 6 May 1988.
23. Underlined by A. Hetherington, *News, Newspapers and Television*, London, Macmillan, 1985.
24. Erikson *et al.*, *Visualising Deviance*, p. 348.
25. Chibnall, *Law and Order News*, p. 35.
26. Erikson *et al.*, *Visualising Deviance*, p. 349.
27. Whitaker, *News Ltd.*
28. Chibnall, *Law and Order News*.
29. Hall *et al.*, *Policing the Crisis*, p. 58.
30. Chibnall, *Law and Order News*.
31. S. Chibnall, 'The Metropolitan Police and the News Media' in S. Holdaway (ed.), *The British Police*, London, Edward Arnold, 1979.

32. P. Cohen, 'Race Reporting and the Riots' in Cohen and Gardner, *It Ain't Half Racist Mum*.
33. M. Fishman, 'Crime Waves as Ideology' in Cohen and Young, *The Manufacture of News*, p. 24.
34. Ibid., p. 16.
35. Ibid.
36. Ibid.
37. Ditton and Duffy, 'Bias'; S. J. Smith, 'Crime in the News', *British Journal of Criminology*, vol. 24, no. 3, July 1984; Burgess, 'News from Nowhere'.
38. Hall *et al.*, *Policing the Crisis*; S. Box, *Power, Crime and Mystification*, London, Tavistock, 1983.
39. Ditton and Duffy, 'Bias', and Smith, 'Crime in the News'. Both discuss the major role of news in the dissemination of information about crime as a general category.
40. S. Cohen and L. Taylor, *Prison Secrets*, London, Radical Alternatives to Prison/ National Council for Civil Liberties, 1978.
41. Independent Broadcasting Authority, *Attitudes to Broadcasting in 1985*, London, IBA, 1986.
42. Ditton and Duffy, 'Bias'; Smith, 'Crime in the News'.
43. Personal interviews with local journalists, June 1989, Edinburgh.
44. Ibid.
45. Ibid.
46. *Evening Times*, 10 January 1984.
47. *Glasgow Herald*, 11 January 1984.
48. *Daily Record*, 11 January 1984. It is important to note that the circulation figures for the *Daily Record* are 757,146 throughout Scotland, 13,000 outside Scotland, and the paper claims 42 per cent household coverage in Scotland (figures for January 1990).
49. *Evening News*, 10 January 1984.
50. *Glasgow Herald*, 11 January 1984.
51. *Daily Record*, 11 January 1984.
52. *Glasgow Herald*, 11 January 1984.
53. *Evening Times*, 31 October 1986.
54. *Evening Times*, 10 January 1984.
55. Ibid.
56. *Daily Record*, 11 January 1984.
57. *Glasgow Herald*, 11 January 1984.
58. *Evening Times*, 10 November 1986.
59. *Daily Record*, 11 November 1986.
60. *Evening Times*, 11 November 1986.
61. *Daily Record*, 11 November 1986.
62. Ibid.
63. *Evening Times*, 11 November 1986.
64. *Evening Times*, 12 November 1986.
65. Ibid.
66. Ibid.
67. *Glasgow Herald*, 12 November 1986.
68. *The Guardian*, 12 November 1986.
69. *Daily Record*, 13 November 1986.
70. *Glasgow Herald*, 13 November 1986.
71. Ibid. and *Daily Record*, 13 November 1986.

72. *Evening Times*, 13 November 1986.
73. *Daily Record*, 14 November 1986.
74. Ibid.
75. *Glasgow Herald*, 14 November 1986.
76. Ibid.; *The Guardian*, 14 November 1986.
77. *Daily Record*, 14 November 1986.
78. *Daily Record*, 15 November 1986.
79. Ibid.
80. *Daily Record*, 11 November 1986.
81. *Evening Times*, 14 November 1986.
82. *Glasgow Herald*, 14 November 1986.
83. Ibid.
84. Ibid.
85. Ibid.
86. *The Scotsman*, 14 November 1986.
87. Ibid.
88. Ibid.
89. *Sunday Mail*, 16 November, 1986.
90. Ibid.
91. *The Observer*, 16 November 1986.
92. *Daily Record*, 30 September 1987.
93. Ibid.
94. Ibid.
95. *Evening Times*, 30 September 1987.
96. Ibid.
97. Ibid.
98. *Daily Record*, 1 October 1987.
99. Ibid.
100. *Evening Times*, 1 October 1987.
101. *The Independent*, 2 October 1987.
102. Ibid.
103. *The Scotsman*, 1 October 1987.
104. *The Sunday Post*, 4 October 1987.
105. *Scottish Sunday*, 4 October 1987.
106. *Glasgow Herald*, 5 October 1987.
107. *Sunday Mail*, 4 October 1987.
108. *Sunday Express*, 4 October 1987.
109. *The Scotsman*, 1 October 1987.
110. *The Independent*, 1 October 1987.
111. *Glasgow Herald, The Scotsman, The Guardian* and *The Independent*, all 3 October 1987.
112. *The Sunday Mail*, 4 October 1987.
113. Ibid.
114. *The Observer*, 4 October 1987, p. 5.
115. *Daily Record, Today*, and *The Times*, all 10 November 1987.
116. *The Guardian*, 25 February 1987.
117. *Glasgow Herald*, 27 April 1988.
118. *The Scotsman*, 28 April 1988.
119. *Glasgow Herald*, 7 May 1988.
120. *The Scotsman*, 10 May 1988.

121. *The Guardian*, 28 February 1987.
122. From private interviews with local journalists, Edinburgh, June 1989.
123. Ibid.
124. D. Leigh, *The Frontiers of Secrecy*, London, Junction Books, 1980; Hollingsworth, *The Press*.
125. See P. Hillyard and J. Percy-Smith, *The Coercive State*, London, Fontana, 1988, on changes under the Thatcher government, such as the 'Meeting of Information Officers' Cabinet Committee', established in 1981.
126. Interviews with local journalists, Edinburgh, June 1989.
127. See Chibnall, 'The Metropolitan Police' and Hollingsworth, *The Press*, on political 'vetting' of journalists; see also *The Late Show*, BBC Television, 5 October 1989, on politics and broadcasting.
128. Interview with Robbie Dinwoodie, previously of *The Scotsman*, now with *Glasgow Herald*, June 1989.
129. Ibid.
130. Ibid.
131. Ibid.
132. Ibid.
133. Ibid.
134. Ibid.
135. Ibid.

CHAPTER 7

The future of long-term imprisonment in the United Kingdom

You can never understand. I can't even boil a kettle for myself, I wouldn't know what to do with money, what does it feel like? Walking on grass would be a new experience, children would terrify me. I haven't seen an animal, except snarling dogs for years, and years. And supposing someone ordinary should be polite to me? What would I do? I've forgotten. I've had no love, no social niceties for so long, I couldn't handle it. I'm finished, institutionalised, and there is nothing I can do.[1]

This book has been concerned primarily with exploring the feelings and attitudes of a group of male long-term prisoners. As Chapter 1 noted, the experience of such prisoners has been marginalized in official inquiries, media reports and sociological analyses of imprisonment in the United Kingdom. While state servants, academics and journalists have frequently talked about the crisis in the prison system, those who have been at the centre of its genesis and at the sharp end of the state's response have remained unheard, invisible in the official quest for the prison Camelot of stability, tranquillity and acquiescence. Prisoners' complaints about the quality of life in long-term prisons – the alienation and boredom, the rigorous enforcement of petty rules, the psychological desolation through lack of outside contact and the fear and reality of violence – have never been taken seriously nor openly discussed by the managers of the system. Chapter 6 demonstrated how this marginalization has been compounded by the sensationalist images of prison life conveyed by the media with their populist emphasis on violent events, dramatic pictures and human interest (read prison officer) stories. The close interrelationship between prison managers and media personnel has been important in neutralizing serious debate and informed discussion about the purpose and goals of imprisonment. It has been a powerful force in constructing specific discourses around long-term prisons in general and explanations of disorder in particular.

As this book has shown, however, there is another history, an alternative reality which needs to be explored if the long-term prisons are not to lurch from one crisis to another. Accounts by prisoners are a central part of this history. Reading such accounts, which stretch back to the second half of the nineteenth century, it is striking how few of the writers claim that they are innocent. Rather, the writings are imbued with a sense of inevitability, the sentence seen as punishment for unacceptable behaviour. What links these accounts across time is not only a general acceptance of the state's decision but also, and as importantly, their demand for justice and due process from a system built on maximum discretion and minimum accountability. It is the power relationships which flow from this axis, and the detrimental impact on their daily lives, which prisoners have challenged.

The major disturbances at long-term prisons over the last two decades, from the prisoners' perspective, have been a *rational* response to both the arbitrary use of power which confronts them every day and the misanthropic smothering of what they regard as legitimate complaints about the system. In a sociological sense, the disturbances can be understood as conscious and structured resistance to penal domination rather than as pathological responses to a regime which is fair, just and benevolent.[2] As Frances Fox Piven and Richard Cloward have argued:

> people experience deprivation and oppression within a concrete setting, not as the end product of large and abstract processes, and it is the concrete experience that moulds their discontent into specific grievances against specific targets . . . it is the daily experience of people that shapes their grievances, establishes the measure of their demands, and points out the target of their anger.[3]

Further, it is important to acknowledge that when the secrecy surrounding prisons has been fractured, prisoners' claims about the unaccountable, and often violent, power of the state have been sustained. After the major disturbance in Hull maximum security prison in August 1976, black and Irish prisoners were picked out by prison officers and subjected to severe and humiliating beatings. As noted in Chapter 1, the official accounts and denials of brutality were challenged and eventually subverted by the National Prisoners' Movement, whose independent inquiry upheld the prisoners' allegations. In April 1979, eight prison officers were found guilty of conspiring with others to assault and beat prisoners and were given suspended prison sentences, one of which was overturned on appeal.[4] Two years later, prisoners' accounts of the circumstances surrounding the brutal death of Barry Prosser in the hospital wing of Winson Green were sustained when an inquest jury returned a verdict of unlawful killing.[5]

Such gaps in the fabric of prison secrecy are rare. What is not rare, as previous chapters have shown, are the continuing demands by prisoners for their claims to be taken seriously. These demands, and the conflicts around them, stretch back to the birth of the Howard-inspired reforms of the 1770s.[6] The Peterhead demonstration in November 1986 which forms the basis of this book was the latest in this long history of disturbances and came towards the end of two decades of intensive strife and disorder. From the late 1960s the state responded to the disorder by developing and consolidating different strategies aimed at regaining control and reinforcing discipline. They included: the use of solitary confinement and segregation; the introduction of the 'cages' in Scotland and the sensory deprivation of the control units in England; the development and consolidation of the paramilitary Minimum Use of Force Tactical Intervention Squad; the use of drugs, particularly in women's prisons; and the refinement of psychological profiles to test for, identify and control 'anti-authority' personalities. By the early 1980s, while these strategies were still developing, it was clear the state had failed to impose discipline and control onto the fragile social order of the long-term prisons. In 1983 the appointment of Leon Brittan as Home Secretary brought an intensification in the search for a set of policies aimed at reasserting the state's authority to manage. The 'restoration of order' was the pivot on which all prison-related issues was to turn.

THE MOMENT OF BRITTAN

Nineteen eighty-three was a highly significant year for long-term prisoners in the United Kingdom. The first half of the year was dominated by conflict and demonstrations. In January and March two assistant governors were taken hostage at Parkhurst and at Wormwood Scrubs. It was the fourth such incident in Wormwood Scrubs in 13 months. During the year, 12 people were taken hostage in different prisons. In March, five hundred prisoners at Albany and Parkhurst took strike action. They were demanding the same privileges as prisoners in Northern Ireland, including three hours' association each evening, weekly packets of food and toiletries, the use of their own clothing and the introduction of private cash to supplement prison earnings. There were further strikes at Gartree and Wakefield. In May there was a major demonstration at Albany. It lasted for six days and resulted in £1 million damage to the prison. In June two prisoners climbed onto the roof of Wandsworth and caused considerable damage. In the same month, prisoners and prison officers clashed in the top security wing at Wormwood Scrubs. The wing was recaptured by prison staff using staves. In July the Deputy Director General of the Prison Service highlighted the 'alarming increase' in the number of escapes by prisoners. There had been thirty escapes in just six months. In August, there was another disturbance at Wormwood Scrubs, this time in the remand wing. According to press reports, almost half of the seventy prisoners in the wing were involved. In September, 18 prisoners and staff were injured when they clashed at Brixton prison. In the same month 38 prisoners escaped from Long Kesh in Northern Ireland.

Finally, in October, 15 prison officers were injured at Peterhead when fighting broke out between staff and prisoners. The Scottish Council for Civil Liberties pointed out that it had written to the Scottish Office the previous year warning of '"a complete breakdown of control"' . . . after disturbances among prisoners'. The organization also complained about the conduct of some prison officers towards the prisoners, but it had been met with '"stonewalling" from the Scottish Office'.[7] Overall, between 1972 and 1983 prisoners had caused damage worth £4.3 million in 11 separate incidents. The majority were in male, maximum-security dispersal prisons.[8] It was against this political and penal background that Leon Brittan rose to address his first Conservative Party Conference as the minister responsible for law and order. His speech in Blackpool on 11 October 1983 marks a crucial moment in the state's response to the crisis of containment in the long-term prisons and to the future direction of penal policy for the confined.

Brittan set the parameters for the debate by resurrecting and focusing on the construct of 'the violent society'. He maintained that violent crime was rampant in Britain:

> In our first term of office the fight against the evil of inflation was the Government's most fundamental task. I believe that in our second term the fight against crime is the key task for us all. There is today a great wave of anger against the wanton violence which disfigures our society. That anger is not confined to this Conference and this Party. It is real, it is genuine. I share it to the full.[9]

Brittan deliberately utilized the populist idea that specified crimes of violence – the murder of police officers and children and murders by terrorists – were escalating. The psychopathic stranger stalking the streets was the folk devil around whom the Home Secretary built his case. In doing so he conveniently ignored the uniqueness of violent crime in relation to the overall number of crimes reported and recorded in England and Wales. Official statistics for the previous year, for example, indicated that over 95 per cent of crimes recorded were offences against property, many of which were comparatively trivial. Despite this, violent crime was the central focus of attention:

> Ideologically and symbolically the violent crimes which he highlighted became crucial for his general argument. A society which allowed such things to happen needed to be disciplined and a sense of order, respect for authority and appreciation of stability restored.[10]

This critique of Brittan's speech, however, is not an argument in support of official criminal statistics. Clearly the range of sociological work published over the last twenty years has challenged the view that 'official statistics' reflect the reality of crime in the United Kingdom.[11] Further, and more fundamentally, this critique is not intended to marginalize the physical and psychological impact of violence against women or the racial terrorism directed towards black people. For it is some indication of the endemic nature of sexual and racial violence in British society that, despite repeated political and media calls for 'curbs' on violent crime, both categories remain neglected by the 'law and order' lobby.[12]

The critique and 'decoding' of Leon Brittan's speech drew criticism from the self-styled 'new realists' within criminology. Throughout the 1980s 'new realism' became established as the 'voice of reason' within Labour Party politics.

It enabled the mainstream of the Party to regroup the Kinnock–Hattersley leadership on the basis of purging 'militancy' or 'ultra-leftists' from the membership. Within so-called 'radical' criminology new realists similarly attempted to distance themselves from those to whom they ascribed the label 'left idealists'. In setting up this debate the 'new realists' criticised 'idealists' for their Marxist reductionism, their economic determinism, their simplistic analysis and – the cardinal sin – for not considering violent crime to be 'much of a problem'.[13] This generalized critique against the 'straw person' of 'left idealism' presented a convoluted logic which was compounded by sociological reductionism:

> If certain sections of the middle-class radical intelligentsia wish to challenge this fact [the seriousness of crime as a problem] then they end up . . . echoing the sentiments of the – also middle – and upper class and male professional elites which operates the state apparatus.[14]

The significance of 'new realism' is that it caricatured the research conducted and interventions made by radical criminologists since the early 1970s.[15] Further, in their rush to judgement the 'new realists' missed the obvious point that Brittan's proposals were never intended to deal with the structural dynamics of institutionalized racism and sexism which provide the context and legitimacy for violence against the powerless. As Radical Alternatives to Prison pointed out at the time of the speech:

> The 'great wave of anger' to which he claims to be responding is something which, if it exists at all, he and his political allies have deliberately created. They have done so by painting a grossly distorted picture of 'crime' with a highly selective emphasis on certain forms of violence; by perpetuating the myth that the British penal system is lenient when it is, by West European standards, outstandingly harsh; and by implying in the face of all evidence that the supposed leniency is a major cause of the supposed upsurge in violence. The Home Secretary's proposals will further reinforce these misconceptions. Nothing that we say is intended to belittle the real impact that violence and the fear of violence make on people's lives, and particularly the lives of women and black people. We are also concerned about forms of violent crime that are often not recognised as such, e.g. the injuries and deaths that result from breach of industrial safety regulations and from the use of excessive force by police. The Home Secretary's proposals have no relevance to any of these problems, and the Government's economic policies are making them worse.[16]

Brittan's proposals for reform, therefore, were not designed to challenge or deal with the structural dynamics that underpin violence against the marginalized and the powerless. Neither was he concerned with the violent and devastating crimes committed by the powerful. Rather his reforms were geared to the consolidation of a political project built on tightening still further the disciplinary screw of imprisonment. This becomes clear where his proposals are examined in greater detail.

PROLONGING CONFINEMENT

Brittan announced a number of changes both in relation to sentencing and to the parole system. He maintained that sentencing was of 'vital importance' and should reflect 'society's deep abhorrence of violent crime'. Lenient sentences, on the other hand, undermined confidence 'and so [weakened] the whole criminal justice system'.[17] He proposed introducing new measures to combat what he saw as over-leniency in sentencing procedures: no life sentence prisoners would be released except by the Home Secretary; in some cases life would mean life; those who murdered police officers, prison officers and children would serve 20 years; those who engaged in armed robbery or committed terrorist murders would also serve 20 years. He had three further proposals to make in relation to crimes of violence. First, he increased the maximum sentence for carrying firearms in the furtherance of theft, from 14 years to life. Second, he proposed introducing legislation to allow the Attorney-General to refer over-lenient sentences to the Court of Appeal. Finally, in what he regarded as the most important step, the parole system was to be changed so that individuals sentenced to more than five years for an offence of violence to the person would not be released except for a few months before the end of the sentence. Similarly, drug traffickers sentenced to more than five years would 'be treated with regard to parole in exactly the same way as serious violent offenders – they should not get it'.[18]

In November, a month after the Blackpool speech, Brittan tightened the procedures still further by announcing the abolition of the joint committee of Home Office and Parole Board officials who until then had decided the date on which the review of a life sentence prisoner's case would begin. Under the new system, the Home Secretary would decide the date for the first reference of a lifer's case to the local review committee of the Parole Board.[19] This package, in conjunction with the biggest building and refurbishment programme for a century, had an immediate impact on the prisons. The changes exacerbated the already tense situation inside as well as contributing to the escalating population of long-termers. That escalation, as Stan Cohen and Laurie Taylor have pointed out, has been continuing since the 1950s and reflects 'the continuing predilection of English judges to hand out longer and longer sentences'.[20] A close analysis of prison statistics for the last 30 years supports Cohen and Taylor's case.

In 1957 the number of male lifers was 140. By March 1988 the number had increased to 2500. In 1987 alone, 250 individuals were sentenced to life. In the same period life sentences were increasingly used for offences other than murder. In February 1980, there were 20 such offences, ranging from murder through grievous bodily harm to using firearms to resist arrest. Those prisoners who received minimum recommendations were also contributing to the build-up in the long-term male prison population. Between 1964 and November 1987, 244 sentences with minimum recommendations were passed by the courts. In only seven cases were prisoners released before the minimum time expired.[21] The build-up in the long-term prison population was compounded by Brittan's changes. In 1982, 39 per cent of the parole decisions affecting prisoners serving five years or more were successful. By 1987, this figure had declined to 23 per cent. In its review of the parole system published in November 1988, the Carlisle Committee pointed out:

> There has also been a knock-on effect in the 2–5 year bracket with favourable parole decisions coming down from 61% to 54% between 1982 and 1987. In his statement of 20th March 1988, the Home Secretary acknowledged that the overall effect of the tighter policy on parole had been to increase the prison population by about 2,000, all but wiping out the gain from extending parole to short-term prisoners.[22]

For Tony Taylor, a prisoner in Wakefield, the changes were profound. He committed suicide after serving eight years of his sentence. Four days before his death he was informed that his name would not even go forward to a local parole review committee for 17 years. He told his sister:

> I just can't believe it or understand it. I am to serve a minimum of 20 years. Hanging I would much rather face. I would walk to the gallows with a smile on my face rather than face what lies ahead.[23]

Brittan's sentencing and parole changes were supported by another significant policy development announced the month before his Conference speech. In September 1983 he established the Control Review Committee. It was chaired by Anthony Langdon, the Prison Department's Director of Operational Policy. Its remit was to 'review the maintenance of control in the prison system including the implications for physical security with particular reference to the dispersal system and to make recommendations'.[24] The Committee reported in July 1984 and was welcomed by the Home Secretary in the House of Commons:

> I regard the report of [the] committee as an extremely important document. I am glad to have had the opportunity to welcome it and to set some of its proposals in action. By enabling better control of the small number of difficult and disruptive prisoners in the prison system, the life of prisoners and staff will be greatly ameliorated.[25]

A central theme in the report, and one which had been repeated for over a century, was that there was a 'disruptive population . . . of the order of 150–200'.[26] The Committee called for the introduction of five or six 'long-term prisoner units' to cater for those who were seen to present control problems. This group ranged from the 'highly disturbed to the calculatedly subversive'. Additionally, a further three or four units were to be established for prisoners 'who present control problems of other kinds'.[27]

The Committee recognized that the dispersal system had failed in one of its two fundamental objectives, namely the control of disorder. Indeed, Annex D of its report listed the major demonstrations that had occurred between 1969 and 1983. There had been ten in five of the dispersal prisons. In addition to the small units, for what its members saw as the recalcitrant minority, the Committee argued for the construction of 'new generation' prisons based on principles developed in the United States. While the report pointed to the fostering of better interpersonal relationships in these prisons, this was underpinned by the concern with control:

> In the furtherance of these management objectives many of the contem-
> porary designs that have been developed in the USA have adopted plans
> that do away with cell corridors – and instead arrange the cells around a
> central multi-use area in each unit. Since each cell opens directly on to the
> central area, staff can observe all the cells without having to move about in
> a consciously patrolling manner. It is claimed that these designs have been
> very successful in simultaneously improving surveillance and encouraging
> control of inmates through the development of good inter-personal
> relations.[28]

At a meeting of prison governors in November 1984, the Home Secretary expressed the 'greatest interest' in the proposals. He told the governors that he was sure 'we are now going in the right direction'.[29] Following the report's publication a Home Office Working Party visited the United States. Its findings were published in December 1985 under the title *New Directions in Prison Design*. The working party concluded that 'the new generation approach provided a workable solution and a third option to what had hitherto been assumed to be a straightforward choice between the concentration and dispersal of maximum security prisoners'.[30]

The final element in the new generation trilogy was the establishment of the Research and Advisory Group on the Long-Term Prison System (RAG). It met for the first time in November 1984 with a remit to advise the prison department particularly on 'the planning, co-ordination and evaluation of the proposed long-term prisoner units'.[31] The report contained a summary by the prison department which indicated the 'progress' that had been made in implementing the Control Review Committee's recommendations. This included the construction of two new local prisons in Milton Keynes and Doncaster which were 'being designed on "new generation" lines'.[32] The summary went on:

> subject to satisfactory financial appraisal of these projects, other new
> prisons in the building programme are likely to adopt similar design
> principles. When the new dispersal prison at Full Sutton is open and there
> has been further experience of the special units in operation, the Depart-
> ment will consider the implications of the 'new generation' designs for
> long-term maximum security prisons.[33]

The RAG had its own vision of a special unit system which members wished to see created by 1992. It included special units in Lincoln and Hull prisons which would have 'specialist assistance of a *psychological* nature'.[34] The RAG emphasized that there would be no prisoner participation in the running of these units. Finally, the report pointed to the special units the RAG hoped to see established in Frankland and Milton Keynes. Its members, however, were undecided about how the regime would operate – whether it should be supported by specialist assistance of a psychological nature or by specialist assistance of a sociological and social psychological nature. Here the group mentioned the experience of Grendon Underwood, the Barlinnie special unit and the Annexe at Wormwood Scrubs as providing the 'inspiration' for the regime if the second option was implemented.[35]

Given the long-established hostility to the Barlinnie special unit and more recent complaints about overcrowding and understaffing in Grendon Underwood,[36] the RAG's hope for a truly therapeutic regime would appear to be over-optimistic. Security and control, underpinned by individualized psychological assessment, remain the cornerstones of long-term prison policy in England and Wales. The proposals for the new generation prisons simply reinforce these tendencies for the regulated surveillance of the individual. The use of sophisticated technology in monitoring prisoners' most personal actions has replaced, or intensified and extended, the older forms of regulation in these institutions.

RESISTING BRITTAN

The package of proposals announced by Leon Brittan and the subsequent reports by those advocating the new generation style of confinement were not endorsed overwhelmingly as the panacea for the crisis inside. Indeed, a range of commentators raised a number of significant questions about the proposals and expressed doubts about their efficacy and viability. Brittan's speech was denounced by a senior member of the Parole Board in a letter to *The Times*. He also resigned from the Board. There was public criticism from two former chairpersons of the Board as well as critical statements from the National Association of Probation Officers, the Prison Officers' Association (POA) and the Parliamentary All-Party Penal Affairs Group. Additionally, 'many other members of the prison service [voiced] their personal disquiet at the prospects for prisoners' morale and prison discipline in establishments for long-term, life sentence prisoners'.[37] Prisoners also engaged in direct action by taking their case against the changes to court. After a series of convoluted court hearings the case was lost in the House of Lords. In a unanimous judgement five Law Lords, including Lords Scarman and Diplock, ruled that the Home Secretary had not acted unlawfully in introducing the policy, 'based on a category of offence and was not in breach of the law by thwarting the prisoners' expectations of release'.[38]

The concept of new generation prisons was also severely criticized. Andrew Rutherford argued that '"new generation prisons" could be as repressive and brutal as "old generation prisons"'.[39] Vivien Stern commented:

the idea that good architecture alone will produce a good prison is a total and dangerous illusion. The contrary assumption, that reasonably humane prisons cannot exist in bad old buildings is also misguided. A humane and decent prison system will not emerge inevitably from sorting out old bad management and industrial relations practices or from building modern new establishments with brightly coloured curtains and telephone booths.[40]

Other critics turned their attention to the US experience. At the annual conference of the POA in May 1985, John Bartell was scathing about the Home Secretary's plans. He saw the proposals for new generation prisons as emanating from a 'balance sheet mentality' in that it was cash limits rather than any new developments in penal philosophy which lay behind the proposals. He maintained that the Control Review Committee had not told the POA that prisoners who refused to cooperate would be detained in a prison 'where they did not leave their cell until they were wearing handcuffs and leg irons'.[41] When Gerry Northam went to the United States to investigate the prisons he found that the Home Office team who had visited had seen only the more positive side of new generation philosophy. There were other prisons, built on new generation lines, which clearly had failed. At Mecklenburg, Virginia, the Director of Corrections referred to prisoners as 'hogs' and 'took pride in the size of his officers'. Prisoners complained of systematic brutality. The American Civil Liberties Union was receiving more than thirty complaints a week from prisoners concerning the prison. Prison officer brutality was confirmed when 'the prison's own TV monitoring system [provided] dramatic evidence in the cases against officers accused of brutality'. Northam argued it was not the architecture that was important but the people managing penal policy and its administration. He pointed out that Home Office officials had privately expressed doubts, with one civil servant talking about 'the danger of creating a monster'.[42] The American Civil Liberties Union also warned against being 'dazzled by new technology into constructing the most repressive and damaging institution of this century'.[43]

In March 1986 the theme of the importance of interpersonal skills, as opposed to architecture, was taken up by Mike Fitzgerald in a paper delivered to the Cropwood Conference called to discuss the new generation proposals. Fitzgerald sketched an alternative proposal to the narrow conceptualization of the Control Review Committee. He maintained that any new proposals for the prison system could only be successful if the prison population was reduced and sentencing policies were changed. He argued for a different conceptualization which would start from the problems faced by those on the ground. From the point of view of long-term prisoners this meant that there 'should be the explicit recognition that the major problem facing those sentenced to long-term imprisonment is the *fact* that they have been so sentenced, rather than the regimes and conditions in which they serve that sentence'.[44] Serious consideration should be given to prisoner and staff accounts and experiences of prison life, with prisoners having fundamental rights to health, recreation, visiting and association. In new generation prisons, prisoners would still have privileges which could be removed via 'the one-sided discretion of individual staff or institutions'.[45] Finally, Fitzgerald called for management to be made accountable for any major decisions taken:

> Visibility and accountability should be provided, for example, through the guarantee of legal rights for prisoners . . . Independent public enquiries into outbreaks of serious disorder, or proposals for major shifts in penal

policy should ensure that all interests are able to take part in debates about penal affairs. [46]

These critiques are important as they raise fundamental questions about the viability of a project which is based more on political expediency than on any serious planning concerning the role and goal of imprisonment in the UK. The reasons for the failure of the dispersal system, both in terms of the philosophical basis of long-term imprisonment and in the context of sentencing policies that are arbitrary and misconceived, have been marginalized in the drive to find a reform which satisfies prison managers and placates the law and order lobby. In this drive, two further fundamental flaws in new generation thinking have been ignored. First, the new generation practice of constant surveillance and inter-personal staff–prisoner contact already operates in prisons for women. The policies and practices in these prisons have not alleviated the distress and deterioration felt by many prisoners, nor have they dealt with the individual and environmental destruction in which the women engage. The philosophy of the regime is regarded by many critics as the cause of the prisoners' problems, [47] a point well made by Dobash et al.:

> in the Scottish system, aspects of prison design at Cornton Vale seem to resemble closely 'new generation' thinking, and small units, purporting to foster 'relationships', are in fact used effectively for the surveillance, control and manipulation of prisoners. It is ironic, but perfectly in the tradition of the treatment of women in prison, that designs developed for high-security-risk, long-term male prisoners, should be suggested as appropriate for women who are supposedly in need of psychiatric assessment or treatment, most of whom, far from being long-term prisoners, are actually on remand. Moreover, the ordinary prison regime with its framework of prison rules, and in women's prisons the particularly close surveillance and control exercised, allow almost no individuality or autonomy and ironically no scope for collective expression. [48]

The second major flaw in the Home Office argument relates to the view that trouble in prisons stems not from the alienation and brutalization of current regimes but from a hard core of disruptive prisoners. As previous chapters illustrated, this explanation has been used, without foundation, to explain the disturbances in Scotland's prisons. Similarly, the spectre of the disturbed individual or subversive group has been raised repeatedly by prison managers throughout the nineteenth century and into the twentieth as the official explanation for the wave of disturbances inside. [49] This view became institu-tionalized in the 1960s. Since that time prison managers have argued that a new breed of prisoner has emerged, more recalcitrant and subversive than his predecessors. However, as Roy King has noted, there is little evidence to suggest that this is the case. This official line of analysis is used

> regardless of whether long-term prisoners are more dangerous and more troublesome than they used to be. We are dealing with perceptions of changes, rather than, or as well as, the changes themselves, and the

perceptions become the mainspring for action in Prison Department policy.[50]

As Chapter 1 indicated King goes on to point out that this view is not only erroneous but self-defeating:

Probably the most widely held view, both inside and outside the Prison Department, is that the worst control problems have been generated by comparatively few peculiarly difficult, recalcitrant and dangerous prisoners, some of whom may be psychologically disturbed. These prisoners are typically thought of as including terrorists, strong-arm men and leaders of criminal gangs, serving very long sentences of imprisonment; men who are as dangerous inside prison as they are outside. . . . It would be irresponsible and naive to deny that such men exist. Of course they do. But I do wish to argue that conceptualising the control problem as the product of 'difficult' or 'disturbed' individuals, and developing a reactive policy towards them, has been both partial and self-defeating. Partial in that it ignores all the structural, environmental and interactive circumstances that generate trouble, reducing it to some inherent notion of individual wilfulness or malfunction. Self-defeating in that the policy itself becomes part of those very circumstances that generate the trouble; it is likely that among those who get defined as troublemakers there are some who are made into troublemakers as a result of the way they are dealt with in prison. Just as there are some who come to prison as troublemakers.[51]

More recent events in England and Wales appear to confirm King's critique. Between April 1986 and July 1988 there were widespread disturbances in a number of prisons. These included: disturbances at 22 prisons and £4 million worth of damage to Northeye prison on 30 April 1986; a disturbance at Risley remand centre the next month in which 27 people were hurt; a disturbance involving 40 prisoners in Bedford prison in March 1988; disturbances at Rollerstone prison in May 1988 and at Haverigg the next month which involved 120 prisoners including 25 who escaped; disturbances in Amersham police station in July 1988 involving 16 remand prisoners and at Lindholme in the same month when six prisoners escaped. Between April 1987 and March 1988 there were 42 acts of concerted indiscipline, 25 roof-climbing incidents and 245 escapes. Finally, 1192 prisoners absconded in the same period.[52] The intensity and ferocity of the 1990 protest at Strangeways, together with the widespread demonstrations at other prisons, showed clearly that the 'bad apples' thesis is not sustainable. Yet in the aftermath of Strangeways that is clearly the 'logic' that has been adopted.

The development of new generation institutions is, however, not restricted to England and Wales. In Scotland, the state has responded to the crisis of containment with similar proposals. As will be illustrated below, these proposals are also philosophically flawed and will do little to alleviate the problems in Scottish prisons.

PRISON PROTEST IN SCOTLAND: INTERPRETING THE STATE'S RESPONSE

In the final section of Chapter 1 the discussion focused on the response of the Scottish Prison Service to the major demonstrations and disturbances in its prisons. Apart from sweeping changes in senior personnel and new initiatives in management and initial officer training, 'discussion papers' were published to develop a 'corporate philosophy' for the Prison Service. As outline in that chapter the second report, *Assessment and Control*,[53] was geared to the establishment of a comprehensive policy for the handling of male long-term prisoners, particularly those identified as engaging in disruptive behaviour. While not wishing to repeat the earlier discussion, it is important to return to the main emphases of this report as they reflect the established official discourse and analysis of prison disturbances. The priorities of this discourse were evident early in the report:

> the Department finds difficulty in accepting that there is a single factor or combination of factors behind the history of recent incidents. It seems more probable that each incident was triggered by a different combination of factors and circumstances. However, this makes it more difficult for the Prison Service to identify where the future incidents are likely to arise and take appropriate action to defuse the situation. It suggests perhaps that rather than looking to changes in the way in which the Prison Service as a whole goes about its task (although clearly this is an area which must be kept under review) a more productive approach may be to concentrate attention on the individual personality and 'repertoire' of particularly disruptive and violent inmates.[54]

Following this logic, procedures would be introduced through which profiles of Scottish 'control risk' prisoners, of which there were between one hundred and two hundred, could be constructed. This positivist qualification, as with all theoretical explanations, had an important converse: the introduction of a social policy built on a series of interlocking maximum security units structured around new generation principles. The prison department would proceed with plans for the 'early provision of a new maximum security unit', designed to 'complement the existing small units at Inverness and Barlinnie and those under construction at Shotts and Perth'.[55] Additionally, the department would review the possibility of introducing another two units of similar size. The report concluded:

> there is a need to review arrangements for the assessment and identification of potential trouble-makers; facilities for holding inmate[s] who prove unwilling or unable to settle in the mainstream; and overall procedures for the initial assessment and continued sentence planning of all long-term prisoners as a group.[56]

While the 1990 document, *Opportunity and Responsibility*, toned down the commitment to such units in favour of the development of small-scale regimes based on a 'new approach' to the needs of long-termers, the central issues concerning the general operation of regimes, the punitive and fear-inducing climate of many prisons, the lack of prisoners' rights and institutional accountability and the entrenched traditions of strident staff cultures remain unchallenged.

Again, it is important to acknowledge that the problems of control identified by state servants occurred in the context of a major rise in the long-term prison population in Scotland. By the end of 1987 long-term prisoners formed over 40 per cent of the total number in custody.[57] The Chief Inspector of Prisons even developed a category known as very long-term prisoners (VLTPs) which, in his 1986 report, he argued had 'steadily increased and current views are that an upward trend is likely to continue.'[58] This position has been compounded by the 'knock-on' effect of sentences which have minimum recommendations attached to them. These numbered 46 between 1965 and 1985 and were supported by the use of indeterminate sentences for crimes other than murder, of which there were 12 in the same period.[59]

At the other end of the penal spectrum, large numbers of individuals were sent to prison for non-payment of fines. Five hundred and forty-eight women and men were imprisoned in 1986 for having outstanding fines of less than £25, while 4857 individuals were imprisoned for non-payment of fines of more than £25 but less than £100. This expansion of prisoners has been paralleled by a concomitant rise in spending on the prisons. Total gross expenditure in the financial year ending 31 March 1986 was £48,743,000. As with the police, the majority of this expenditure went on staff costs (80 per cent), while a paltry proportion (3 per cent) was devoted to welfare considerations such as education, training, recreation and assisted visits. In cash terms this welfare expenditure amounted to £632,000. In the same year, the prison department spent £1,072,000 on travelling and removal expenses for prison officers.[60]

The proposal for new generation prisons has been supported, in Scotland, by a range of other policies designed to isolate and discipline those individuals deemed to be responsible for disturbances. The internal regime at Peterhead was rationalized in the wake of the 1986 disturbance. In November 1987 one prisoner wrote to a national newspaper describing how

Body-belt manacles which secure hands directly at the stomach level, have been in use for years in Peterhead. Prisoners in segregation at Peterhead are escorted by up to six warders carrying baseball-bat-size clubs; have been for years. It's permanent policy. No one denies it.

The lock-down system went into effect immediately after Peterhead's most recent incident. It is now a permanent segregation prison. Only sex offenders and a small number of short-termers – all of whom have recently been ghosted into service (clean and fetch) are not in permanent segregation 23 hours a day.

There are cells in Peterhead which have sheets of steel-welded box-steel frames covering the entire window area; small holes have been drilled to allow air in (there's no glass); but only barbed wire can be seen through a hole your finger couldn't pass through.[61]

The Scottish Council for Civil Liberties highlighted the existence of a linked series of maximum security units which contained

the 'Cardboard Cells' of A Hall where there is a mattress on the floor of the cell and cardboard furniture which is removed at night while the hall is patrolled by officers in groups of 12 or 14 carrying riot sticks, the 'Ten Cell Unit' from which there has been total silence but which appears to be used for taking the most 'difficult' prisoners out of the system long-term and which is thought to have a psychiatric control function, the infirmary, which, it is claimed, is used as an isolation unit, and the old punishment block which was refurbished several years ago. We now know of plans to turn B Hall into a Maximum Security Unit, while in the longer term work has begun on building a new high security prison within the existing perimeter.[62]

This 'Chinese Box'[63] includes a silent cell described as a 'cube of concrete within another cube of concrete'.[64] The cell has a bare concrete floor and walls, and a two-inch platform on which the prisoner sleeps without a mattress. The only 'furniture' is a plastic chamber pot. These units have been supported by the introduction of a range of different tactics to deal specifically with sieges, including: bartering for food; the management of information through temporary news black-outs; keeping reporters at a distance; the creation of special squads involving police and prison officers which draw on the expertise of Scotland Yard's Anti-Terrorist Squad; the drawing up of a new manual setting out siege tactics; the use of sophisticated electronic equipment for eavesdropping; as indicated above, the use of the SAS to end one of the demonstrations.[65]

As previously noted, these developments are based on the unsubstantiated assertion that the control problems have been generated by a hard core of difficult prisoners. This emphasis can be clearly seen in the Scottish Office report of October 1988 discussed above, especially in its bibliography. There are eight books and reports listed, the majority of which support the view that individual 'bad apples' are responsible for disorder. Among the eight which the Scottish Office has consulted is *Prison Violence*, edited by Cohen, Cole and Bailey. This book contains an article by Professor Kenneth Moyer which emphasizes the biological basis of violence. In order to control this violence, Moyer advocates the use of radios which could be bolted to the subject's head:

An electrode could be placed in a suppressor area of the brain, just as Delgado did with the Boss monkey. It could be brought out to a radio, which is bolted to the subject's head. His brain could then be activated by a transmitter and the patient could then range as widely as the area that the transmitter will reach.

There are problems with this approach. Since the radio has to be bolted to the skull, it means that the bolts have to go through the scalp. This is a constant possible source of irritation, and a source of infection. There are also psychological problems. People tend to report that they feel conspicuous with radios on their heads. However, one woman fashioned a wig so that she was able to cover her radio adequately.[66]

Utilizing such literature and the testimony of academic 'experts' not only reinforces individualistic explanations of deviance but also ignores the historical evidence, discussed in Chapter 1, which demonstrates that disturbances and protests have been an integral and consistent element in Peterhead's development. In addition, structural questions concerning sentencing, parole, regime, philosophy and accountability are ignored. This individualization will be intensified with the introduction of new generation regimes. However, a close examination of long-term women's prisons provides clear evidence that those who advocate new generation policies are supporting a philosophy which is likely to deepen the sense of outrage and frustration inside and to push prisoners into further confrontation with the system.

LIFE IN THE PRISON SUBMARINE: LONG-TERM IMPRISONMENT FOR WOMEN

On 30 June 1987 the population of adult women prisoners in England and Wales reached 1160. This was 21 per cent higher than the previous year and far outstripped the rate of increase for male prisoners (9 per cent). The increase was due almost entirely to women serving medium to long sentences, particularly those serving over 12 months. As the prison department pointed out, this reflected:

> the large rise in the last three years in the numbers received with medium or long sentences. In particular there was a rise of over 100 in the population sentenced to over 3 years. It reached 320, more than three times higher than the population ten years earlier. As a result, since 1977 this group rose from 13 per cent to 27 per cent of the total adult female sentenced population, . . . most of the increase occurring since 1984. There was also an increase of 65 between mid-1986 and mid-1987 in the population sentenced to over 18 months up to 3 years. By 1987 this group represented 25 per cent of the total adult female sentenced population. This was only slightly higher than 1986 when the proportion showed a sharp increase compared to earlier years when it was around 20 per cent.[67]

Women were also being sentenced to longer periods inside. In 1987, the average length of sentence (excluding life) was 13.2 months – 'about 1.8 months longer than in 1986 and higher than in any of the previous ten years'.[68] In Scotland, there was a similar trend. While the Scottish Home and Health Department does not provide the same detailed breakdown by gender as its counterpart in England and Wales, state servants have pointed to the rise in women prisoners since the mid-1980s. In November 1986, it commented on the 'significant rise in the female element' of the prison population most of which was 'among adult females serving direct sentences'.[69] In September 1987, it pointed out that the 'average daily population of females almost [reached] 200 for the first time'.[70]

The experiences of women prisoners in general, and long-termers in particular, have rarely been considered in the majority of official and sociological publications on the subject. Indeed, the Cropwood Conference, mentioned above, which explored the future of long-term imprisonment in the UK, did not consider the relationship between new generation prisons and women. In the collection of papers published after the conference under the general title of the *Cambridge Studies in Criminology*, the editors indicated that the Control Review Committee Report was confined to male prisoners. Consequently, 'it was inevitable that the great majority of the papers at the conference would, therefore, concern the problems of handling male long-term prisoners'.[71] While they hoped that a paper on long-term women prisoners would be presented, this did not materialize. They recognized that 'this is a significant omission from the volume'.[72] This collection was simply following a long line of other publications which either marginalized or ignored women completely. From the Mountbatten Report in 1966, through that of Radzinowicz in 1968, to the May Report in 1979, women have been invisible. Indeed, May's 342-page report, the most important inquiry since the Gladstone Report of 1895, did not once mention the situation of women prisoners in general or long-termers in particular.[73] The neglect of this prison experience reflects the more general omission of women from social science research. As Deborah Cameron and Elizabeth Frazer have pointed out, that omission has been underpinned by the nature of sociological research which, under the guise of objectivity, has been simply 'sexist research, beginning from partisan, masculine assumptions and presenting its equally partisan conclusions as "the truth"'.[74]

Within criminology, this neglect has been challenged significantly by the publication of a number of books and articles focusing on women's imprisonment, beginning with Pat Carlen's pioneering study *Women's Imprisonment*, published in 1983. The book was a highly rigorous dissection of the lives of women prisoners in Cornton Vale, Scotland's only women's prison, and the deeply sexist, often patronizing and grimly authoritarian criminal justice process with which the women were confronted. The same year saw the formation of the pressure group Women in Prison (WIP). This group has been committed to raising the specific issues which affect women prisoners, among them 'sexist and racist discriminatory practices which result . . . in them receiving fewer opportunities, closer surveillance and much greater control by drugs than male prisoners'.[75] WIP has called for the replacement of the parole system for lifers and for the introduction of half remission on all sentences. Additionally, it argues that lifers should have access to a sentence review panel after completing seven years of their sentence.[76]

Since 1983, there have been a number of other publications which have analysed the position of women in the penal system and the experiences of long-termers within that general population.[77] The most powerful and poignant of these have been based on accounts by prisoners themselves and have particularly concentrated on the regime and conditions in H Wing in Durham, which holds many of the women serving the longest sentences. The wing was initially opened in 1961 as a special security block for men. It was condemned as 'uncivilized' and 'intolerant' by Lord Mountbatten in 1966 and was closed in 1972. It was reopened in 1974 and was designated for 'Category A women prisoners, for life sentence and long-term prisoners at the beginning of their sentences and for women who have proved a control problem in other establishments'.[78] Constant surveillance, poor conditions, individualization and electronic monitoring are the cornerstones of the regime:

> All women there are kept under constant and mind-numbing surveillance, and they never leave the unit. One hour's exercise (monitored by closed circuit TV) is taken in a small tarmac yard caged in by a 20 foot high wire fence topped with barbed wire and patrolled by guard dogs. Only three women at a time are allowed to gather together in a cell and then the cell door must be left open. Work and education facilities are extremely basic. Cell doors are electronically locked at 8 pm and are not opened again until 8 am the following morning. They have no access to night time sanitation and have to endure the degrading prison practice of slopping out. The lavatories for day time use have only half doors, denying women any privacy. The numbers of visits women can receive are restricted as the visiting room can only take 3 visitors at a time. Prisoners are often refused visits particularly at Christmas when many people want to visit. Regular strip and cell searches take place. One woman told us that after several years of once or twice weekly searches no unauthorised article had been found. Prisoners from Durham's H wing have said that the physical and psychological effects of being imprisoned in such conditions are considerable and include loss of hair, disorientation, debilitating depressions, apathy, loss of weight, and sight problems.[79]

Within the long-term women's population particular groups are the subject of special attention. Those in the highest security category A are continually searched, before and after work and before and after visits. Every week or ten days prisoners have a complete cell and body search. They are also subjected to complete wing searches, usually on a Saturday, which is their own time:

> You're locked in and they bring men over with dogs. They search everything – toilets, showers, landings, everything. You hear them running up and down stairs, and you hear the dogs barking. Then they go to the cells, one after the other, and they take everything out but the bed: they can't get that through the doors without dismantling it and only the inmates know how to do that. Everything in your cell's pulled out on the landing, and the whole thing takes a day. You have to eat all your meals in the cell and you lose an entire day.
>
> If the staff get bored and all the girls are getting on, they don't like it, so they start going round stirring up trouble: divide and rule. Some of them do like trouble because it makes the time go quicker and they're so fond of telling us that they are doing a sentence as well. It's a well-known fact.

They'll go into a prisoner's room, say something and leave that prisoner with that thought and then it'll start trouble. [80]

Such searches inevitably involve the use of strip searching, which is a central aspect of women's imprisonment. It can be used disproportionately on particular prisoners. Martina Anderson and Ella O'Dwyer, who were remanded in Brixton in July 1985 on Category A, were continually subjected to strip searching. Martina Anderson had one search after an internal gynaecological examination and both she and Ella O'Dwyer experienced strip searches on average 25 times a month. Ella O'Dwyer described it in the following terms:

I stand like an embarrassed child watching her dangle my bra and panties about. For increased effect I am ordered to turn around slowly to give them a peep at everything. They order me to lift the gown that I have been given to wear. I have only been allowed to wear this gown since September. Before that I had to stand naked while they checked my clothes. Prison Officers rub my hair and ears and like an animal I have to lift my feet so they can inspect them too. The awful dread is that I will be touched so I am stiffened to resist. They have told me that they can lift my breasts forcibly if they decide to and even probe my body folds. They can touch any part of me at all. It is horrible to have four eyes staring at me over the top of a blanket. While two other officers stand behind this blanket another may stand in front. I know that every part of me is being touched accidentally or deliberately since I arrived here. Normal physical contact has become a challenge. The gown I was wearing slips off when I fumble, sweat and rush into my clothes. [81]

As discussed earlier, many of the principles which lie at the heart of new generation prisons are already practised in women's prisons. These regimes have led to suicides, attempted suicides, arm and wrist slashing and the further demoralization of already damaged individuals. The converse of these processes has been the continuing reliance on force to maintain order through segregation, male prison officers, the use of drugs and the sexist application of psychiatric labels such as 'personality disorder'. Women's prisons provide a clear illustration of the philosophical weaknesses lying at the heart of new generation philosophy. At the same time, they indicate the bankrupt nature of penal philosophy in the UK and the continuing domination of punishment and retribution which are at the core of this philosophy. The prison system in Northern Ireland provides further evidence for this argument.

POLITICS AND LONG-TERM IMPRISONMENT: THE CASE OF NORTHERN IRELAND

Since 1968, and directly related to the political situation in the six counties,[82] there has been a significant increase in the numbers of people imprisoned in Northern Ireland. By February 1988 the rate of imprisonment was higher than any other member state of the Council of Europe, at 125 per 100,000 of

150

population.[83] This increase was matched by a massive increase in expenditure. In 1980 the British state spent £255 per prisoner per week, but by 1986–7 this figure had escalated to £933. By 1986–7 there were 17 prison officers to every ten prisoners and 83 per cent of the prison budget was allocated to staffing costs, while ' "inmate occupation" such as education and prison industries [accounted] for a mere four per cent of the total budget'.[84]

During the 1970s the number of long-term prisoners rose significantly:

> Of all men sentenced in 1977, for example, 29% (or 647) received terms of four years or more, including 304 who were given 8 years or over and 80 who received life sentences. Since that peak year both the number and proportion of long-term prisoners has declined. In 1986, there were 150 new long-term prisoners, representing 6% of all males receiving prison sentences that year.[85]

As Bill Rolston and Mike Tomlinson have noted, in order to understand the make-up of Northern Ireland's prison population it is necessary to draw a distinction between those who are serving short-term sentences for non-political offences and the long-term population sentenced for mainly political offences. In March 1986 the average length of a long-term sentence was over ten years. Rolston and Tomlinson also pointed to the expansion of the lifer population. In 1980 there were 377 lifers; this figure had climbed to 449 by March 1987, when the lifers 'made up 28% of the sentenced prison population or 40% of all political prisoners'.[86] They concluded that the prison population in the six counties 'is unusual by any standards' and identified three important features of this population:

> Firstly there is a rapidly expanding number of people entering the prisons to serve brief sentences for fine default. While this is changing the character of the short-term population, short-termers remain quite distinct from the long-term population. Secondly, . . . the sentenced population continues to be dominated by political prisoners serving lengthy sentences. Thirdly, the political prisoner population itself is made up of two groups, those serving determinate and indeterminate sentences. The large number of life sentence prisoners has continued to rise during the 1980s but may now be declining.[87]

The overwhelming majority of long-term prisoners are men. In 1986 the average daily number of female prisoners was 30. Like their counterparts in England, Wales and Scotland, these women experience the prison regime in ways which uniquely affect them. Strip-searching has been a particularly emotive issue and, as noted above, it is used disproportionately against women prisoners. In Armagh between November 1982 and November 1985 'the average number of strip-searches per prisoner per month was approximately 2.5'.[88] As Rolston and Tomlinson pointed out:

> The thousands of searches which have been conducted since 1982 have not been entirely successful as a deterrent against smuggling but they have

netted a few items. In April 1983, 15 Vallium and 2 sleeping pills were found under a prisoner's foot in the search cubicle. In September, a £5 note and a small phial of perfume were discovered, and in October the searchers found an uncensored letter. Two years later in June 1985, 47 assorted Librium, Libraxan, and Ativan were found among prisoners' clothing and in the reception area.[89]

In 1986 women prisoners were moved to a new maximum security prison at Maghaberry. The prison was constructed on new generation principles, with intensive security and technological surveillance integral to its operation. This takes many forms: electronic doors; television monitors; fish-eye mirrors; observation cameras; control rooms with 'banks of switches and lights'. These are contained in a 'soulless, low complex of buildings wired in and fenced in on an eerie, featureless, stretching plateau'.[90] Technological surveillance, and the isolation and disorientation that it generates, is intensified in the allocation of six women to each wing. Previously the women prisoners were housed together in one wing. When the women meet together for association they are under constant surveillance by prison officers and thus given 'no opportunity for privacy or relaxation'.[91] Furthermore, they continue to be 'strip-searched at every possible opportunity including trips to and from hospital'.[92]

There is also a significant number of Irish prisoners in British prisons (1050 in 1987). For those convicted of political violence the position is stark. Their heavy sentences are compounded by being placed on Category A, and their movements are heavily restricted. Constant surveillance is a central part of the daily routine, as are sudden and unexpected transfers between prisons. Paul Hill, one of the Guildford Four, was transferred 48 times in fourteen years. He spent 1438 days in solitary confinement:[93]

> I view solitary confinement as an attempt to destroy me mentally and psychologically, so if ever the time comes when we're exonerated and we are released, we will not be in a condition, a lucid condition, that we'll be able to tell things as they were, and explain exactly what happened to us. I'm a Category A prisoner, which is the highest categorization, which is one where your escape is dangerous to the police, the security of the State and the general public at large. I've been informed in the last month that my visiting conditions are, to put it bluntly, to become more brutal. I've been informed that I must send a sterile set of clothing to the visits 24 hours before I have a visit. I must then go to the visiting area. I enter one room where I'm stripped in sight of two prison officers. I leave that room naked, I enter the other room, where I put on the sterile set of clothing which has been sent from the day before. I then proceed along the corridor, which is thirty yards, with the two prison officers, and then I'm stood on a box about 8" off the ground, a wooden platform where I'm rubbed down – I'm searched again physically, which is totally absurd in view of the fact that I've just been strip searched. I then enter a visiting-room about 6' by 5' wide which is basically a table, two chairs one side, two chairs the opposite side. There's a partition travelling the length of the room under the table,

and there's a board – a swing door – at the side. I'm told that I can embrace my visitors before the visit and after the visit. For the previous thirteen years my mother has sat beside me, and I've sat beside my girlfriend, and I've been able to engage in family discussion whenever possible. A prison officer is within four or five feet and can observe the whole visit. Now I've been told that a prison officer has to be in the room, one on my side of the partition, one on my visitor's side of the partition, which makes family conversation or anything personal completely impossible. I have a daughter who was born whilst I was on remand who because of the circumstances is pretty fraught. She's only seen me in a succession of prison visiting areas. I haven't been able to have one personal word with my daughter in thirteen years.[94]

Accounts by long-term prisoners, both in Northern Ireland and in Britain, reveal the ongoing conflict around social order. Dirty protests, hunger strikes, and demonstrations have been part of the repertoire of responses mobilized by prisoners to protest against the terms and conditions of their confinement.[95] Violence has been central to this conflict:

I've been assaulted on several occasions in prison, three times pretty severely. I was assaulted in Hull prison, in the aftermath of the Hull disturbance in 1976, when I was forced to run a gauntlet of prison officers from my cell while collecting my breakfast, and I was beaten back along the same gauntlet. On being removed to another prison I was beaten down a flight of stairs and placed in a cell. I was removed to yet another prison, where I had a period of constraint, where I was lodged in the strong-box, naked, with a body belt. A body belt consists of a broad leather belt around the waist about 4" broad with handcuffs either side, and a padlock on the front. This was kept on for a considerable period, several days, during which my food was just pushed into my cell and I had to lie sideways on the floor and eat off a dish. This wasn't removed even when I went to the toilet, which made my toilet physically impossible.

I was also assaulted in the aftermath of disturbances at another prison in 1983, during disturbances that I had no involvement in whatsoever. I was removed by a MUFTI squad to the reception area where I was taken in a van to a nearby prison, and in the van, going the short distance to that prison, a towel was placed around my neck from behind, and I was forced into a corner in the back of the van. It was difficult to breathe and I was punched and kicked in the back of the van. I was brought into the prison where they stopped between the gates and the hospital. I was driven to the hospital, where I was bundled along a landing, which is the same landing where people are housed whilst they are waiting transfer to Broadmoor or Park Lane. I was lodged in a strip cell, I was threatened, I was stripped, I was again put in constraint.[96]

The build-up in the long-term prison population in Northern Ireland's prisons is likely to be compounded by changes announced in November 1988.

Remission is to be cut from one-half to one-third for those convicted of political violence and sentenced to more than five years. In addition, any person released on remission after serving more than one year who is then convicted of another offence 'within the expiry date of the previous sentence will have to serve out the unexpired portion before serving the new sentence'.[97]

These changes are directly related to the continuing struggle to maintain order, not only inside the prisons but also beyond the walls. As Rolston and Tomlinson concluded:

> it has become clear that those responsible for the prisons are almost entirely wrapped up in the problem of how to control political prisoners and the contribution this can make to the defeat or containment of political violence outside the prison. Few should be in doubt about the centrality of these concerns or the determination with which they are pursued. . . . At the heart of penal policy . . . stands the British government's continuing attempt to criminalise the unresolved violent political struggles over the North of Ireland's relationship to Britain. All policies affecting the running of the prisons, right down to the most trivial of matters, have this political element attached to them – witness the litigation over the confiscation of Gaelic Bibles in October 1987, or the general policy against the Irish language and games.[98]

CONCLUSION

The issues central to the development of long-term prison regimes in recent years need to be situated within a wider political context. In particular, there are two important dimensions to be considered before arriving at a full and analytical understanding of the future role and direction of long-term imprisonment in the UK. The first dimension relates to the continuing expansion of the prison system and the system's capacity to detain citizens in increasing numbers. This was a significant development in penal politics during the late 1980s. The second dimension concerns the reasons *why* the system is expanding at this historical moment. To understand the reforms which have been introduced by successive Home Secretaries, it is necessary to explore the relationship between prisons, the state and the maintenance of social order. Taken together, both dimensions raise profound questions about the role of the prisons in the exercise of social authority and political power in the last decade of the twentieth century.

Sustaining prison growth

In June 1988, the Council of Europe released prison statistics which covered its 20 member states. These figures were based on detention rates per 100,000 of the population as at 1 February 1988. With a detention rate of 98.2 per 100,000, the UK was ahead of countries such as Greece and Turkey and second only to Luxembourg in relation to the number of citizens incarcerated. When the figures were further broken down, Northern Ireland and Scotland occupied the top two places with England and Wales in fourth place behind Luxembourg.[99] This high rate of incarceration has been supported, particularly in England and Wales, by the prison building programme announced by Leon Brittan in October 1983. By March 1988, this programme was costing £1 billion, making it 'more expensive in relation to gross domestic product than any other developed country'.[100] The number of new prisons under construction climbed to 26 by the beginning of 1988. According to the Home Office, this programme is 'expected to provide over 22,000 places by the mid 1990s'.[101] Additionally, prison managers expect the daily average prison population to reach 67,400 by 1995. The number of long-term and life sentence prisoners is also expected to rise. In 1969, those serving over four years and less than life constituted 3.2 per cent of the average population in custody; by 1995 it is expected to be 14.3 per cent. Similarly, lifers constituted 0.7 per cent of this population in 1969; by 1995 this figure may climb to 3.4 per cent.[102]

The number of prison staff has also continued to rise. The projected figure for 1989 was approximately 29,000.[103] As the Home Office has pointed out, 'the long-term trend is towards more [prison] officers per inmate. Forty years ago there were about 6 inmates per officer. In 1987–8 the ratio was approximately two and a half inmates per officer'.[104] In contrast to this massive growth, the government is proposing to build nine new bail hostels which will provide only two hundred new places. Between April 1987 and March 1988 the Home Office expenditure on the probation service was £9.7 million, a rise of £1.7 million on the previous year.[105] This increase is small in the context of the £1 billion prison building programme.

These figures raise significant questions about how the prison budget is allocated and spent. In 1987–8 total cash expenditure, including new prison buildings, was £775 million. This was '£77 million (11 per cent) more than in 1986–1987 in cash terms and £40 million (5.4 per cent) in real terms'.[106] The bulk of this expenditure related to the pay, allowances, overtime and super-annuation of prison staff and to the running costs of the prisons. Prisoners and their needs come low on the expenditure ladder. For example, prisoners were paid £5.63 million in 1987–8, an average weekly wage of £2.23. In contrast, the prison department spent over £6 million on transferring officers between prisons and a further £5 million on detached duty, travel and subsistence. While the department spent £10.8 million feeding the prison dogs, just over £30 million was allocated to catering for the *entire* prison population.[107]

Since mid-1984 in England and Wales the prison population has grown by 3500 per year. This compares with a growth rate of 600–700 per year over the previous ten years. The expansion of the long-term prison population has been particularly significant. Between 1977 and 1987 the proportion of adult male prisoners sentenced to over four years rose from 20 per cent to 31 per cent. Similarly, 'the proportion of the adult female population sentenced to up to 18 months fell from 67 per cent to 48 per cent, whilst the proportion sentenced to over three years increased from 13 to 27 per cent'.[108]

This situation has been compounded by executive decisions taken by the Home Secretary. Since 1987 the power to set minimum terms for life sentence prisoners has rested with this minister, who has the power to approve, cut or lengthen recommendations made by trial judges. In the six months between April and September 1988 ministers considered the cases of 106 lifers. They agreed with the judges' recommendations in 34 cases and cut the jail term in a further nine. However, in 63 cases (59 per cent) they ruled that the prisoner should spend a *longer* period inside than that recommended by the trial judge. According to the *Daily Mail*, 'no details of individual cases have been released but minimum recommendations that a prisoner should serve at least 12 years may have been lengthened by three years'.[109] Andrew Rutherford has analysed this expansion in terms of the 'dualistic role' of imprisonment. This refers to the system's capacity to

> incapacitate very serious offenders for long periods but also to provide brief and salutary prison sentences for minor offenders. With regard to both groups there is considerable elasticity, and under conditions of expansion the incapacitation net is stretched to include persons other than those convicted of serious offences. Habitual property offenders and institutional trouble-makers become likely candidates for inclusion. At the same time, the custodial threshold is lowered to include persons who earlier would have been fined or dealt with by some other non-custodial means.[110]

Why did the expansion occur during the 1980s? Answering this question involves moving beyond the obvious and traditional goals of imprisonment – the deterrence, rehabilitation, punishment model – to an analysis which considers the dialectical relationship between prisons, the state and social order. The dual role of imprisonment, to which Rutherford refers, emanates from this dialectic.

Power, politics and prisons

Between 1979 and 1985, successive Conservative governments introduced a number of Acts, Orders and Bills which increased the power of the state to intervene and determine policy in a range of areas affecting the lives of individual citizens.[111] Since 1985, this process has continued.[112] Table 6 indicates some of the important changes within the criminal justice system since that time. These changes, the direct result of the election of three successive Thatcher governments, have extended and intensified the power of the state to regulate, discipline and control the lives and experiences of increasing numbers of citizens in the UK. In terms of pursuing trade union activities and political activism, including the right to demonstrate, these powers are draconian.

Coincidentally, however, the state has *withdrawn* from policing the activities of the economically powerful and politically influential, whose fraudulent and

156

Table 6   Changes to the criminal justice system, 1985–9 [113]

Act/Order/Bill	Year	Effect
Interception of Communications Act	1985	Allows the Home Secretary to issue warrants for telephone tapping without reference to a court.
Public Order Act	1986	Gives police substantial new powers to restrict peaceful demonstrations.
Animals (Scientific Procedures) Act	1986	Anyone disclosing information on experiments involving live animals will be open to prosecution.
Emergency Provisions (Northern Ireland) Act	1987	Perpetuates the non-jury Diplock courts, army powers to detain and the power to intern without trial.
Criminal Justice Act	1988	Restricts the right to jury trial and the right of defence to challenge jurors. Removes safeguards in extradition proceedings.
Local Government Act	1988	Section 28 criminalises activities by local authorities which promote homosexuality.
Immigration Act	1988	Restricts the right to appeal against deportation.
Order of Parliament	1988	Removes the right of silence for those under police interrogation in Northern Ireland.
Security Services Bill	1988	Empowers the security services to burgle homes and tap telephones if Home Secretary authorises it, with no form of accountability to Parliament; MI6 is excluded entirely.
Official Secrets Bill	1988	Excludes public interest defence for those who discover fraud, negligence or unlawful activity by the state.
Local Government and Housing Bill	1989	Restricts the rights of local government officers to stand for election, to canvass, to speak, or to write publicly on party political matters.

violent actions have a devastating impact on the lives of the powerless. Between 1981 and 1985, for example, 739 individuals were killed on building sites. According to the Health and Safety Executive, 517 of these lives (70 per cent) could have been saved if the minimum safety standards had been observed. It pointed out that 'bad habits, sloppy practices and poor management and organization seem endemic'. Occupationally, the construction industry was the most dangerous with a death rate twice that of agriculture, the second most dangerous.[114] Similarly, those who own and control businesses regularly break the laws concerning wages. In 1987, 4443 establishments were found to be underpaying workers. There were but nine prosecutions. Since 1979 the number of wages inspectors has been cut by more than half while 9½ million workers earn less than the Council of Europe's decency threshold.[115] In 1987 the cost of defrauding social security was £500 million resulting in 14,000 prosecutions. The cost of income tax fraud in the same year was £5 billion but there were only 20 prosecutions.[116] The state is also withdrawing its protection of women not only by removing protective legislation, abolishing the maternity grant, allowing women's average earnings to fall and undermining local authority women's committees but also through withdrawing support for women's refuges. One-third of the 150 refuges in England and Wales are likely to close if the government's board and lodgings payments are withdrawn.[117]

Taken together, these reforms represent a political project designed to establish a much more integrated and less informal process of justice in the UK which will confront the problems of crime, disorder and 'subversion' rationally, professionally and, it seems, ruthlessly. Leon Brittan recognized this when he became Home Secretary:

> on taking office I decided that we needed a strategy which would enable us to pursue our priorities and objectives in a deliberate and coherent way. Such a strategy is now in place. It covers all the main areas of the Department's work, both general policies and specific legislative or administrative objectives. We shall be reviewing it regularly. Our principal preoccupation is, and I believe ought to be, the criminal justice system which incidentally I wish to see treated in all that we do as a system.[118]

Douglas Hurd carried this project further through the changes discussed above. The specific reforms which have been proposed for the prison system are integral to this project. The building programme, electronic tagging, new generation prisons, the proposals for privatization and changing the working practices of prison officers can be seen not as a benevolent restructuring of the penal estate but rather as part of what Stuart Hall has called 'regressive modernization' in which state institutions are being reformed in 'the attempt to "educate" and discipline the society into a particularly regressive version of modernity by, paradoxically, dragging it backwards through an equally regressive version of the past'.[119] The modernization of prisons is part of this process, working not just at economic and political levels, in terms of disciplining marginalized black youth in particular,[120] but also at the cultural and ideological level. This connects with what Giles Playfair has called the 'punitive obsession' which resides in the popular culture and consciousness of wider society. As Hall has pointed out:

> The language of law and order is sustained by a populist moralism. It is where the great syntax of 'good' versus 'evil', of civilized and uncivilized standards, of the choice between anarchy and order, constantly divides the world up and classifies it into its appointed stations. The play on values and on moral issues in this area is what gives to the law-and-order crusade much of its grasp on popular morality and common sense conscience. But it also touches concretely the experience of crime and theft, of the loss of scarce property and the fears of unexpected attack in working-class areas and neighbourhoods; and, since it promulgates no other remedies for their underlying causes, it welds people to the need for authority which has been so significant for the right in the construction of consent to its authoritarian programme.[121]

Leon Brittan's reforms, discussed above, are a clear representation of Hall's argument in terms of the construction of an 'ideological inclination' designed to win consent for particular policy initiatives.[122]

As this book has shown, it is also important to recognize that the state retains a monopoly on the use of *legitimate* violence which, as Nicos Poulantzas has pointed out, occupies a determining position in state practices.[123] In prisons this monopoly allows state servants at all levels of the hierarchy to play key parts, either in the actual use of violence or in defending its use through depicting the confined as pathological and desperate. Operational policies and practices formulated within prisons and, therefore, institutionalized have been neglected by liberal democratic theories of the state. Where they have been addressed they have been explained in terms of a small number of 'excessive' individuals, the 'bad apples', who must be removed before spreading the disease to the general body of responsible state servants. As Chapter Three noted, violence in Peterhead was much more complex and widespread than indicated by this superficial construction at the heart of official discourse. As Poulantzas recognized, violence is institutionalized within the state and operates not simply in terms of physical repression but also through strategies 'about which people seldom talk: namely *the mechanisms of fear*'.[124] Chapter 3 also showed that fear was a central element in the lives of the Peterhead confined. It is this combination of the actual and the threatened use of force which reproduced the domination of the Peterhead regime and its imposition on the daily lives of the prisoners.

Also, it is important to note that the liberal democratic rhetoric which holds individual state servants responsible for transgressions misses the more fundamental political point that the state (and, by extension, its employees) 'often transgresses law-rules of its own making by acting without reference to the law, but also by acting directly against it'.[125] Consequently, the rule of law does not override the state, thereby making state institutions accountable. On the contrary, it is the state 'as the practitioner of legitimate violence which takes precedence over law'.[126] Thus prisoners, as state captives, do not receive the protection of the law in liberal democracies, and state institutional practices, based on coercion, transcend the rule of law.

Finally, it is important to note that alternative formulations, different penal strategies which are not based on power and domination, do exist. A large prison population, long prison sentences and 'high-tech' institutions are not natural events but are socially constructed priorities. Consequently, like any social construction, they can be deconstructed, and then reconstructed, to fulfil functions which empower rather than discipline or regulate. This process is complex, for it involves applying what Antonio Gramsci called 'good sense' to the analysis of crime, criminal justice and the state. This means challenging the previously established common-sense understanding of these constructions by employing a political perspective that neither patronizes nor reinforces existing power networks. As he noted, 'it is not a question of introducing from scratch a scientific form of thought into everyone's life, but of renovating and making "critical" an already existing activity'.[127]

Introducing 'good sense' into the prison debate means moving beyond the idea of reforming an antiquated system of punishment to a position which raises the possibility of abolishing prisons in their present form. There is now a body of literature which highlights the need for radical reform whose introduction will lead eventually to the dismantling of the present system.[128] This radical restructuring includes the control of sentencing policy by breaking the assumed but fallacious link between long sentences and declining crime rates; decarceration and the construction of alternative institutions to deal with damaged individuals; the institutionalization of legal, medical and welfare rights for prisoners; and the strict regulation of state discretion with a concomitant increase in internal and external accountability.[129] Such strategies are designed to empower prisoners and contrast sharply with current practices in the UK which not only depress and brutalize but also infantilize prisoners by denying them autonomy and rationality. The accounts by the prisoners in this book have only underlined the brutality of institutionalization and the daily pain of existing inside what Jimmy Boyle has called 'the dinosaur of a system'.[130] The extinction of this particular dinosaur would herald the start of a new epoch in the treatment of the confined.

NOTES

1. Judith Ward, 'H. Wing, Durham', in T. Hadaway (ed.), *Prison Writers; An Anthology*, London, Iron Press, 1986, p. 33.
2. Recent sociological and historical work in a number of substantive areas has emphasized this point, and the need to understand the diverse nature of resistance within capitalism. See, in particular, S. Rowbotham, *Hidden from History*, London, Pluto, 1973; S. Humphries, *Hooligans or Rebels?*, Oxford, Blackwell, 1981; P. Gilroy, *There Ain't No Black in the Union Jack*, London, Hutchinson, 1987; M. Ward, *Unmanageable Revolutionaries*, London, Pluto, 1983.
3. F. F. Piven and R. Cloward, *Poor People's Movements*, New York, Vintage, 1979, pp. 20–1.

4. National Prisoners' Movement, *Don't Mark His Face*, London, National Prisoners' Movement (no date); J. L. Thomas and R. Pooley, *The Exploding Prison*, London, Junction, 1980.
5. C. Coggan and M. Walker, *Frightened for My Life*, London, Fontana, 1982.
6. See J. Sim, *Medical Power in English Prisons*, Milton Keynes, Open University Press, 1990.
7. *The Guardian*, 18 October 1983. The account of previous events was compiled from the following: *The Guardian*, 6 January 1983; *The Guardian*, 22 March 1983; *The Guardian*, 20 July 1984; *The Guardian*, 2 March 1983; *Daily Mail*, 24 May 1983; *The Guardian*, 20 June 1983; *The Guardian*, 17 June 1983; *The Guardian*, 28 July 1983; *The Guardian*, 3 August 1983; *South London Press*, 23 September 1983.
8. *Hansard*, 11 July 1983, col. 215.
9. Conservative Party News Service, *Extract from the Speech by the Rt Hon. Leon Brittan* QC, MP, 11 October, 1983, p. 2.
10. J. Sim, 'Working for the Clampdown: Prisons and Politics in England and Wales' in P. Scraton (ed.), *Law, Order and the Authoritarian State*, Milton Keynes, Open University Press, 1987, p. 199.
11. S. Box, *Deviance, Reality and Society*, London, Holt, Rinehart and Winston, 1971; R. Hall, *Ask Any Woman*, Bristol, Falling Wall Press, 1985.
12. See E. Wilson, *What Is To Be Done about Violence against Women?*, Harmondsworth, Penguin, 1983; P. Gordon, *Racial Violence and Harrassment*, London, The Runnymede Trust, 1986.
13. R. Kinsey, J. Lea and J. Young, *Losing the Fight against Crime*, Oxford, Blackwell, 1986, p. 58.
14. Ibid., pp. 72–3.
15. M. Ryan and T. Ward, 'Law and Order: Left Realism against the Rest', *The Abolitionist*, no. 22, 1986, pp. 29–33; J. Sim, P. Scraton and P. Gordon, 'Crime, the State and Critical Analysis' in Scraton, *Law, Order and the Authoritarian State*.
16. Radical Alternatives to Prison, *Brittan's Proposals – A Discussion Paper*, London, Radical Alternatives to Prison (no date), p. 1.
17. Conservative Party News Service, *Extract from the Speech by Brittan*, p. 4.
18. Ibid., p. 9.
19. *The Guardian*, 1 December 1983.
20. S. Cohen and L. Taylor, *Psychological Survival*, Harmondsworth, Penguin, 1981, p. 10.
21. Figures cited in Sim, *Medical Power*, ch. 5; Home Office, *Prison Statistics England and Wales*, Cm 547, HMSO, 1987, p. 11.
22. Home Office, *The Parole System in England and Wales: Report of the Review Committee* (Carlisle Report), Cm 532, HMSO, 1988, p. 12.
23. *The Guardian*, 24 January, 1985.
24. Home Office, *Managing the Long-term Prison System: The Report of the Control Review Committee*, HMSO, 1984, p. 1.
25. *Hansard*, 19 July 1984, col. 499.
26. Home Office, *Managing the Long-term Prison System*, p. 15.
27. Ibid., pp. 17–21.
28. Ibid., p. 7.
29. *The Listener*, 18 April 1985.
30. T. C. Platt, 'New Directions in Prison Design', paper presented at the 18th Cropwood Conference, University of Cambridge, March 1986, p. 2.

31. Research and Advisory Group on the Long-Term Prison System (no date), *Special Units for Long-term Prisoners: Regimes, Management and Research*, Home Office, Introduction.
32. Ibid., p. 45.
33. Ibid.
34. Ibid., pp. 41–2 (emphasis in original).
35. Ibid., pp. 42–3.
36. *The Guardian*, 23 January 1984.
37. A. K. Bottomley, 'Custody and Community: The Question of Parole', paper presented at Howard League Seminar Series, Thinking About Crime, Westminster Cathedral Conference Centre, London, 21 March 1984, p. 3.
38. *The Times*, 16 November 1984.
39. Cited in V. Stern, *Bricks of Shame*, Harmondsworth, Penguin, 1987, p. 237.
40. Ibid.
41. *The Guardian*, 24 May 1985.
42. G. Northam, 'Can We Learn any Lessons from Death Row?', *The Listener*, 18 April 1985, p. 7.
43. Ibid.
44. M. Fitzgerald, 'The Telephone Rings: Long-term Imprisonment', paper presented at the 18th Cropwood Conference, University of Cambridge, March 1986, p. 17 (emphasis in original).
45. Ibid., p. 20.
46. Ibid., p. 22.
47. P. Carlen, *Women's Imprisonment: A Study in Social Control*, London, Routledge and Kegan Paul, 1983.
48. R. P. Dobash, R. E. Dobash and S. Gutteridge, *The Imprisonment of Women*, Oxford, Blackwell, 1986, p. 213.
49. Sim, *Medical Power*, chs 2–6.
50. R. King, 'Control in Prisons' in M. Maguire, J. Vagg, and R. Morgan (eds), *Accountability and Prisons*, London, Tavistock, 1985, p. 191.
51. Ibid. p. 189.
52. *The Observer*, 24 July 1988; *The Guardian*, 9 August 1988; Home Office, *Report on the Work of the Prison Service, April 1987–March 1988*, Cm 516, HMSO, 1988, p. 12.
53. Scottish Prison Service, *Assessment and Control: The Management of Violent and Disruptive Prisoners*, a Discussion Paper, Scottish Office, October 1988.
54. Ibid., para. 2.11.
55. Ibid., para. 8.3.
56. Ibid., para. 1.6.
57. Scottish Home and Health Department, *Her Majesty's Chief Inspector of Prisons for Scotland Report for 1987*, HMSO, 1988, p. 15.
58. Scottish Home and Health Department, *Prisons in Scotland: Report for 1986*, Cm 223, HMSO, 1987, p. 14.
59. P. Scraton, J. Sim and P. Skidmore, 'Through the Barricades: Prisoner Protest and Penal Policy in Scotland', *Journal of Law and Society*, vol. 15, no. 3, Autumn 1986, p. 249.
60. Scottish Home and Health Department, *Prisons in Scotland 1986*, p. 28.
61. *The Guardian*, 2 November 1987.
62. Scottish Council for Civil Liberties, *Some Documents and Observations on the Scottish Prison System: A Discussion Document following a Hostage Taking at Saughton and Peterhead*, Glasgow, SCCL, 1986, p. 9.

63. S. Cohen, 'Prisons and the Future of Control Systems: From Concentration to Dispersal' in M. Fitzgerald, P. Halmos, J. Muncie and D. Zeldin (eds), *Welfare in Action*, London, Routledge and Kegan Paul/Open University Press, 1977, p. 220.
64. *The Observer*, 16 November 1986.
65. *The Independent*, 6 October 1987.
66. K. Moyer, 'Biological Substrates of Violence' in A. K. Cohen, G. F. Cole and R. G. Bailey (eds), *Prison Violence*, New York, Lexington Books, 1977, p. 37.
67. Home Office, *Prison Statistics England and Wales*, Cm 547, HMSO, 1987, p. 86.
68. Ibid., p. 87.
69. Scottish Home and Health Department, *Statistical Bulletin*, no. 5, 1986, p. 3.
70. Scottish Home and Health Department, *Statistical Bulletin*, no. 6, 1987, p. 2.
71. A. E. Bottoms and R. Light, 'Preface' in A. E. Bottoms and R. Light (eds), *Problems of Long-term Imprisonment*, Aldershot, Gower, 1987, p. viii.
72. Ibid.
73. M. Fitzgerald and J. Sim, 'Legitimating the Prison Crisis: A Critical Review of the May Report', *The Howard Journal*, vol. XIX, 1980, pp. 73–84.
74. D. Cameron and E. Frazer, *The Lust to Kill*, Cambridge, Polity, 1987, p. xi.
75. P. Carlen (ed.), *Criminal Women*, Cambridge, Polity, 1985, p. 187.
76. Ibid., p. 189.
77. Ibid.; Dobash *et al.*, *Imprisonment of Women*; A. Mandaraka-Sheppard, *The Dynamics of Aggression in Women's Prisons in England*, Aldershot, Gower, 1986.
78. Women's Equality Group/London Strategic Policy Unit, *Breaking the Silence*, LSPU, 1986, p. 164.
79. Ibid.
80. U. Padel and P. Stevenson, *Insiders*, London, Virago, 1988, pp. 119–20.
81. Women's Equality Group/London Strategic Policy Unit, *Breaking the Silence*, p. 161.
82. K. Boyle, T. Hadden, and P. Hillyard, *Ten Years on in Northern Ireland*, London, The Cobden Trust, 1980, ch. 7.
83. Council of Europe, *Prison Information Bulletin*, no. 11, June 1988, p. 20.
84. B. Rolston and M. Tomlinson, ' "The Challenge Within": Prisons and Propaganda in Northern Ireland' in M. Tomlinson, T. Varley and C. McCullagh (eds), *Whose Law and Order?*, Belfast, Sociological Association of Ireland, 1988, p. 189.
85. Ibid., p. 170.
86. Ibid., pp. 171–2.
87. Ibid., p. 173.
88. Women's Equality Group/London Strategic Policy Unit, *Breaking the Silence*, p. 161.
89. Rolston and Tomlinson, ' "The Challenge Within" ', p. 175.
90. R. Ardron, 'Soulless Isolation – Maghaberry', *Troops Out*, June 1987, p. 8.
91. Ibid., p. 9.
92. Ibid.
93. *The Guardian*, 4 January 1989.
94. Cited in K. Smith, *Inside Time*, London, Harrop, 1989, p. 222–3.
95. D. Beresford, *Ten Men Dead*, London, Grafton, 1987. For an excellent historical analysis of these processes see D. Hayden, 'The Imprisonment of Irish Prisoners in Ireland and Britain: From Colonial State to Free State', unpublished MA dissertation, Edge Hill College of Higher Education, 1988.
96. Smith, *Inside Time*, p. 221.
97. *The Guardian*, 23 November 1988.
98. Rolston and Tomlinson, ' "The Challenge Within" ', p. 188.

99. Council of Europe, *Prison Information Bulletin*, no. 11, June 1988, p. 20.
100. *The Guardian*, 30 March 1988.
101. Home Office, *The Work of the Prison Service*, p. 39.
102. Home Office, *The Parole System in England and Wales*, p. 145.
103. *The Guardian*, 21 January 1988.
104. Home Office, *The Work of the Prison Service*, p. 36.
105. *The Guardian*, 21 January 1988; Home Office, *The Work of the Prison Service*, p. 26.
106. Home Office, *The Work of the Prison Service*, p. 41.
107. Ibid., pp. 16 and 84.
108. Home Office, *Prison Statistics England and Wales, 1987*, Cm 547, HMSO, 1988C, pp. 7–10.
109. *Daily Mail*, 23 February 1989.
110. A. Rutherford, *Prisons and the Process of Justice*, London, Heinemann, 1984.
111. J. Sim, 'Working for the Clampdown', pp. 200–203.
112. P. Hillyard and J. Percy-Smith, *The Coercive State*, London, Fontana, 1988.
113. *The Guardian*, 24 January 1989.
114. *The Guardian*, 14 June 1988; *The Observer*, 6 November 1988.
115. *The Guardian*, 4 July 1988.
116. *The Observer*, 23 October 1988.
117. *News at Six*, BBC Television, 11 August 1988.
118. Cited in the Foreword to Home Office, *Criminal Justice: A Working Paper*, Home Office, May 1984.
119. S. Hall, *The Hard Road to Renewal: Thatcherism and the Crisis of the Left*, London, Verso, 1988, p. 2.
120. S. Box, *Power, Crime and Mystification*, London, Tavistock, 1983, ch. 6.
121. Hall, *The Hard Road*, p. 55.
122. Ibid., p. 281.
123. N. Poulantzas, *State Power Socialism*, London, New Left Books, 1978, pp. 76–92.
124. Ibid., p. 83 (emphasis in original).
125. Ibid., p. 84.
126. Ibid., p. 85.
127. A. Gramsci, *Selections from Prison Notebooks*, London, Lawrence and Wishart, 1971, pp. 330–1.
128. T. Mathiesen, *The Politics of Abolition*, London, Martin Robertson, 1974; H. Bianchi and R. Van Swaanigen (eds), *Abolitionism*, Amsterdam, Free University Press 1986; various editions of *The Abolitionist: The Journal of Radical Alternatives to Prison*.
129. J. Sim, 'Long-term Prisons and the Politics of Abolition', paper presented at a One Day Conference on Prison Reform, Long Lartin Prison, 1 March 1989.
130. J. Boyle, *The Pain of Confinement*, Edinburgh, Canongate, 1984, p. 311.

APPENDIX 1

The questionnaire

2–4 ABBEYMOUNT,
EDINBURGH EH8 8EJ.
Tel: 031-661 0982

5th February, 1987

Dear

PETERHEAD INDEPENDENT INQUIRY

Following the recent disturbances in Scottish Prisons, all of which seemed, in one way or another, to relate to Peterhead Prison, we held a Public Meeting here at the Gateway Exchange. A panel of politicians chaired by an eminent QC heard information from a packed audience about conditions and treatment in the prison, that worried them. The outcome of this was to call for an independent public inquiry. This was followed by various Members of Parliament raising the issue in the House of Commons. The call for such an inquiry was rejected by the Secretary of State. He opted for Her Majesty's Chief Inspector of Prisons. The overwhelming majority of people at our Public Meeting have little faith in this office in the light of the report made about the Glenochil suicides.

We now have our committee who will take evidence from a wide range of people about Peterhead and they will be responsible for writing up a report which will then be published and widely circulated. As part of this process we are sending you a questionnaire and we hope that you would co-operate by filling it in and returning it to us. A stamped addressed envelope will be included.

The committee comprises of a lawyer, politician and criminologist. They will send you a copy of their report when it is completed.

I would like to make it clear that if you feel that participating in this project will bring pressure on you then please do not do so. All of us appreciate there can be no confidentiality as your questionnaire will obviously be read by the prison authorities. I can assure you that we will treat it confidentially at our end.

In conclusion, if there is any other prisoner or ex-prisoner, family member etc. who would be interested in giving evidence then please let us know.

Yours sincerely,

JIMMY BOYLE

AGE ....

SENTENCE ....

WHEN IMPOSED ....

BACKGROUND INFORMATION

(1) Marital status (please tick as appropriate)
    single/married/divorced/widowed
    If married – would you be living with your wife if at liberty? YES ... NO ...

(2) Do you have children? YES ... NO ...
    If YES: How many?..................................
    What are their ages..........................

(3) Which of your close relatives visit you regularly? ....

(4) Which town/city are you from?......................

FAMILIES *USE for Q3.*

(1) Have your families experienced any problems visiting you? YES ... NO ...
    If YES: What were the problems? (tick as appropriate)

    Distance...................................
    Expense ....
    Childcare ....
    Lack of Privacy ....
    Humiliating conditions ....

(2) Do you get enough visits to maintain effective contact with
    your family? YES ... NO ...

    Please comment:

(3) When you have a visit, do you think it is long enough? YES ... NO ...

    Please comment:

(4) Do you get visits from anyone else apart from family? YES ... NO ...
    If YES: Who? (tick as appropriate)

    Lawyers ....
    Doctors..
    Social Workers ....
    Others (please specify) ....

(5) Have you experienced problems with outgoing/incoming
    mail? YES ... NO ...
    If YES: What were the problems? (tick as appropriate)

    Withholding mail ....
    Censorship of mail ....
    Public comments made by staff regarding mail ....
    Others (please specify) ....

(6) Can you afford canteen letters?   YES ... NO ...

QUALITY OF LIFE

(1) To assist in trying to understand your view of the quality of
    life in prison can you tell us whether you find the following
    satisfactory or unsatisfactory? (please tick as appropriate)

	Satisfactory	Unsatisfactory
General hygiene	....	....
Washing	....	....
Food	....	....
Clothing	....	....
Laundry	....	....
Bedding	....	....
Medication	....	....
Heating	....	....
Sanitation	....	....

Other comments:

(2) Do conditions give you enough privacy?   YES ... NO ...
    If NO: Why not? please comment:

(3) Do you feel safe in prison?   YES ... NO ...
    Please comment:

CAROLINE

(4) Is fear a predominant factor in your daily life?   YES ... NO ...

(5) What type of work do you do?
    Briefly describe what you do:

    What do you think of the wages? (tick as appropriate)

    Excellent ....
    Good..
    Poor ....
    Awful...

(6) What do you think of the work provided at Peterhead?
        (tick as appropriate)
    Interesting ....
    Useful upon release..
    Helps you pass the time ....
    Boring ....
    Useless ....

(7) Is there adequate opportunity for you to speak to:
                        YES   NO
    Psychiatrist   ....
    Psychologist   ....
    Doctor   ....
    Teacher   ....
    Social worker   ....

(8) What do you do for recreation?
Please comment:

(9) How often do you get recreation? (tick as appropriate)
Once/twice/three/four/or five times a week.
Estimate how many hours each week:

(10) What is your view of the following facilities?

	Satisfactory	Unsatisfactory
Recreational	....	....
Educational	....	....
Physical training	....	....

Comments (if any):

(11) How long do you spend locked in your cell?

Week-days........
Week-ends........

How do you pass the time when locked-up?
Comments:

(12) Would you like access to phones as in Saughton?   YES ... NO ...
If YES please comment on how this would help you.

(13) How have conditions in Peterhead changed since you have
been there? (please tick as appropriate)

improved ....
same ....
worse ....

RELATIONSHIP WITH STAFF

(1) How would you describe your relationship with staff?

good ....
bad ....
indifferent ......

Please comment:

(2) How would you describe the way staff treat you?

good ....
bad ....
indifferent ......

Please comment:

(3) What aspects of the behaviour of staff

(a) annoy you ....
(b) please you ....

(4) Have you ever been physically assaulted by staff?   YES ... NO ...
If YES: please describe circumstances

(5) Have you ever witnessed anyone else being assaulted by staff?   YES ...   NO ...
If YES: (a) please describe circumstances
        (b) were you asked for a statement?   YES ...   NO ...
           If YES: by whom (tick as appropriate)
              Police.................
              Lawyer ....
              Prison staff ....

(6) If you have been assaulted or have witnessed an assault on someone else, have you used the official channels to complain?   YES ...   NO ...
If NO: Why not?

If YES: please give details (including outcome and tell us whether you felt happy with the outcome)

(7) Do you think relationships between prisons and staff are better now than when you arrived at Peterhead?   YES ...   NO ...

(8) Have you been placed on report?   YES ...   NO ...
If YES: What for?

How often?

What was/were the punishment/s?

(9) Do you think the discipline system is fair?   YES ...   NO ...
Comments (if any)

(10) Apart from the question of physical assaults, have you used the official channels to raise matters which have bothered you?   YES ...   NO ...
If YES: What happened?

(11) How have the parole changes affected you?
Please comment:

How have the parole changes affected the prison?
Please comment:

Have you been considered for parole?   YES ... NO ...
If you have been considered for parole, when was this?
Please comment:

What was the outcome?

When can you next apply?

(12) Have you ever experienced:
    (a) Solitary confinement?   YES ... NO ...
        If YES: What for?

        How long?

    (b) Silent cell?   YES ... NO ...
        If YES: What for?

        How long?

    (c) The 10 cell unit?   YES ... NO ...
        If YES: What for?

        How long?

    (d) Have you ever experienced the 'B' Hall?   YES ... NO ...
        If YES: What for?

        How long?

(e) The prison authorities say the 10 cell unit is an alternative
regime and not a punishment unit.
Do you agree with that?   YES ...   NO ...

(13) The public often think that the Inspector of Prisons is an
independent watchdog.
We would like to ask a few questions about his role.
(a) Are you given due warning of his visits?   YES ...   NO ...
(b) Have you ever been interviewed by him?   YES ...   NO ...
     If YES: Did you feel you could speak openly and freely? YES ...   NO ...
              Did you think it was a worthwhile thing to do?   YES ...   NO ...

(14) Do you think that his visits and conversations with prisoners
will lead to a true picture of what is going on?   YES ...   NO ...
Comments:

(15) Have you ever been informed in advance of the Under
Secretary of State's visit to the prison:
(a) that he was coming   YES ...   NO ...
(b) that you could speak to him about grievances?   YES ...   NO ...
If YES to either: Please comment on the results.

(16) Do you feel your experience in prison will make you more
(YES) or less (NO) prepared for life outside?   YES ...   NO ...

(17) What improvements could you suggest for Peterhead?
Please comment:

If you wish, give us any comments you have on any of the topics covered above or
anything not covered which you think is important.
Thank you for your co-operation.

APPENDIX 2

Letter from T. J. Kelly, Scottish Prison Service, to Jimmy Boyle, April 1987

James Boyle Esq
Gateway Exchange
2–4 Abbeymount
EDINBURGH
EH8 8EJ   2 April 1987

Dear Mr Boyle

I have been asked to reply to your letter of 23 February to the Secretary of State in which you suggest that there has been a breach of the European Convention on Human Rights and our own Rules in relation to correspondence of your organisation about an intended 'inquiry' into conditions and treatment of prisoners at one establishment. You had also written to the Governors of Peterhead and Inverness Prisons on 4 March asking why letters from your organisation had not reached, at that time, prisoners to whom they had been addressed.

Your understanding of the position in relation to prisoners' correspondence is incorrect. The need for a degree of control over prisoners' correspondence is recognised in the Prisons (Scotland) Rules 1952, the Prison (Scotland) Standing Orders and the European Convention on Human Rights. In particular Standing Order M, which deals with correspondence, is drafted specifically in the light of provisions of Articles 8 and 10 of the European Convention on Human Rights. These Articles of the Convention safeguard 'respect' for correspondence and freedom of expression but recognise that intervention may be necessary 'in accordance with the law' and 'in the interests of national security, or public safety' and 'for the prevention of disorder or crime' or 'for the protection of the rights and freedoms of others'. It is reasonable, therefore, that any unusual intervention should be very carefully considered in relation to the appropriate provisions.

Until you wrote to the Secretary of State on 23 February neither we in the Department, nor Governors of individual penal establishments, had received any notification that it was the intention of Gateway Exchange to obtain views of prisoners in various penal establishments or to conduct an 'inquiry'. In the literature we have received, there was no indication as to who would conduct your 'inquiry' nor any indication as to whether any attempt would be made to seek corroboration of any affirmative responses to a number of questions under the heading of 'Relationships with Staff' which imply criminal conduct. Neither do you indicate whether your inquiry results are to be published. Other organisations, including bona fide academic researchers or representatives of the media, put proposals for access to us in the first instance and this enables us to consider what would be appropriate and acceptable on the merits of the individual proposal. We cannot be expected to reach an early conclusion if we become aware of a survey or 'inquiry' only by chance.

In recent months, allegations, whether well-founded or not, have given rise to unrest in a number of penal establishments in Scotland. It is only reasonable, therefore, for the Department to consider the effect which questionnaires inviting prisoners to make general allegations would have on the security and good order of penal establishments, on the interests of prisoners and on the interests of staff. The Secretary of State had already invited Her Majesty's Chief Inspector of Prisons in Scotland to make a special investigation into complaints about conditions and treatment of prisoners at Peterhead Prison following incidents there and at Edinburgh Prison last year and his report will be published in due course. As you say, the Secretary of State has not agreed to a general inquiry about Scottish prisons. But it appears that your organisation's 'inquiry' is narrower in scope and less balanced in approach than the very thorough investigation which the Secretary of State had already requested.

For the reasons I have indicated, we take great care about any proposal from an organisation or individual appointing itself to carry out an 'inquiry' involving prisoners. If prisoners have legitimate complaints to make, it is in their interests and that of the public at large, that these should be made to those who have the necessary powers and authority to investigate such claims thoroughly. We are prepared, after careful consideration to allow your 'questionnaire' to be admitted to those prisoners to whom it is addressed on the basis that any replies are subject to the normal, limited, restrictions on prohibited material or material intended for publication in outward correspondence from prisoners.

We appreciate that the consideration of these issues has delayed receipt of your 'questionnaire' by individual prisoners. As I have explained, however, we had not been forewarned of your intentions and, in the circumstances, careful consideration was needed before we felt able to conclude that your 'questionnaire' should be passed to the prisoners to whom it was addressed.

Yours sincerely

T. J. KELLY
Deputy Director

Index